ALL UNDER HEAVEN

DARRYL ACCONE

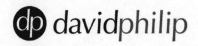

First published in 2004 in southern Africa by
David Philip Publishers. an imprint of New Africa Books (Pty) Ltd
99 Garfield Road, Claremont 7700, South Africa

Second impression 2006

ISBN 10: 0 86486 648 8
ISBN 13: 978-0-86486-648-6

Cover designer: Toby Newsome
Text designer: Odette Marais
Editor: Rina Minervini
Proofreader: Jennifer Stastny
Typeset in 11,7/13,5 pt Bembo by Jenny Wheeldon
Printed and bound by CTP Book Printers, Duminy Street,
Parow. Cape Town, South Africa

To my ancestors

ACKNOWLEDGEMENTS

Throughout the many years that this book was thought about rather than written, one person, Jewel Accone, tended the flames of memory. Without her personal recollections, some set down in writing, my task would have been almost impossible. Alongside those memoirs, she maintained another wonderful resource: clippings files on the Chinese in South Africa. I am deeply grateful to her for preserving and honouring so much of her family's story, as well as that of the South African Chinese, and for many long and memorable conversations during the writing of the manuscript.

If Heidi Holland and Adam Roberts had not asked me to contribute to *From Jo'burg to Jozi*, their celebration of Johannesburg, it is possible that *All Under Heaven* would still be an idea. *Kum Saan*, the 1 000-word piece I submitted to them, drew the attention of Sharon Hughes, then commissioning editor at David Philip.

In the writing, I was sustained by extraordinary support. My wife Shayleen was loving and patient even when I was most trying, and brought her humaneness and sensitivity to numerous readings of the manuscript. Shay and David Medalie were instrumental in setting up a writing group that gave considered and caring advice on the manuscript. My thanks to them and the other members of the Gang: Cecily Singer, Geoff Sifrin, Renos Spanoudes, Michael Holm and Damon Garstang.

I owe further gratitude to David for his encouragement and generous spirit. His reading of the final manuscript saved me from egregious errors and it was he who found the way to a fitting ending for the story.

Emma Chen offered valuable suggestions and, most importantly, kept a rigorous eye on the various Chinese aspects of the story. Any errors that remain are, of course, mine. Emma's help extended to interpreting my many senses of Sky, Sea, Earth and Fire and translating them to the Chinese characters that announce each part of the book.

Thanks to Celeste Vinassa and Sean Kenselaar for their careful scanning of priceless family photographs.

My appreciation to Karen van Eden, commissioning editor of David Philip, for her alert reading of the drafts, smoothly managing the production process and kindly consulting me on many matters, even down to typeface preferences.

It was a great pleasure to have Rina Minervini as my editor, renewing a working relationship that began as newspaper confrères. Her acuity and subtle sensibility led to many refinements of the manuscript.

To misuse a famous quotation, I managed to write this book only because I stood on the shoulders of giants, the shoulders of my family and of my ancestors. My deepest debt is to them.

My primary sources were the newspaper clippings compiled by Jewel Accone, which contain cuttings from the *Rand Daily Mail*, *Sunday Times*, *Sunday Express*, *Pretoria News* and *The Star*.

I consulted *Chinese Science and the West*, edited by Basil Clarke (Nile & Mackenzie Ltd: 1980), on the subject of shipbuilding.

Valuable in checking Chinese history in South Africa was *Colour, Confusion and Concessions*, subtitled *The History of the Chinese in South Africa*, by Melanie Yap and Dianne Leong Man (Hong Kong University Press: 1996).

The epigraph to Sea is taken from Stephen Mitchell's translation of *Tao Te Ching* (Macmillan London Limited: 1989).

The epigraph to Fire is taken from *The Nine Songs, A Study of Shamanism in Ancient China* by Arthur Waley (George Allen & Unwin Ltd: 1955).

AUTHOR'S NOTE

To reflect the usages of the time when the events in this book took place, Chinese names have been rendered in the older form of Romanisation, Wade-Giles, rather than in Pinyin, the system for transliterating Chinese that was adopted in 1958. Thus, for instance, readers will encounter Canton, Kwangtung, Hong Kong and Mao Tse-tung instead of the current Guangzhou, Guangdong, Xianggang and Mao Zedong.

The same adherence to historical usage applies to place names such as the Transvaal, Lourenço Marques, Portuguese East Africa, etc. and to the mind-boggling nomenclature invented by successive South African governments to categorise and classify the peoples of the country. Derogatory terms such as Coloured, Native and Non-White are used only to accord with historical realities.

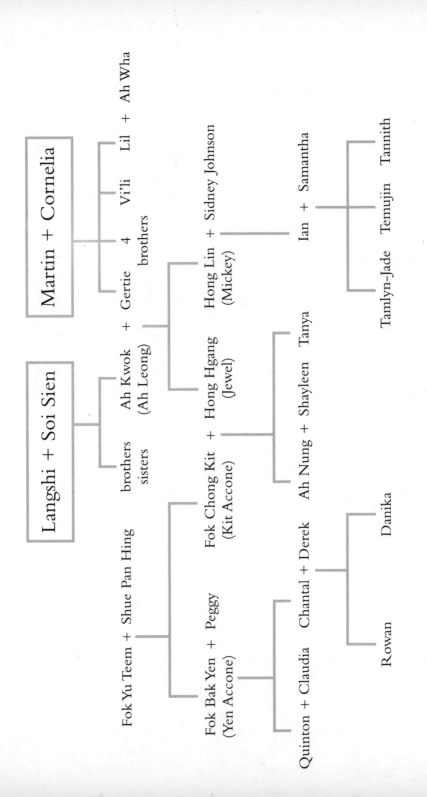

PROLOGUE

The gravestone cast a long shadow, the sun bright even at this early hour of the day. Ah Nung began to feel dizzy as he looked at the thicket of compacted vertical, horizontal and diagonal characters chiselled into its granite face. A wisp of incense caught at his nose, insistent in its acrid sweetness.

'When can we go, *Mo ts'an?*' he asked his mother, who was arranging a bunch of white carnations in the flower-holder at the foot of the grave.

'*Yat koh tsz* – five minutes,' she said, brushing a strand of jet-black hair from her ivory-hued face. She was perspiring lightly, a sheen coating delicate features lit by the direct rays of the new sun.

Father, struggling with some rank *khakibos* that had sprung up behind the headstone, squinted into the sun as he looked towards the eastern reaches of the cemetery and the cypresses that bordered the main road.

'*Foo ts'an*, whose grave is this? It is not anyone from our family. Perhaps it is one of the *Ying-Kwok yan? Foo ts'an?* Please. Why are we here? What are we doing at this grave?'

Ah Nung's father chuckled. 'No, *tsai*, this is not *Ying-Kwok yan*, not an English person. The man buried here is *T'ong yan*, one of us, Chinese. He did a very sad thing, hurting the community, and then a very brave thing to win his honour back. And that made them all ashamed for not sticking by him, despite what he did, because he was one of us – and what he first did, he did with good intentions.'

'What did he do, *Foo ts'an?* If he is *T'ong yan*, why is his grave so far from the others? Why is it facing the other way, with its back to the morning sun?'

'Come, Ah Nung, we'll tell you on the way home,' said the boy's mother, brushing red dust and dead grass from her skirt before joining her hands and inclining them three times towards the tombstone.

1

When they had left, the freshly tended grave kept its eternal vigil, look-ing in vain for the rays of the morning sun to stroke its head and caress the name and inscriptions scored into its grey stone.

CHOW KWAI FOR
1885–1907
Gave his life for the community that abandoned him
Rest in peace and honour

From the Chinese of the Transvaal, grieving that they drove
a countryman to pass so early from this world

As they strolled down the grassy slope towards the main gate of the ceme-tery, Mother and Father explained to Ah Nung, as simply as they could, about Chow Kwai For. This is the story they told.

As you know, Ah Nung, in South Africa black people are made to carry Pass Books wherever they go, books with their names and pictures and the places they are allowed to be in. We are more fortunate, we have only to carry ordinary identity books.

One day, many years ago, the government said that the Chinese, too, would have to carry Pass Books – identity documents that 'Non-Whites', but not Whites, had to keep on themselves at all times. The Chinese refused.

The Chinese Consul-General and local community leaders spoke out against the Pass Book. The community stood fast against the government. There were street protests and the famous lawyer, Mohandas Gandhi, stood in solidarity with the Chinese.

But Chow Kwai For had just arrived from China; actually, from Heinan Island, south of the mainland. He was hoping to work in Kum Saan, the gold mountain of Johannesburg, in the land of Namfeechow, this South Africa of ours. He did not want to cause trouble. He believed that one should obey the law, even more so in a foreign country. So Chow Kwai For went to the government office and got his Pass Book. He had his fin-gerprints taken and put in the book, as well as into the central records. He left the government offices smiling, sure that his stay would be trou-ble-free because he had followed the rules.

Somehow, perhaps because he spoke a different dialect of Chinese, he had not known of the community's position. When he found out, he was embarrassed but gave it not much thought: he could not break the law. He wanted to fit in to this new country, this very different society.

But just as they say that blood is thicker than water – that family are closer than friends – so it is with nationality. The Chinese felt betrayed by Chow Kwai For. They thought he had valued fitting in to this uneven society, where Chinese had few rights and no respect, above remaining faithful to his community.

Also, because one Chinese had a Pass Book, it could have meant all Chinese would have to. So angry were the Chinese that they would not have anything to do with the unfortunate young man. No one would speak to him. They refused to sell him goods, food, clothing, herbal medicines. There was no place in Chinatown that would accept him as a lodger.

In hope – because the young always have much hope – Chow Kwai For carried on, believing that at some time he would be forgiven. But even though the government could not force the Pass Book on the community, Chow Kwai For's crime was not forgotten. He was not forgiven. An outcast, he struggled on for a few years but the loneliness, the hatred and the shame in the eyes of the community were too much for him.

One day, in his dingy room in a corrugated iron shack, he hanged himself. He left behind a note saying that he hoped his death would cancel the community's dishonour and that his family name would no longer be held in disgrace.

Still, Chow Kwai For was buried far from other Chinese, because he was regarded as bad luck. Vengeful elders said that in the traditions of this new country where they lived, the grave should face westwards, like those of murderers, who did not deserve ever to see the rising sun. Chow Kwai For, they said, was as bad as a killer because of the way he had put the community in danger. That is why the grave is so far from the other Chinese.

But then, because community and country are closer than adopted home, the Chinese felt very guilty at how they had driven one of their own sons to leave the world so soon. After a while, the community understood that the shame, dishonour and disgrace were theirs. So they put up a tombstone to honour the young man who had wanted just to fit in. And they remembered that fitting in is what all people who come to new and strange lands want to do, in some or other way.

上天

S K Y

All Under Heaven

Popular synonym for
China in the era
of the Warring States,
475–221 BC

SKY

ONE
Sha Kiu village, southern China, 1911

'Fit in!' 'Keep faith with home!' 'Assimilate!' 'Resist!' Such are the age-old siren-calls to immigrant communities, tempting and perturbing generation after generation of settlers. To the young Ah Nung, fitting in meant keeping his balance, learning to bend with the changing winds, as his forebears in South Africa had found. In the first generation to come over had been his great-grandfather Langshi and grandfather Ah Kwok from his mother's side of the family. On a spring morning in 1911, they set off from Sha Kiu village in Kwangtung province, with wooden trunks crammed with clothes and food, on the first stage of their journey to Africa. Ah Nung's great-great-grandfather Tian walked with them for the first ten *li*, a wispy presence between his vigorous son and the wide-eyed boy. He had dressed in his best white silk jacket and trousers, and savoured each step in the company of his son and grandson. A shallow, flat black skull-cap contrasted with the old man's long but thin white beard, the latter belying his vocation in life, for he was not a venerable philosopher-scholar but an aged fish farmer who loved poetry and the epic novels of Chinese literature. And as well as he knew the intricacies of the *Romance of the Three Kingdoms*, he knew too the webs of life that could entrap his kin, holding them forever in foreign lands. Already, he had lost three brothers to Mei-kwok, the big country of America, halfway across the world from the motherland, Chung-kwok.

Melancholy though he felt, Tian put a gloss on the morning and talked about far-off Namfeechow, where men white and black in colour lived. 'They say, *tsai*,' he said to his son, 'that some of those *bak-gwai*, those white devils, fought a great war against the *bak-gwai* from Ying-kwok. But there were too many soldiers of Victoria, the *wong-hau* of that little island, and the English queen's forces won in the end. They

7

say that the war was because of the gold that they found in Kum Saan, where you are going.'

'True, *foo t'san*,' said Langshi to his father. 'But we do not go for gold. Ah Kwok and I will tend to our people, the *T'ong yan* community, in the city of the gold mountain. Many of them there are, but none are miners.'

Walking along beside his elders, Ah Kwok recalled the stories he had heard about the labourers who had gone to work on those mines. They had been an earlier wave of Chinese migrants, indentured workers who tunnelled and shovelled underground by day, slept in overcrowded rooms by night, and when off-duty were penned in compounds like beasts and denied even basic recreational facilities. At first they brooded and endured their lot. But when requests to improve their conditions were met by ears that would not hear, they rioted in protest, broke out of their cages and killed a number of guards. The violence of the reaction was mitigated when the miners' horrific living conditions became public knowledge, and in a seemingly inspired and humane response, the men had been sent home. Chinese miners were never again employed in the goldfields of Johannesburg or elsewhere in the Transvaal province.

A bright eleven-year-old, the eldest of eight children, Ah Kwok had certain advantages over other children in the village. Both his grandfather and father could read and he was learning new Chinese characters every week, for he would need to master at least 5 000 if he was to have any hope one day of entering the imperial administration. Many of the hopes nursed by Ah Kwok's *Kongkong*, his grandfather, had been realised in his father Langshi, whose name meant bright scholar. Not merely literate and expert with the abacus, Langshi had also become a traditional Chinese herbalist, and it was this skill that he was exporting to set up a practice for the burgeoning Chinese community in the mining town of Johannesburg, founded only 25 years before. Father and son would work very hard to send money home, planning all the while to follow it back before too long. The plan was for Ah Kwok to keep up his Chinese studies while in Africa, come home and prepare further for school examinations, and acquire sufficient knowledge to sit entrance exams for higher education or government administration. But in truth, despite the adventure that beckoned, Ah Kwok would rather have stayed home as spring yielded to the

long days of familiar summer with its liquid fruits and fairs and visiting
theatre troupes and musicians and snakes slithering everywhere, waiting
playthings for brave and patient boys to catch and sell at the local market.

Namfeechow, on the other hand, was a great unknown. What colour
rivers would this strange-sounding country have? Were they wide and
deep for swimming? Did the mist cover the mountains in the early morning and then rise off the water to reveal towering tops, resembling the serrated teeth of dragons or the elongated forehead of Shouxing, the god of
long life? What sort of *T'ong yan* boys and girls were there in Kum Saan
– would they look just like those at home in Sha Kiu and its neighbouring rival Ma Kiu?

'*Naam-tsai*, my boy,' Ah Kwok heard his grandfather call as they put
down their heavy trunks. They had reached a ridge that dipped and rose
in a series of troughs and peaks as far as the eye could see. Along this
spine, a ribbon of sand unfurled between the surrounding verdure. It was
the road to the north and the river flowing to the market town of Lok
Chung, from which they would travel to Canton, the great and ancient
port, capital of the province of Kwangtung and chief city of southern
China. It was from here that hundreds of thousands of Cantonese left for
new countries, to trade or to work.

And it was from the top of the ridge that one could look down into the
valley and just make out the roofs of Sha Kiu, and at its northernmost edge
the carp ponds, on the dark bottoms of which drifted the liquid stock built
up by grandfather's lifetime endeavours. Testimony to those efforts were
Tian's hands, as rough and hardened as the bark of an old ginko tree, and
knobbly at the knuckles and joints. As a young child, Ah Kwok had
thought his grandfather's gnarled hands were enormous: so big, that they
reminded Ah Kwok of the mountains in the story of Stone Monkey,
mighty peaks that the proud primate flew between only to discover they
were Buddha's fingers and that the mist-shrouded valleys below were his
palms. While Tian's hands had been broadened by work and time, his body
was slim as it had been when he was in his twenties. But if anyone wondered about his age, his face, sculpted by wind, water and sun, supplied a
ready answer. It had been eroded by the years as much as his hands had
been roughened by them. Working in all weathers in the rice fields and

the fish ponds had left him with a sunken face so that his flattish nose presented only the merest suggestion of nostrils. His cheeks were concave inlets and his eyebrows were exaggerated by the indentations scoured out above them. Despite his sprightly demeanour and the vitality of his speech, Tian's face acknowledged each of his 75 years, though when he smiled he had the mischievous look of an errant schoolboy.

It was down at the ponds that Tian smiled most, and especially in the summertime, as the cool of evening began to grapple with and subdue the day's humidity. These were special times for Ah Kwok, who would sit at the pond and eat lychees, peeled by his *Bobo*, his grandmother, while *Kongkong* fed his fish and cracked open lychees by precise applications of his teeth. As June gave way to July, it was time for the little red fruit *longyan*, the luscious 'dragon's eye'. Fruit was more than a seasonal aspect of life for Ah Kwok; it meant being at the core of the family. That very morning, as the three men of the family had said goodbye to *Bobo* and Ah Kwok's mother, *Bobo* had laughingly said that she hoped to see Ah Kwok in time for pineapple season in October or, at the latest, a month later when Sha Kiu's bananas would ripen and put to shame for yet another year those shrivelled-up excuses for a fruit that they grew over in Ma Kiu. Ah Kwok had known it was going to be wrenching to leave, but this reminder of the bounty of summer had brought a liquidity to his eyes and a tremble to his voice.

Of course he and his father Langshi would return, with gifts for *Mama*, *Bobo* and *Kongkong*, as well as for Li Mudan, the pretty ten-year-old daughter of their neighbours, the Lis, and her brother Ni Qiu. Parting from his two great companions earlier in the morning had scarcely been easier for Ah Kwok than bidding farewell to his mother and grandmother. Ah Kwok loved Mudan's daring, her easy laughter and smiling face, the last reflecting the beauty of her *ming* name, her personal and familiar name, which was Peony in English. And as for Ni Qiu: the twelve-year-old boy had been named, daringly but not irreverently, after Confucius's original first name, Ni Qiu being the hill on which the great philosopher's parents had prayed for a son. Childless after seven years, the Lis of Sha Kiu had climbed the hill overlooking their valley, the same one on which Ah Kwok's grandfather had just called to him, and entreated the gods for a child. Ten months later a boy was born to them and they could not resist giving him the *ming* Ni Qiu, the more so as only family and close friends call people by their *ming*. Like Confucius, whose public or 'style' name was Zhong Ni, the Ni Qiu from Sha Kiu had another name, Ah Wa.

'My boy, *lai ni-shue*,' his grandfather called again. 'Come here.' Snapping out of his reverie, Ah Kwok turned to the old man. Tian had set down the trunk containing Ah Kwok's possessions, a weight that he had shouldered with the ease born of a lifetime's hard work. He had carried it with a mixture of willingness and morbidity, for maybe it would be the last direct service he rendered his grandson. But it was certain that the time for goodbye was upon them. 'Remember this proverb above others always, and live by it,' Tian said to Ah Kwok. 'Respect and cherish written words.' Then, from the recesses of his frayed cloth knapsack, Tian withdrew two objects. First, he placed a book in his grandson's hands. 'This is *Shiji*, the history book written by Sima-Qian, who lived more than 2 000 years ago, during the Han Dynasty. As you know, it is the early history of "All Under Heaven", and our people have loved and cherished it since it was first printed, some decades after Sima-Qian died. In it you will find as well scores of the proverbs that mark our everyday speech. Being familiar with those is important not only for cultured conversation but because their apt use will distinguish you as a person of learning and wisdom.'

'*Toh tse*,' Ah Kwok replied, thanking his grandfather. He had listened, rapt, to his grandfather and father reading from *The Historical Record*, and now he had his very own copy. Emperors and assassins, princes and kings waging war, cunning eunuchs and wily ministers hatching court intrigues, murders, suicides, great physicians – *Shiji* was an anthology of deeds and gallery of villains and heroes to captivate anyone's imagination. But Ah Kwok had learnt also that beneath its bloody surface, the book was a distillation of past experience, expressed in instructive and eloquent maxims that guided one's way in the present and the future.

The second gift was a red silk cord. 'This cord will bind you in Namfeechow to us in Chung-kwok,' said Tian. 'It symbolises holding kin together. It is a lifeline to your family that will never break. It will bring you back again. Take care, Ah Kwok.' At this, the tears that the young boy had held at bay all day came on like a sudden tide. Sobbing, he grabbed his grandfather's thin but wiry waist and clung on, hoping to fight the rising foreboding that this voyage would reduce him to being merely a vagrant in a foreign land. Tian gently tilted the burrowing head away from his chest and brushed away the boy's tears. 'They say there are bananas yellow and bursting with taste where you are going. You will find many other things to remind you of home. And you must not forget that wherever in the world you are and will be, Sha Kiu will always be your old family home. It cannot be otherwise, for here you have spent the first years of your young life. No village, no town, no city can take its place. Sha Kiu has your heart and you have its, forever.' Ah Kwok forced himself to smile, and nodded. Then he stepped back from the encircling arms and their comforting folds of silk and began unclasping the hasps of the wooden trunk, to store his precious gifts.

Turning to Langshi, Tian said, 'Remember this boy is worth educating.' It was an appeal and an instruction. Langshi nodded, as determined as dutiful, and Tian nodded at him solemnly, before placing his hands firmly on Ah Kwok's shoulders. A far-away look held in the old man's eyes, as though it were the future he could see and not the undulations of the way to the market town on the river to which Langshi and Ah Kwok were headed. Perhaps Langshi guessed what was going through his father's mind at that moment. Tian was seemingly robust and healthy, but Langshi had in recent seasons noticed an infinitesimal decline as the old man tended his fish and helped with rice growing. To feed the fish, snails and weeds had to be gathered from the streams, river and small lake east of the village. Collecting weeds was more onerous than it sounded, as the best growths, which Tian insisted on as stock food, grew under four or five feet of water, and were situated some distance from the lakeshore. Last summer the old man had harvested fewer weeds, his capacity to dive in and stay under water not what it used to be. Langshi had managed to help from time to time, and the fish had in the end been well fed, but what would happen this summer? And what of the staple of life? He would not be there to help his father to pick rice seedlings, harvest the rice and prepare the fields anew. Who would dig the ditches without which the crop would be ruined?

'*Ngoh kam-maan tsoi lai*,' announced Tian. He was going back to the village. On the way down, he would be able to see his son and grandson for
quite a while, but when the track into the valley dipped into the long
zigzag, they would be out of sight.

'*M-ho hui*,' Ah Kwok blurted out, imploring him not to go.

'*Ngoh hui faan-kung*,' Tian said gently, indicating he was going to work.
'The pond needs to be cleaned, and I want to look at the lychee tree. And
you two have a long way before you. Your father has told me you'll stop
at a good inn and eat some *char siu* with rice, and lettuce soup. You have
never had *char siu*, a wonderful honeyed roast pork, so already you have
much to look forward to. Now go, boy, and make me proud with stories
of your doings in a new place.' Quickly, before another round of tears
could begin, Tian spun on his heel and walked off.

'Grandfather!' shouted Ah Kwok. But the white-robed figure would
not be halted. As Langshi held his son back, Tian strode away. Ah Kwok
was howling now, gusts of tears buffeting his cheeks. When Tian was a
few hundred yards away, he turned quickly and stood for the briefest of
moments, his right hand held palm upwards, commanding the boy to stop
the commotion, but also imparting a benediction and a goodbye. As
quickly, he turned around and resumed his march homewards.

Despite the azure day, Ah Kwok felt himself pitched into darkness. He
had known this moment would come and had prepared himself for
months, ever since the letter from abroad had arrived at the village. But
anticipation of parting is one thing, the reality of separation quite another. At first blush the chance to go to Kum Saan was very exciting: a city
of gold, where everything was new and anything possible. As his father,
mother and grandparents discussed the venture, Ah Kwok was swept
along by their enthusiasm and sense of possibility. It would be an adventure for the boy, the adults concurred; an opportunity to see some of
China and a whole new world too. Surely it would stand him in good
stead. Nor were he and Langshi going forever. This would be a short-
term working excursion, to a land not so distant as America. Best of all,
it was at the invitation of the community elders in this Johannesburg, and
Langshi would be the first properly trained herbalist to practise among
the Chinese there.

Mastering himself, Ah Kwok said, 'Father, I will be all right now.' He untangled himself from Langshi and picked up the red silk cord from the top of the trunk. A hand at each end, he stretched the cord to its full length, then relaxed his arms, bringing his hands together, then extended them once more. Hands apart, hands together, separated, joined – he began to understand the meaning of the cord and was soothed by the rhythmic motion of his hands. As he held the silk, Ah Kwok had a sudden image of his grandmother plucking mulberry leaves and placing tiny silkworm eggs on them. When they hatched, tiny black worms emerged and began nibbling at the leaves. As the silkworms grew, so did the sound of their eating. Fatter and fatter and whiter and whiter they grew (though he loved best the two-tone, black-banded tiger worms) until one day they spun themselves into cocoons from which the fine and lustrous silk was coaxed. These recollections, so immediate and full, competed with the very real image of his grandfather receding as he returned to Sha Kiu. Raising the extended cord above his head, Ah Kwok whispered a goodbye to the speck of brilliant white among the greens and browns of the surrounding hillsides. Slowly he lowered his hands, folded the cord and placed it reverently in the trunk. Looking up, he caught his father smiling approvingly.

'Let us continue, Ah Kwok. The road is long and we have many *li* to walk before we can sleep.' Langshi bent over his son's luggage, scooped it off the ground and lowered it on to the boy's shoulders. Ah Kwok gasped at the sudden weight. It astonished him to think his grandfather had managed this bulk so easily. Glancing across at his father, he grimaced and said, '*Kongkong* is very strong.'

'Yes, he is,' Langshi replied, suppressing his own unease about his father's diminished vigour. 'So must we be on this walk, but at least a fine *faan tan kuun* awaits us, an inn that serves excellent *char siu* and refreshing lettuce soup. Come, let us go on and I will tell you about the ferry of the Tanka people and of Canton and Kum Saan.'

Two
Kwangtung province, southern China, 1911

Langshi had the upright bearing of his father, unusual among rural Chinese, whose labours tended to encourage a hunched and beetling ambulatory style. His hands did not have the weathered and gnarled look of Tian's, however, for they were employed in a vocation that dictated subtle manual work. From an early age, Langshi had shown an interest in the herbal medicines his mother Andong used whenever one of the family was unwell. It was fitting that hers were the healing hands in their home, for her name stood for peace (An) and flowing (dong). But his *Mama*'s knowledge was limited and eventually there were questions she could not answer. At about that time, a young man in the neighbouring hamlet of Ma Kiu set up as a herbalist, having returned from an apprenticeship in the northern mountains with a Taoist hermit. Although the two villages had a history of rivalry, on occasion spilling over into enmity, the young Langshi found an affable teacher in Low Bun Kee, who had studied the life of Bian Jue, the celebrated physician whose life story is related in *Shiji*. It was Bian Jue who employed acupuncture to bring a man in a coma back to consciousness. And it was he who developed diagnostic approaches such as taking the pulse, and noting the complexion of the face and condition of the tongue.

Langshi learnt much about medicine and pharmacology during his three years with his master. Each day he would walk the seven *li* from Sha Kiu to Ma Kiu, looking out for herbs, leaves, roots and fruits used in the preparation of traditional remedies. He watched the older man select and chop up stems and roots until he was entrusted with such tasks. Mortar and pestle became familiar to Langshi, as did the sensitive scale that measured the tiniest quantities with accuracy. He learnt the causes of illnesses, how to diagnose them, and their remedies. Low Bun Kee showed him

15

how to read health from the pulse, and what to look for in the texture and colour of the tongue. Chopping, grinding and weighing each prescription's many ingredients was delicate and demanding work, calling for nimble fingers and sure hands. This was manual labour far removed from the toil of the fields. Langshi's hands did not broaden and thicken but retained their slimness and a certain smoothness. Tian and Andong were pleased that their first-born would not be a peasant farmer.

So too was Soi Sien, whose family lived on the eastern fringes of Sha Kiu, near the lake. Five years younger than Langshi, Soi Sien had been bound to him for much of her short life. It had begun when, at the age of six, she had wandered off on her own down to the lake. Her parents, like the rest of the village, were gathering the rice crop on the steep terraces that surrounded the village. The bright green of the young rice plants had given way to straw yellow, the sign that the grains were full and firm and ready to be harvested. Lines of bamboo-hatted villagers advanced steadily through the paddy fields, their sickles slicing off the drooping, ripe heads of the plants. Soi Sien played at the water's edge, looking at her reflection as it blurred and distorted each time she dropped a stone into the shallows. The cool nibbling at her toes delighted her and she decided to wade in a little more, up to her knees. First, she leaned over to hitch up her light cotton dress so that it would not get wet. In that instant, the soft shelving mud under her feet gave way and she fell, head first, into the dark blue water. Soi Sien had opened her mouth to scream, but that had the effect only of forcing water into her lungs and turning her view of the world into an opaque rippling high above her. Rays of light intersected the water and fell towards her, but whatever warmth they held did not reach Soi Sien. Thrashing around, she found the world of light and air receding and then, suddenly, all was blackness.

In the paddy fields, drained of water to enable the harvesting, there was hard, hot work on the go. As the sun arced towards its noonday zenith, thirst became more insistent. Pouring the last of the water from their bamboo bucket, Tian offered it around his family harvesting group, and then sent Langshi to the lakeshore to draw more. Relieved to be heading for the shady fringes of the lake and the refreshing touch of its lapping waters, the boy raced along the rows of rice, clambered up the dike wall and set off uphill on his errand. As he emerged from the reeds that edged the lake at that point, he was confronted by the sight of a girl child drifting face down on the water's placid surface. Langshi dropped the bucket and dived into the water. As he doggy-paddled towards the body, however, he was seized by a terrible fear. Almost recoiling in the water, he remembered that baby girls were sometimes drowned, because families prized boys. Girls were just mouths to feed, not worthy of educating and an expense when it came to dowries and marriage. At other times, mothers left their newborn daughters in the forest, where predators or exposure, the gentler form of nature, would take the infants' lives. Panicked now, Langshi was on the point of turning back but his inelegant swimming style had been too effective and the next stroke of his right hand thudded not into water but the inert body he had seen. Gasping, he looked down and saw instantly that this was no infant, and then his mind chided him sharply: hurry, perhaps she is still alive. Turning her over, he recognised beneath the greyish-blue pallor seeping into the features the familiar face of Soi Sien. Propping her up on his outstretched arms, Tian kicked out behind him and made for the shore, struggling to keep both their heads above water. Time and distance seemed to elongate but after what was actually less than a minute, Tian felt sticky mud against his knees. Bracing himself, he rose out of the water, slipped back a little and then, in two strides, was on solid ground at last.

'Father! Help! Soi Sien is filled with water! Help!' he shouted as he raced downhill towards the fields. As Langshi's words reached them, the harvesters dropped their sickles and sprinted to meet him. In the frantic bounding that marked Langshi's progress, Soi Sien was jolted into retching consciousness, her lungs giving up the unwelcome water that had flooded them. It was from that moment of awakening that Soi Sien was indebted to Langshi. In truth, it was from then on that she was in love with him. For his part, Langshi was very fond of Soi Sien and of her name, which aptly – and eerily too, he thought – connoted a fragrant and beautiful white water flower.

Langshi remembered that long-ago moment as he walked ever farther from Soi Sien and their home. It was both comforting and saddening to recollect their life together, their partnership that would have to endure this break in the cause of future prosperity.

'Father, how many *li* before we reach the inn?' asked Ah Kwok, abruptly bringing Langshi back into the present, and the glare of the early afternoon sun.

'Another twelve *li* my boy, but two travellers always shorten a walk and the road will seem shorter yet if I tell you about the Tanka people. We will see them later on this journey and have occasion to be served by their mighty strength. They live on boats. It is said they are born, live and die without ever putting a foot on land. When we reach the river flowing north, we will see their rafts and houseboats. In Canton, they ferry passengers from the shore to the ships waiting to sail down the estuary to the sea. What makes them special is the way they do this. In the shallows, near the dock, the strongest men pull the ferry by ropes crossed over their shoulders. From the back, other Tanka men and women push the vessel out into the stream. Sometimes you will see women with infants on their backs, strapped into wooden harnesses that can keep the young ones afloat in case they are torn free from their mothers. When the craft is in deeper water, those in front continue pulling, by swimming ahead of it, with those ropes biting into the skin of their backs. It is hard work, but bitter in winter, when it is not unusual for some of these boat people to die from colds and other ailments.'

'Father, if there is sickness among these river people every winter, why then do we not go there to live and work? We would not be very far from *Kongkong* and *Bobo* and we could be together as a family – you, *Mama* and me. Please, *foo t'san*, why not?'

'These people are very poor. They live from what the river or sea provides. There is little money for medicine. If we were to live among them, we would go hungry too. You must know that we are fortunate. There is the rice, fruit and grandfather's carp. Although we have little, we have never starved: not to have known extreme hunger is a blessing that very few people, whether they live under heaven or in other lands, can claim.

'You and I are going to this land far to the west so that I can work among our people there, who have much more money than we here back home. The goldfields in Namfeechow are the richest in the world, they say. They are new and more and more veins of gold are being found all the time. To such a place many thousands will come, much money will be in circulation and our people will slowly be able to sustain themselves better and better.

'For the present, we *T'ong yan* will live close by and support each other. One day, that will change. But by then we will be back home, you and I. You will be in Peking sitting your examinations for the imperial administration and I will be passing on my knowledge of medicine to a younger man. In the evenings your mother and I will think of you and remember your grandfather, if he is not with us then. All of this will be possible because of the few years we will spend across the sea.'

Ah Kwok did not ask another question, for by now the weight of the trunk was beginning to tell. The green canvas that covered the wood and its bamboo struts was dark and wet with the young boy's sweat. His neck and back were sodden, and his blue shirt clung to his body. Passing breezes sent a chill through Ah Kwok as they cooled the films of perspiration coating his body. Luckily it was not summer, when the humidity that made the Sha Kiu bananas such fine eating tormented the villagers with its clamminess. Taxing Ah Kwok further was the footpath, which began to drop steeply down the hill. Narrower now, the way was a twisting surface of loose stones and slippery sand, unpleasantly yielding to each footfall. At least, he consoled himself, the thick vegetation that ran down the hillside would catch him if he fell off the track. Breathing heavily, he followed his father down another incline, each step taking him farther from home, *Mama*, *Bobo*, Mudan and Ah Wa.

The three youngsters had planned many escapades for the summer. He and Ah Wa wanted to catch the long black river snakes and sell them at the local market. They had managed to get hold of a new sack, made of hemp, to store their sleek captives. Its rough surface felt reassuring and the two boys had been certain that it would bring them luck as they burrowed away at snake holes in the river bank with their long bamboo sticks. Ah Kwok thought he would buy Mudan some fabric for a new dress with the money made from selling the snakes to those in the food trade. The middlemen who haggled with Ah Wa and Ah Kwok would take their sinuous cargo to restaurants in market towns, where the snakes would be kept alive until chosen by a diner. Killed and skinned almost on the spot, the snake could be prepared in up to 30 different ways – no surprise, as the Cantonese had 50 ways to prepare chicken. But such entre-preneurial adventures would have to wait for another summer, and not even next year's, if his father's words were true. It seemed it would be many seasons before they would return, at least all the cycles of two whole years before Ah Kwok could look down on the mulberry trees and rice fields of home. But at this moment he was able to see only the trail, with its puffs of dust sent up by his father's feet.

Langshi moved ahead on the scrabbly pathway, checking his stride so that he was not too far in front of his son. He was worried about Tian, and concerned for Ah Kwok. It would not be easy for the boy to be away from his grandparents and mother; and perhaps it would be most difficult for him to be parted from his friends. Langshi had watched the easy com-panionship between the three grow into something more fundamental. At night he and Soi Sien had often spoken about the prospects of Mudan and Ah Kwok marrying, and of the boys being brothers-in-law. They had not raised the matter with the Lis, their neighbours, but it was a question that could not indefinitely be postponed. On a particularly cold night last win-ter, as Soi Sien enjoyed the warmth of their bed and the cosy partnership it implied, she had asked Langshi when the best time would be to broach the futures of Ah Kwok and Mudan with the Lis. Langshi was not averse to initiating discussions. Recalling their own courtship, he pointed out how fortunate he and Soi Sien had been, for not only had the arrange-ments between the families gone smoothly but they had been in love. To be enamoured of one's arranged spouse was a luxury, a boon unexpected and rare. It seemed that Ah Kwok and Mudan were blessed in the same way, for their friendship was as close to love as it is possible for an eleven-year-old boy and a ten-year-old girl to know. 'Tomorrow, after I have plucked elephant's ear fungus in the forest, I will go and speak to Mudan's parents,' Langshi declared. Soi Sien hugged her husband and curled con-tentedly against him, contemplating the bounty that the new day held.

On that next day, the letter from Kum Saan arrived, offering Langshi an opportunity unthought and undreamt. Langshi's cousin Ah Sin, the eld-est son of the brother in America that Tian was fondest of, had heard good things about this land of a newish gold rush. Wearied by life in one Gold Mountain, he was tempted by a new beginning in another. So he had set off from San Francisco, crossed Mei-kwok by rail and sailed first to England and thence to Durban in South Africa, where he arrived in early 1910. A hot and dry railway trip had brought him from the coast to the tents, shanties and score of buildings that were Johannesburg, on the Witwatersrand, the ridge of white waters. In a very short time – the letter said just over six months – Ah Sin had saved more money than in several years in San Francisco. Slowly his missive reached its purpose. Would Langshi, it asked, perhaps consider coming out to South Africa to provide sorely missed herbalist's skills to the community? It would, of course, be for a short while only, two or three years at most.

At first Langshi and Soi Sien were perturbed. Their happiness had been focused suddenly and sharply on the potential in Ah Kwok and Mudan's being married. Life in Sha Kiu was good for the extended family: there was food enough and more importantly, they had cultivated their minds with learning and their son was each month enhancing his reading ability by becoming familiar with new characters. Then again, could this be a chance to achieve their dreams of an early ease from the rigours of rural life? Perhaps, too, the idea of Ah Kwok entering government administration was misguided. After all, the boy would have to learn Mandarin, with its soft sounds and sing-song accent. 'Mind you,' Langshi pointed out, chortling for a while, 'it has only four tones to Cantonese's nine, so it should be half as hard to speak.'

'Don't joke,' Soi Sien said in reply. 'You have heard what happens when men go to the goldfields and railroads of America. You must remember the folk song of our province about the Gold Mountain of America:

"If you have a daughter, don't marry her to a Gold Mountain man.
Out of ten years, he will not be in bed for one.
The spider will spin webs on top of the bedposts,
While dust fully covers one side of the bed."

'If you go to this other Kum Saan, I may become one of those women. I do not want that. Not now, not at my age.'

'Come now,' Langshi replied, 'that will never happen. I love you too dearly to be away from home for long.'

'But why go at all?' she asked. 'Life here is livable, even though we cannot save much for the future. We will be all right. This province is fortunate, with its climate; we do not have the harshness of the north, the dryness of the west. And we have one another, we are a family: three generations in one village.'

'Yes, all that you say is true. But would it not be very fine if we could be at ease in old age? If we were able to sit back and savour time, not be its slave? You know well that here we cannot put aside anything substantial for the future, except husbanding the fish and seed for next year's catch and crop. In Kum Saan I will be able to save much — look at what Ah Sin has achieved in less than a year. The money he has made there may not enable him to retire a wealthy man in Namfeechow, but in Kwangtung, and especially in Sha Kiu, with such an amount he would be able to feel secure against all but war.

'If I work very hard for a short time, live frugally and set aside money to send home, soon we will have accumulated the wherewithal to live comfortably. We are growing older and in some years' time I may not be as hale and able to undertake demanding daily work of the sort that I am sure awaits me in this gold-prospecting place across the seas. So, release me and Ah Kwok for a few years. I promise that his studies will not be neglected. And above all I vow to return to you and Sha Kiu and to our life together, a life that will be the more satisfying for what I manage to do in the time away.'

Soi Sien was not convinced immediately by her husband's argument. But as winter wore on and the matter was discussed again and again, she came round to accepting that Langshi and Ah Kwok would be leaving in the spring. Eventually, as hints of spring drifted in the sharp morning air, she found herself comforted by Langshi's repeated and confident assurances. Any forebodings she still harboured she kept to herself, or confided to her mother-in-law as they went about the business of the house.

So, the decision was made that saw Langshi and Ah Kwok trudging down towards the river valley and the old wayfarer's inn at the base of the hill, where Ah Kwok's first taste of honeyed roast pork awaited.

THREE
Kwangtung province, southern China, 1911

As the inn came into view, Ah Kwok marvelled at the bustle of travellers, pack animals and livestock that thronged the clearing in front of the rectangular two-floored wooden building. There was a blur of low-slung life: pigs nuzzling the ground, chickens and geese sending up feathers and a cacophony from the crates in which they were being transported. In counterpoint to the clucks and cackles was raucous human conversation, punctuated by the strident word endings characteristic of Cantonese. You could tell merchants, travellers and peasants by their different manner of dress. Ah Kwok was accustomed to market days, but those had been near Sha Kiu, where the merchants were not as grand as those gathered at the inn. Here, a group of about four or five sat on facing benches around a table under the shade of a spreading tree, eating small dumplings and drinking tea. They were resplendent in light jackets of beautiful white cotton, fastened down the middle by wooden toggles on the right of the jacket which were passed through loops on the left. The cool ease of the merchants impressed Ah Kwok, all the more as his grimy shirt clung to him. He remembered, too, his frayed trousers and the well-worn rope that hitched them up and kept them in place, as he glanced appreciatively at the light but strong weave of the traders' cotton pants and their silk sashes.

'Ah Kwok, stop staring,' chided Langshi quietly. 'Come, let us find a place to leave our trunks and then order something to eat.'

The two made their way through the press of bodies human and animal, with a score of diverse smells assailing them. There was a whiff of farmyard faeces underfoot, subdued by the altogether more welcoming aromas issuing from within the inn. Once inside, the bustle without seemed almost calm in comparison, for here food was being consumed at

23

a rate that outstripped its production. Shouting was the order of this hot and steamy world, from the curses and demands emanating from the kitchen to the complaints and orders of the diners. It was not, Ah Kwok soon realised, that anyone was angry. Everyone was hungry and hurried and harried by being on the road; those not spending the night at the inn were eager to resume their journey as speedily as possible. Langshi observed the initial, slightly wide-eyed puzzlement of his son with amused empathy. He was pleased when after a further while, Ah Kwok remarked, 'Father, all here seem to be enjoying the noise. They like to make more noise themselves.'

Just then, Langshi called to a serving man nearing an adjacent table. When he came over, he asked, 'What does Sir want to eat, Sir?'

Langshi asked first for a cup of tea. He then ordered steamed rice, *char siu* and lettuce soup. 'And make it quick,' he ended, winking at Ah Kwok as he barked those final words. Never one to raise his voice, Langshi nonetheless was given occasionally to fitting in to his immediate sur-roundings. He wondered at that moment whether this Union of South Africa would be as easy to adapt to as Ah Sin made out in his letter. There it would not be a matter of barking out in Cantonese to expedite one's needs, but of learning the rules and regulations, protocols and customs of a foreign culture. And the language – but then maybe Ah Kwok could be relied on to master enough English to get them by. Of another language, Ah Sin had also written: it was, he said, descended from the tongue of Hoh-laan, Holland, and spoken by many of the whites in Kum Saan. There were many other languages still, those of the black people of the country, between which sounds Ah Sin could not yet distinguish.

During Langhsi's contemplation, Ah Kwok had been looking around at the food on the other tables. Much of it he recognised: white steamed buns filled with either pork, chicken or black-bean paste; clear-steamed fish; and mouthfuls of fish or pork wrapped in opaque white parcels shaped like a small squid with its tentacles cut off, all a-swim in delicious soup base. There were some dishes entirely new to him. Looking at steaming soups and odd shapes on plates, Ah Kwok recalled that he had heard that the Cantonese enjoyed wild cats, prepared in various ways. Particularly, Ah Kwok recalled something that Tian had once told him,

Ah Wa and Mudan about the ways that the masked palm civet was captured and used as one of the main ingredients in an expensive dish called
dragon-tiger-phoenix soup. 'There are no dragons or tigers any longer,'
Tian had sighed nostalgically, 'and of course the phoenix is a mythical
bird. But this civet, which has a white line running from the crown of its
head down to its snout, and white fur in its wide ears, is still with us and
on our tables. The rich people who eat this soup enjoy the shreds of civet
and of snake in it, and the whole is flavoured with petals from the
chrysanthemum flower.' Not wishing to spoil his appetite, Ah Kwok
thrust such stomach-churning recollections from his mind and glanced
around, hoping to fix on a dish of *char siu*. Sure enough, being borne
towards him, was a plate of such pork. Of all the things he spied, none
filled him with greater delight than this dish, which his father had promised and then ordered, and a preview of which he had from the sliced
pieces now placed on the next table. While it was by no means exotic
fare, Ah Kwok had never sampled pork at home. Meat was expensive and
the villagers could not afford to eat it regularly. But in his household it
was not so much necessary frugality as other priorities that had dictated
that whatever small amounts of money accumulated at the end of each
harvest went towards a new book. And there was also his grandmother's
love of pigs, a strange affection in a region renowned for devising numerous ways of preparing and eating animals. *Bobo's* attitudes meant that no
pork was consumed in their household and Ah Kwok could only listen
to Tian and Langshi talking of the delicacy and texture of the meat, and
of its quality of being both sweet and salty.

When their *char siu* arrived, Ah Kwok darted at the nearest piece with
his chopsticks. 'No! Do not ever forget your manners, whether hungry or
excited,' Langshi upbraided Ah Kwok. Then, softening, he chuckled and
added: 'This food will not run away. I hope that you will never develop a
taste for food that has to be eaten quickly because it is still alive. You will
have to depart far from our family's practices to be that way; and you will
have to be very rich, in which case it would be an abuse of your wealth.
But I am spoiling this experience for you: what does the pork taste like?'

Despite being checked in his enthusiastic lunge for the *char siu*, Ah
Kwok did not feel overly chided. And that first taste of the sweet and

tangy meat, with its tiny coverlets of fat topping each slice, was a revelation. He wondered out loud: 'Father, I am not certain if I will be able to resist eating pork ever again.' Then he picked up a second piece, and dropped it into his mouth.

'Well, we shan't tell your grandmother. In the letters we will send home, we will write that we are managing well enough on a diet of *dofu*, Chinese mushrooms and greens. I will relate that we are thriving on monk's food, that vegetarian dish that she loves so much. But this will be our secret – one I am sure your grandmother suspects but will play along with.'

The soup greens were crisp, having been sweated in hot oil and then added to the clear broth. They refreshed and revived father and son, but the deep weariness of an emotional day summoned them to the hard beds and dirty linen in their room upstairs from the dining area. Ah Kwok was repulsed by the greyish-brown excuse for a sheet that lay creased and uninvitingly on his pallet. 'What manner of people are these innkeepers, father, that they cannot keep their guestrooms clean?'

'Ah Kwok, we shall have to live with this, and not only here. You know that on the *Foh shuen*, the steamship, we are travelling steerage – on deck, open to the elements, the rain and wind of the skies, the fire of the sun. Things shall not be very sanitary there. This little room with its dirty beds is luxury before what is to come. So, perhaps remove the sheet and cover the straw mattress, which might be dirtier still, with your jacket. But sleep you must, for we have another long day before us, on the river, and it is one that you will, I think, enjoy better for being rested. Tomorrow we reach Lok Chung and sail with the Tanka people on a *T'eng-tsai*, a small boat, to Canton. Thereafter we make for Hong Kong and our passage to Kum Saan.'

Looking glumly again at the sheet, Ah Kwok followed his father's advice and withdrew from his wooden trunk a jacket of dark-blue cotton. He remembered watching how the fabric was warped on the loom and then the cross-threads of the weft woven in, and how the tailor who visited the village twice a year had cut and sewn this large, formless piece of cloth until, almost miraculously, it had sprung from his table as a jacket, with pockets inside and out, and a collar that fitted snugly around Ah

Kwok's neck. This pride of his wardrobe the boy placed reluctantly on the bed because it was his biggest garment and would cover the largest area, and shortly after lay down on it, thinking of summertime escapades to keep at bay the imagined horrors of the straw mattress and its smelly cover.

As he battled to fall into sleep, he thought how good it would have been to go on a last snake hunt with his friends, and imagining turned to dreaming.

It was a lazy, warm, sunny afternoon. The goats and water buffaloes had been fed, the fish attended to, the women were home from the rice fields and preparing supper for the evening, the men had gone into town for *yum cha*, the young girls were caring for the babies and the boys were plotting.

Ah Kwok, Ah Lai and Ah Sek were among the mulberry trees, three scruffy boys with short-cropped black hair, slim bodies clad in patched clothing so often mended that one could not tell what the original colour was.

'What shall we play?' asked Ah Lai.

'Skimming pebbles on the water,' answered Ah Sek.

No word from Ah Kwok, leader of the trio.

A silence.

All three boys stretched out on the tufts of grass under the giant mulberry tree.

A smile passed over Ah Kwok's face. His bright black, intelligent eyes lit up. '*Hei sun, hei sun* – get up, get up.'

'Move, move,' shouted Ah Kwok.

'What? What?' asked the other two.

'We are going to catch snakes,' said Ah Kwok.

'Snakes,' echoed Ah Lai, who was the cowardly one of the three.

'Yes. Snakes,' answered Ah Kwok.

The other boys drew closer to Ah Kwok. 'This is what we must do,' he said. 'You, Ah Lai, go home and get a large, strong bag. Be careful not to be seen by the old folk. And you, Ah Sek, smuggle some good matches from your mother's kitchen. Don't get caught. I am going to get bamboo and cut a stick to hold the snake's head.'

They separated and ran off to do Ah Kwok's bidding, gathering again at the mulberry tree when all the tools of their venture had been collected. There was a feeling of excitement but also of fear. Snakes were no joke. They were dangerous, and more so if they were cobras. And Ah Kwok had decided that a cobra it should be, because it would bring them a good price if captured.

The three went scouring for snake holes in the tall grass. They found rat holes, mole nests and empty holes where the residents had moved out. They were beginning to doubt that there were any cobras.

A shout from Ah Kwok. He had found a snake hole. 'But wait, we must find the exit as well,' he cautioned the other two. They searched through the long grass and at last found the exit. They would trap the snake if it tried to escape.

'Gather dry grass,' said Ah Kwok.

The three collected handfuls of pale grass strands, placed a good quantity in front of both holes and then lit the piles. They forced the burning tufts into the hole so that the smoke would draw into the nest. They went on fanning and soon there was a movement. This was the dangerous moment in the operation.

'Keep fanning,' yelled Ah Kwok. The other two speeded up the up-and-down motion of their hands. Ah Kwok grabbed the sack and told Ah Sek to hold it open. Ah Lai kept fanning the smoke, his face a study in panic.

Just then a snake poked its head out. King Cobra was large and splendid, and drunk from the smoke so that it seemed hardly able to see where it was. Ah Kwok grabbed the bamboo and neatly caught the snake's head under the fork at the end of the stick, shoved and held it down.

'Come! Come! Ah Lai — hold it! Grab the stick!' Trembling with fear, Ah Lai did as he was told.

'Ah Sek — hold open the bag.' Ah Kwok got hold of the snake's head and wrestled with its long body. From the narrow hood he confirmed that it was inded of the species which could grow up to eighteen feet in length. Grimacing as he got purchase on the dark coils, he hoped this particular example would not be as long. It was good the snake was doped by the smoke. Quickly, Ah Kwok pushed it into the bag and twisted the top. 'Rope, rope,' he shouted, almost at the same moment realising that he had not asked for any to be brought.

'Ah Lai, give up the cord of your trousers. Now,' commanded Ah Kwok. Winding the cord around the bunched top of the bag, Ah Kwok knotted it.

'What now?' asked Ah Sek and Ah Lai, the latter's eyes fixed on the writhing sack and evident fury of its unwilling occupant.

'We go to town,' said Ah Kwok.

So, the three dusty figures went walking along the sandy road until they reached town. They made their way through the maze of market stalls selling greens, fish, meat, fruit, ducks, honeyed roast pork, savoury buns and rice cakes. Seeing and smelling this array set their stomachs groaning with hunger.

'Where are we going?' asked Ah Sek.

'When are we going to get rid of the snake?' implored Ah Lai.

'Soon, soon,' answered Ah Kwok. 'I am looking for the medicine man.'

After some searching and asking for directions from the curious vendors, Ah Kwok found what he was seeking. Before approaching the stall, Ah Kwok first shook the bag vigorously, making the snake more agitated.

The medicine man was tall and strong, his hands and arms covered with a cream that was a special antidote to protect against snake bite.

'Good afternoon, sir,' said Ah Kwok.

'Good day little one. What do you want?'

'I have a small snake here and want to sell it,' came the reply.

'Let me see,' said the snake man.

He took the bag from Ah Kwok, opened it and thrust his hand into it, emerging with the hissing cobra. It had tried to bite him, but he was a very experienced catcher and besides, cobras moved less swiftly than other snakes. Ah Lai knew nothing of this, and so he marvelled at the calmness of the medicine man. But even had Ah Lai known that and also that the cobra's fangs are shorter than those of vipers and cannot fold back, and so do not deliver poison as readily, nothing would have persuaded him to get any nearer than the dozen or so feet that he had put between himself and the serpent.

'It's a lovely snake,' said Ah Kwok.

'So it is,' said the man, 'and very cheeky too. Did you perhaps shake the bag?'

'No, no, sir. It was like this all the way,' said Ah Kwok, looking around at the other boys for support. They nodded in agreement.

'It has been twisting and hissing all the way into town, sir,' said Ah Lai, his voice quavering.

'Will you buy it? It is a really fine snake for your medicine,' said Ah Kwok.

'What do you want for it?'

The three friends had no idea of the price they should set. There was a silence, elongated and twisting.

Then the medicine man suggested 20 *sien*.

'No, no,' said Ah Kwok. 'Much more.' He was thinking of all that could be bought, not for him but especially for his mother, who worked so hard.

'Well what then, little one?' asked the medicine man, amused by Ah Kwok's determination.

'Fifty *sien*.'

A pause.

'All right. Fifty *sien*. You drive a hard bargain.'

The snake man placed the cobra in a basket and paid Ah Kwok, a shadow of a smile playing about his face as he did so.

'*Chien, chien*, we have money, money, money,' chanted the three friends.

'What shall we buy?' Ah Lai and Ah Sek wondered.

'First, we'll have sweetmeats,' said Ah Kwok, heading for one of the stalls. They bought themselves some of these delicacies, shared out equally, and some juice squeezed from ripe lychees, for it was June and the hunt and subsequent walk had parched them.

'What with the rest of the money?' asked Ah Sek and Ah Lai.

'Food for the folk back home,' replied Ah Kwok.

Off they went to the roast duck vendor. They bought for three families, and each portion was neatly wrapped in banana leaves and tied with a strand of thick grass.

They reached Sha Kiu as the sun was going down. In Ah Kwok's house the rice had been cooked and his mother was boiling the soup. That was all supper would have consisted of. Ah Kwok came quietly into the kitchen and said, '*Mama*, here is food.'

She was surprised. Her grey eyes opened wide as she undid the banana leaves. '*Gnaap*. Oh heaven! Duck.'

'Yes, *Mama*, for you.'

'No,' she answered. 'We must share with the elders. They come first.' She divided the duck for Tian and Andong and also for First Uncle and family. There was a piece each for Ah Kwok, his father, mother and siblings.

It was a good meal.

FOUR
Pearl River, China, 1911

'Ah Kwok,' called the disembodied voice. There were mists obscuring the face of the speaker, and the sound seemed to be coming from a long distance away. 'Ah Kwok, wake up,' said the voice, and it was accompanied by a pressure on Ah Kwok's right shoulder that rocked him gently into the day.

'It is time to rise,' said Langshi. 'We will eat some *congee* and then set off for Lok Chung. Come boy, make haste, for I have allowed you to sleep until the latest moment.'

Wakefulness reminded Ah Kwok of the snake and the duck and dragged him into the grimy surrounds of the little room. As his nose discerned the sweet odour of the pallet, he snapped upright, swung his feet to the wooden floor and walked over to his trunk. Taking a fresh, much-mended shirt from the pile on the right, he drew it over his head, ran hands through his short hair and slapped himself a few times on either cheek.

'Father, when will we reach Canton? I cannot wait to see the Pearl River.'

'Before this day is out, well before,' answered Langshi. 'I would say that by early afternoon we shall be there. But now, let us be off.'

Shouldering their trunks, which seemed lighter this morning than when they had deposited them on the dusty floor the previous afternoon, Langshi and Ah Kwok made their way downstairs. Eddies of steam came from the kitchen, and also the bubbling sound of breakfast gruel, *congee*, being made ready.

Already the dining room was crackling with Cantonese, raucous and punctuated by the laughter of gruff, early-morning throats as yet not lubricated by tea. Two large bowls of soupy rice, topped with small pieces of meat and fish, were placed in front of Langshi and Ah Kwok by the innkeeper himself, who wished them good morning with a hearty '*T'so shan*' and then asked if they had slept well.

'*Ho ho*, very good,' said Langshi.

'And you go to Canton?' asked their host, grinning.

'Yes, and from there to Gold Mountain,' replied Langshi.

'Ahh … Kum Saan. But, say, which Gold Mountain you go to?'

'Kum Saan in Namfeechow, in Africa. Not the mountain in San Francisco.'

'Aha … but you know that sometimes people land in the wrong country, when they take passage and say only 'Kum Saan'. For there is also a gold mountain in Australia, in the place there they call Melbourne. I have heard it from a Hakka miner that he set off for this Namfeechow but was put on shore in Mei-kwok, America – ha, ha. Said to me it was not enough to say Kum Saan – you must say New Gold Mountain, Soen Kum Saan. Then you must watch which way the ship sails from Hong Kong. If it turns south-east, you are going to Australia; west, you are heading for Africa. So, sir, watch out for the correct way.' The two adults chortled over this story, but to Ah Kwok it was alarming in the extreme: he knew nothing about these other mountains of gold and distinctly preferred the familiarity of the barely known to that of the absolutely unknown.

'*M'koi,*' said Langshi, recovering from his chuckling and thanking the man for this useful information. As an afterthought, he noted to himself that it would not do to land on opposite sides of the world from their destination.

'*M'shai, m'shai,*' smiled the innkeeper, gesturing as well that Langshi shouldn't mention it. Then he looked at Ah Kwok and enquired about the relationship between the two guests.

'I am the son,' answered Ah Kwok.

'*Hai, hai.* What is your name?'

'My name is Ah Kwok.'

'Well, Ah Kwok, this old hostelry man who has never left Kwangtung province wishes you well on your travels. May you return home safe and sound, and rich too. Before you leave, come to the kitchen and I shall give you a little something, for the road ahead.'

'*Yau-sam* for the best wishes and *toh tse* for the food,' said Ah Kwok, demonstrating attentiveness to the niceties of etiquette and language, there being different thanks for help, good wishes and gifts.

'*M'shai, m'shai*,' said the innkeeper, smiling. Then, inclining his head to Langshi, he said: 'The old proverb sits on this one. He is a boy with potential, worth educating. Fare well in Soen Kum Saan.'

Within the hour, trunks a little weightier for the sausages the old man had given them, Langshi and Ah Kwok were on their way to the market town of Lok Chung. Ah Kwok asked his father about the Hakka, for the boy had heard of these guest people who lived in the mountainous north-eastern reaches of the province and were, it was said, not really Han Chinese at all.

'Ah, the Hakka are different. They are wanderers, regarded as refugees or strangers by other Chinese. You can even insult them by pronouncing "Hakka" in a particular way. The nicest way to think of them is as "guest people". It is strange that they have no kinder word to describe themselves than "foreigner", which I suppose is accurate, given their history of uprooting and settling, and uprooting again.'

Langshi stopped, put down his trunk and stretched, advising Ah Kwok to do the same. The sun was climbing higher and it was getting hotter. After fanning himself, Langshi swung the load back on his shoulders, strode forward and continued his history of the Hakka. 'It is said that more than 2 000 years ago, they travelled from the Yellow River in the north to Hunan province in the middle of China. One thousand years after that, they came in wave upon wave of migrations to our province. After the Manchus conquered China, other Hakka travelled further yet, down to the coast of Kwangtung, to Szechuan and the islands of Heinan and Taiwan. They were forced to live their name as refugees 50 years ago, during the Taiping Rebellion, a religious revolt against the Manchus led by a Hakka.

'At about the same time there was terrible fighting between the Hakka and the Cantonese. The latecomers pushed for land and water in areas where our people had lived for centuries. That was when the Hakka were called "guest bandits", during the time when feuds were waged everywhere in Kwangtung, thousands on both sides driven from their homes, villages and fields laid waste. At the end, the Hakka fell back to the north-east, where they live still in the area around Moiyean ... guests still but no longer bandits.'

'But what are they like as people?' Ah Kwok wanted to know.

A rueful smile played over Langshi's face. He paused to consider his answer, and if Ah Kwok had been able to see, he would have noticed a flash of anger light up his father's usually placid brown eyes. Sighing, Langshi began, 'They have different customs to us and we cannot under-stand each other's language.'

After another pause where his intake of breath was more to steady him-self than to fill his lungs, he continued. 'Their food contrasts with ours and their dress is dissimilar. But though they are so apart, they have some very good practices from which we should learn. First, they do not bind women's feet. The women help in the heavy farming by ploughing. Hakka women are regarded in a way that our women are not.'

'Will we see these wandering people, father?'

'Yes, because they too are making their way to Namfeechow. It is like-ly that some will be on the same passage as ours.'

As Langshi said this, they rounded a bend in the road and the first glimpse of the market town was afforded them. Down at the river's edge, Ah Kwok could make out a mass of boats with squat, elongated wooden structures on their decks. They were houseboats, the floating homes of the Tanka people. Canton and the Pei Kiang, the Pearl River, were not far off now, in distance or time. Excited, Ah Kwok quickened his stride and drew level with his father. 'The Tanka – we are here at last, father.'

'Almost,' said Langshi. Another half-hour's walk brought them to the crowded jetties along the river. Tied up alongside or plying the waters were numerous boats of several sizes and shapes. As he looked out over the river, Ah Kwok took in a cluttered view of barges, bamboo rafts and sampans with their single sails, stern oars and little shelters aft of the mast. The rafts ferried piles of cargo, a burden their lowness in the water suggested was too much.

'How unsafe the rafts seem,' Ah Kwok observed.

'Well, bamboo is very light, strong and buoyant,' Langshi began. From the tone of his voice, Ah Kwok knew he was in for another lesson, but how wonderful that, for once, the subject matter should be visible and tangible. As the two settled down on the jetty, the sun bounced a galaxy of light points off the water and it seemed to Ah Kwok that nothing could be as perfect as this moment.

'Our particular type of bamboo, *nan chu*, is a giant species that can grow to 80 feet in height. Its diameter can be as much as one foot. That width makes it ideal to lash together and form a floating surface that can support much weight yet float effortlessly. These rafts can navigate where deeper boats with bigger draughts cannot; they require only a hand's breadth of water in order to float.'

Explanations aside, the bamboo rafts remained a marvel to Ah Kwok. Generally two oarsmen steered and propelled them, and the mass and variety of their loads were remarkable. But their utility and durability, noble virtues, soon exerted less of a spell over Ah Kwok than the sampans. He knew *saam paan* meant 'three boards' but that was a literal description for something far more alluring. The jaunty curve of the sail, with its ribbed sections, the single or double scull at the stern that was twisted to move the boat on, and the small hutch on deck, roofed over with mats: what adventures such a craft promised! From his eyrie on the pier, Ah Kwok saw, huddled under the roof of a passing sampan, an old woman peering into an iron pot from which issued savoury aromas. Beyond her sat a younger woman, cradling a small child in her arms. Of such waterborne domesticity Ah Kwok had never dreamed and it seemed to him that the life of the Tanka, the boat people, was preferable by far to his own. Novelty being a quick seducer, Ah Kwok had no sooner fallen for the sampan when, far out on the river, he caught sight of a junk.

Its lateen sails full blown, the junk was speeding downstream towards the sea. Its profile presented itself to Ah Kwok for just a few minutes, but they were enough to set any young boy's mind to imagining a life on river and sea. Low at the bow, high at the stern, the junk presented a rakish silhouette against the water. Its sails had a gleam that fascinated Ah Kwok, and he asked his father why it was that they shimmered so.

'The sails are made from bamboo matting,' said Langshi. 'Indeed, the whole ship is made of bamboo. And, between the bow and stern are solid partitions running across the boat. That makes it very strong and means also that some of the compartments below deck are watertight.'

Ah Kwok vaguely heard his father but he was distracted, captivated by the cut of the boat's sails and its form. Then a curious-looking vessel attracted his attention because it had no mast or oars. Attached to the side of its hull were two large wooden wheels, much like those on the water mill at the Sha Kiu granary, each partially submerged in the water. Langshi explained that the paddle wheels were worked by treadmills in the hull. 'There is an ancient story that when Wang Chen-O's forces sailed up the Wei River to fight Ch'iang tribes, they went in paddle boats. Because everyone was concealed in the hull, the tribesmen thought they were being met by a ghost army.'

Ah Kwok, though engaged by the new craft, harboured no thoughts of its replacing the sleek and zigzagging junk in his affections. Harnessing the wind seemed so much more elegant than harnessing men up to the paddle wheels. One day, he thought, when he returned to Chung-kwok, he would buy a junk and sail it, just for pleasure.

A prickle of hunger reminded Langshi of the food the old innkeeper had given them. 'Come, my boy, let us eat those sausages – pork ones, I might add,' he said with a hint of a twinkle in his eye. Professionally, he was somewhat concerned that this sudden consumption of pork would affect Ah Kwok's metabolism, but he shrugged off such doubts as being more becoming of an old woman. That reasoning brought an image of his mother to mind, and her attitude – almost piety – towards pigs. Shaking his head, Langshi bit into the rich, fatty sausage. Ah Kwok followed, relishing the different taste from the *char siu*. He found this pork was not lean and clean on the palate, but thickly delicious.

All along the pier, boat people, fishermen and dock workers were taking their midday meal. On the barges tied up alongside the pier, families squatted on deck around small stoves that burnt twigs and peat, providing enough fire to fry or steam whatever food had been gathered. Fish and freshwater crab were the staples of river dwellers. Farther out on the Pearl River delta, near the sea, shellfish and seaweed graced dishes whose ingredients were finely sliced and diced to ensure that many hungry mouths would be fed from meagre quantities.

Sampans too were floating kitchens at this hour: rice and fish steaming, the occasional whiff of soya sauce lacing the air and, every now and then, the suggestion of oyster sauce or the sharp intrusion of pungent fish sauce. A haze of grey hung over the water, the collective cloud from hundreds of pots and scores of woks, and it bore with it the salty, sweet, sour and tangy traces that formed the essence of Cantonese cooking.

'Father, when do we sail for Canton?' Ah Kwok asked, eager to be off the river front and on the water itself.

'We must make our way down the pier and towards the larger boats. We will find a fisherman heading towards the city in his sampan or perhaps a transport junk. Come.'

Some 50 yards along, Langshi stopped opposite a fisherman's sampan. The man was separating his haul into wicker baskets, the fish sliding easily from his hands and plopping one upon the other. Their eyes were cruelly glazed over, thought Ah Kwok, and in that moment a remembrance came of Tian scooping up a fat, dark brown carp from the pond and rapping it sharply on the back of the neck to kill it. No sooner dead, it was scaled and gutted. Within minutes, *Bobo* was rubbing the insides with salt and sesame oil. Then she chopped off the heads of large spring onions, placed those in a dish and put the fish on top. In turn the fish dish was placed in a steamer, beginning its transformation to clear-steamed fish. There were other operations, additions and complementary sauces that were fried quickly in a sizzling-hot wok and then poured over the fish when it was perfectly steamed, but Ah Kwok could not remember that part of the process exactly.

'Where are you sailing?' asked Langshi of the fisherman. He was going to Canton, the man replied. His boat was empty save for himself and his poor catch, which he hoped to sell in the city for a better price than here in the market town. He would be sailing shortly, within a quarter of an hour, if the two of them were bound that way. He asked if Langshi had any money. Langshi confirmed that he did indeed.

'*Yau yung*,' the man shot back; it was useful that they had. The fare would not be much; he could see that they were from a village and not the town, and so he would not charge his usual rate. As it turned out, his fare was somewhat on the high side, said Langshi. Surely the fisherman, evidently a man of some means, could lessen his price a little, for country bumpkins?

'*Ho ho, ho ho*, very good: you bargain with my conscience. And I suppose you want me to take pity on the boy, in his faded shirt? I'll wager that the trunk that he is sitting on contains some fine silk shirts, brocaded to boot.' Just as Langshi was about to retort, the fisherman's mean, narrow face opened out into a wide smile. The harshly furrowed lines seemed to dissolve and he lost the salt-whipped coarseness of his skin in the baby-like set that his face now assumed. 'Come aboard, come aboard, *hai, hai*, we'll come to an agreement. I'll wager the boy is keen to feel the wind whipping the sails and the water under the prow. Come, come, off to Canton we go.'

Relieved by this turn of events, all Langshi could do was utter '*m'koi*' several times and clamber aboard with his trunk after helping Ah Kwok down into the boat. They stowed their trunks on the side of the sampan opposite the fish baskets and settled down to watch the practised ease of the boatman. Sculling in relaxed fashion, he kept up a flow of chatter and a stream of questions about Sha Kiu and Ma Kiu, Kum Saan and Namfeechow. It was, in its relentless inquisitiveness – and cheerfulness, it must be granted – like wooden staff-fighting practice: thrust and response, over and over. But Langshi enjoyed Ah Biu's company and often in the three hours of their little cruise up river they laughed loud and long.

Especially amusing was the story of a recently returned Gold Mountain man, Wing Pak Fah. This very same Ah Pak had been a Ma Kiu contemporary of Langshi. Over the years, they had been living proof of the enduring nature of the inter-village rivalry and its slogan, 'Sha Kiu, Ma Kiu, *da kiu*' – literally, 'Sha Kiu, Ma Kiu, Fight'. Even when Langshi was studying herbalism under Low Bun Kee, the immature Ah Pak sprang any number of malicious tricks on Langshi. There was, of course, no personal reason for this vendetta: it was simply a case of Sha Kiu, Ma Kiu, *da kiu*. And Langshi was by no means blameless, choosing always to retaliate on a grand scale after the accumulation of several little guerilla onslaughts on his person and dignity. The worst revenge Langshi exacted on Ah Pak was to contrive the collapse of the toilet on which the Ma Kiu man was suffering the pangs of terrible diarrhoea, a stomach complaint not unrelated, it should be added, to the perfectly ripened basket of dragon's eye fruit that had somehow fetched up on the threshold of Ah Pak's home and which he had gorged on, it being early July and the beginning of the season for the delectable *longyan*.

What had happened to Ah Pak, the fisherman recounted, was this. He had tired of the grind of farming and determined instead to make a fortune abroad, in the gold fields of San Francisco. It was Ah Biu who had ferried Ah Pak to Canton, some three or four years before, and heard all his dreams of gold. And in the way that life has of fashioning coincidence, it was Ah Biu who brought Ah Pak – less talkative and a good deal more sombre – back from Canton, just three months ago. The unfortunate Ma Kiu man had never made it to California. He had landed on the south-eastern hook of Australia, at Melbourne, after a voyage that was a good deal shorter than he had been told the passage to America entailed. Believing at first that the ship was only putting in to a port of call, Ah Pak was terrified to discover that this was its destination. True, another Chinese told him, there was a Gold Mountain here, but it was different from the old Gold Mountain of San Francisco: this was New Gold Mountain; surely Ah Pak had been told of the difference and knew to which place of gold he was headed? Desolate, Ah Pak held out for a long while but these were not the circumstances that he had dreamt of, for not one of the Ma Kiu boys he thought to meet up with was there. Langshi did not contain his mirth at this tale, but marked down again mentally to make sure of securing berths on a ship sailing for the correct gold mountain: the other new one, in Namfeechow.

As the little craft of three boards with its complement of three drew up in the Pearl River delta, it seemed to Ah Kwok that the air and the light itself had changed. Lush, semi-tropical vegetation lined the banks of the river, which was crisscrossed by tributaries and countless man-made waterways. Ah Kwok was right about the change he felt, for the Tropic of Cancer made its line just north of the city. The vast network of water and greenery that was the delta had at its northern corner the city of Canton, upstream from its port and framed yet further to the north by the White Cloud Hills.

As the river traffic increased, Ah Biu ducked his head into the matted cabin and emerged with a squat bottle and three small glasses. 'To toast you on your way,' he explained, pouring a watery, colourless liquid into each.

'I'm not sure about the boy,' said Langshi, but Ah Biu would have no shirking.

'He goes a boy, he will return a man. He must drink to that, and to Chung-kwok. *Yum seng!*' Ah Biu drained the little tumbler, wiped his lips with the back of his hand and beamed at Ah Kwok. Langshi had followed the fisherman in toasting success and victory in life and Ah Kwok had emulated his father with ease. But now came the moment of realisation. The innocent-looking liquid had started a fire that began at his throat and scorched its way down, concentrating finally in a raging blaze in the pit of his stomach. Had he been able to see it, he would have noticed that his face had reddened furiously; still, he soon had more than an intimation of that as his cheeks also seemed to be alight. Worst, his throat would not allow the passage of words. Ah Kwok wanted to ask his father if he would be all right but could not. Sensing the question, Ah Biu laughed sympathetically and assured Ah Kwok that he would not die; that eventually he would regain his voice; and that this was the finest *sam-shiu* liquor: a triple-distilled alcohol made from fermented rice. Already, added the boatman, Ah Kwok was on the way to manhood, with this powerful tot consumed.

Leaning against the side of the boat to steady himself, Ah Kwok looked at the city of Canton. Most of it stood on the north bank, where he saw the remains of walls that were being pulled down, and an area of crowded houses and narrow streets that were an island surrounded by space and bright new structures and settlements. 'That part, boy, is the old city,' said Ah Biu. 'They are destroying it to make way for these wide avenues. Who knows, soon they will want to move us boat people too.' Shaking his head, Ah Biu adjusted the scull oar and the boat twitched gently towards the pier. Just before they fetched up near the wooden dock, the old fisherman said, 'Don't forget what they say about this place: "Everything new comes from Canton."' Steadying the sampan, he threw a rope to a young boy above, waiting to moor the boat.

Ah Biu turned to his two passengers. 'I never go on shore. Tanka people pride themselves on not setting foot on land. So we part here. *Ts'ing ts'ing*. And remember – to success!'

'*Ts'ing ts'ing*,' Langshi and Ah Kwok chorused in goodbye. Then they climbed up from the sampan and on to the ancient timbers of the dock, and deposited their trunks with the comforting timbre of wood on wood.

FIVE
Canton, China, 1911

Never before had Ah Kwok seen as many people, been surrounded by as many smells and kinetic colours. As he and Langshi made their way into the crowded city, attractions competed with one another. A woman jostled past Ah Kwok, an infant strapped to her back in a red, embroidered baby-sling. Street sellers called out their fare: pickled vegetables here, sugar cane there, Cantonese sausage over at the moon gate off which ran a cobbled alley lined by rows and rows of washing hung out to dry.

'Paper silhouettes! Have your profile to keep! Your silhouette cut in paper, in just three minutes!'

'*Yum cha*! *Yum cha*! Finest tea-house food in Canton! Pork *bao*, chicken pies, black-bean paste *bao*! *Kai dan ko*! Don't have to be marrying to sample our legendary egg-cake! Freshly steamed *kai dan ko* here!'

Old men walked along together, wearing wide, baggy trousers of bright blue, stopping now and then to look in at speciality food shops or tea houses. Younger men hurried by, some carrying wicker baskets on their backs, loaded with food or cloth, fruit or bags of rice. Nothing was still or silent; to Ah Kwok it was as if the whole world had become a whirligig, moving to the accompaniment of atonal noises and sudden bursts of sound.

Langshi asked several times for the location of the steamship offices but despite the enthusiastic directions received, he and Ah Kwok seemed no nearer their destination than when they had climbed off the sampan and on to the pier a few hours before. Night was drawing near, so Langshi thought it best to find a room and then go out for a meal – the last decent one, he warned Ah Kwok, for many weeks. Searching for quarters, they stuck to the old, crooked lanes of Canton and the river-hugging areas where the boat people lived. Had Ah Kwok returned ten years later, he would have been astounded by the changes, and even more so after 25 years. In 1921, the Cantonese demolished the walls on the north bank of the river, and laid wide boulevards. By the 1930s, cars were an everyday part of life and the glimmerings of the development of the south bank of the Pearl River had begun. In decades, this new part of the city had become its commercial heart and housing projects were begun for the boat people. The township that had sprung up on the north bank around 860B.C. had changed orientation completely, but one thing still applied: the new always came from Canton. What the old fisherman had been criticising was but a small, ad hoc development to accommodate yet more Western trading concerns; a hint of the massive changes to come, and imbued with prescience by an old sailor.

At the intersection of a large thoroughfare, Langshi turned right, and they passed through another moon gate and down a lane lit by flickering, smoky lamps. All along, there were places of accommodation, and halfway up Langshi ducked in at a low doorway. 'Are there any rooms to let?' he asked the youth at the counter.

'Yes, there is one, on the second floor,' came the reply.

Mindful of Ah Kwok's squeamishness the night before, but even more conscious of the pittance he had in reserve to see them through the voyage to South Africa and the early costs there, Langshi paused a while before asking to have a look at the room. Beggars such as they could not really afford to be choosy, but who knew what horrors lurked in the rooms of a down-at-heel inn in such a large city.

Following the boy upstairs, they looked into a clean enough room, with two low beds. There did not seem to be any unpleasant odours, so when the boy asked '*Ni-kaan ho m ho ne?*' – is this one all right? – Langshi said it was.

Then Langshi handed over the night's rent in advance, weighing his purse as he did so and mentally calculating what remained of the travelling allowance that had been sent from Namfeechow, an advance against future services he would render. He would treat Ah Kwok to typical Cantonese dishes for dinner, but after that it would be a daily eking out of the food they had brought with them in their trunks. On the voyage, reflected Langshi, they would have an unvaried diet of *naam yu*, a soya-based food, flavoured with fish and a hint of chilli, that they would eat a little of each day with rice. Tonight, though, they should celebrate the easy passage so far.

So Langshi and Ah Kwok stepped out into the humid early spring of a Canton evening and made their way to the restaurant district nearest the inn. At a crowded establishment, the Ya Gai, they wedged themselves between a table of a dozen young men and women and a party of four sailors. Over the hubbub, Langshi ordered a portion of One-Hundred-Flower Chicken, steak in oyster sauce, rice and tea. While they waited, the temptation to teach Ah Kwok something of the history of Canton was irresistible. Ah Kwok always dreaded these didactic moments, when his father would become a 'teach'. After Langshi died, and the lessons were memories rather than vivid recitations of knowledge, lore and learning, Ah Kwok cursed himself for not listening properly, or for believing arrogantly that he would always remember this tale or that hero or those bits of history because they had so often been recounted by his father.

In the lively, smoke-filled Ya Gai — a name that later became famous among Canton's eateries — Langshi was in full swing. 'Legend places the city's founding after a great flood. After the rains, the sky produced something more extraordinary: five sages, each mounted on a goat that held a stalk of rice in its mouth. The wise men instructed the people to live in peace and prosperity and they gave them the rice stalks, the basis for future well-being. Having given the people the seeds of their tomorrows, the sages faded from view as the waters subsided to allow for the planting of the rice. But the goats turned to stone and were revered for countless years in the Temple of the Five Sages, one of the many shrines in Canton that are no longer. Even today, though, the city is known also by names conferred by the legend: it may be called Goat City, Five Goat City or Rice Grain City.'

This was a wonderful story, and one that Ah Kwok never forgot. At that instant, however, their food was brought to the table and the young boy's mind was at once exercised by its exotic nature. He was puzzled by the combination of land and sea tastes in the sliced beef steak and oyster sauce dish, but that inquiry soon dissipated in the delicious melding that his tastebuds experienced. Unforgettable was the One-Hundred-Flower Chicken. This was a dish of steamed chicken with clear sauce, decorated by a circle of chrysanthemums, and looked unlike anything Ah Kwok had ever seen – or tasted. Seven hours in preparation, it was hardly an everyday affair.

Replete, sleepy and satisfied, Langhsi and Ah Kwok wandered back slowly, alternately sniffing at the delicate tropical night breeze and drawing in huge lungfuls of the salty, damp air. When they reached their lodgings, Ah Kwok did not remark on the cleanliness or otherwise of the sheets, but instead lay down and, almost immediately, drifted into sleep.

The next day began early and ended late, and afterwards Ah Kwok could remember only snatches of the many things he and Langshi had done. First they located the steamship office and confirmed their passage. Thereafter Langshi bought some peanuts and preserved fruits as emergency supplies for the voyage. These rations included peanuts that had been soaked in their shells in salt water and then air dried, roasted peanuts and peanut brittle; salt olive, the fruit having been absolutely wrinkled and coated in salt; rolls of small, disc-like wafers of fig; dried lemon skins; sweet and sour olives, and chilli olives; and last, a small portion of that delicacy, dried pips from the Chinese winter melon, the *tong kwa*. It was not the pips that yielded delight but what they contained: their treasure of seeds. These were extracted with difficulty by novices but with ease by connoisseurs, who held a number of pips at a time between the teeth and popped out their seeds.

Satisfied with this frisson of luxury, Langshi indicated to Ah Kwok that it was time to make for the docks and the ferry that would take them out to the transport junk that waited in deeper waters of the estuary to sail for Hong Kong. There, they would board the steamer and travel to Gold Mountain. On the ferry, it was as Langshi had told Ah Kwok about the Tanka people. Wiry but powerful men with ropes slung over their shoulders waited at the front of the ferryboat while at the back some youngsters and women were stationed to push. There was even a young girl with a baby strapped on her back, held in a wooden harness of the type that Langshi had described and explained as an ingenious life-jacket. Between the heaving and pushing, the shouts of encouragement and effort fore and aft, the go-between vessel slid out into the current and glided towards the junk. The Tanka men who had been pulling it, swimming, now shouted goodbye as they paddled for their boats. The swirl of waving from the jetty grew smaller and less distinct and last, the sounds of farewells and good wishes faded and died altogether. It could have been a heady moment for Ah Kwok, but he could not forget the heaviness that had suddenly clutched at his heart as he had stepped off the dock and into the ferry. Something had dragged him back, not wanted to let go of him, from the moment he had left the dusty approach to the pier and set foot on its broad timbers. It was as if in leaving the soil of Canton he had committed some irrevocable action.

They drew nearer to the junk by the minute, and farther from the land. Ah Kwok saw the vastness of China, as the land behind the city disclosed itself. And beyond that, there was more and more: mountains with strange shapes, rivers that ran yellow, gorges so deep that sunlight never touched their depths. He thought of the grandfather rainbow carp, his *Kongkong*'s prize fish, and of the common brown carp and mustachioed barbels in the pond at *Sha Kiu*. He wondered what Mudan and Ah Wa were doing and what his mother was preparing for the evening meal. *Bobo* and *Kongkong* were probably checking the state of the lychee tree.

The thin sheet of grey cloud that had been spreading westwards all morning now reached the edge of the sun and in a few minutes had drawn across the great eye of the sky. A man near Ah Kwok expressed relief at the shade: he was not from Kwangtung and was quite done in, he said, by the day's humidity and constant sun. Ah Kwok wished he too could welcome the cool brought by the shade but he felt uneasy. It seemed to Ah Kwok that a veil had been drawn over all under heaven.

SEA

*All streams flow to the sea
because it is lower than they are.
Humility gives it its power.*

Tao Te Ching

S E A

ONE
On the Daimaru, *Indian Ocean, 1923*

As the waves pitched the ship into another trough, Gertie clutched more tightly to the taffrail and threw back her head, exulting in the wind and spray. Canton was a day's sailing away, the last port of call of the six-week voyage. And though she loved the bucking of the ship and the way plumes of spray whipped off the manes of the waves, speckling her in a thousand droplets, Gertie could hardly contain her excitement at the prospect of China. Father had told her of his home village, south of Canton city, lovingly detailing its rice fields, fruit trees and ancestral hall. It was there that Gertie and her brother Andrew were heading, to be followed by Father, Mother and their five siblings, to live on the soil of what Father always called home.

Gertie cast her soft, deep brown eyes downwards, glancing at the wake of the ship, and then turned to look up at the sky. Hers was a mischievous face, always giving the appearance of an upturned nose and creeping smile, perhaps because of the way she liked to tilt her head. Behind that mask, Gertie was thinking about Namfeechow and Kum Saan, where she was born, and which were now a little distant after what she had experienced in the past weeks. She and Andrew had travelled first by train from Johannesburg to Durban, a journey spread over three days and half a dozen landscapes. At Johannesburg station they had raced along the platform, bounded up the iron steps of the railway carriage and tumbled into their compartment, suitcases and hat boxes in tow. A hug and a kiss for each of them from Mother and Father, and then they were on their own, standing at the wide window and waving goodbye. Soon, the train had left the city behind and was heading south, the weak rays of a winter's late afternoon gently lighting stretches of pale grassland on either side of the tracks. Into the night the train went, stopping at small sidings, disgorging passengers and freight, taking on new travellers and goods.

Around early evening, the ticket inspector opened the compartment door and commanded, rather than asked, '*Kaartjies!*' He was a tall, stringy man, with a thin moustache that drooped comically because of its attenuated length. He smelt slightly of liquor and appeared affronted by two children travelling on their own. Gertie and Andrew showed their tickets, but the inspection was not over. 'Where is your travel permits? Chinese must have a pass to travel from province to province and this tickets says you are going to Durban – that is two provinces you must travel through from the Transvaal. Come, do you have passes? Show me now, don't waste my time.'

They produced the official pieces of paper detailing their names, home address, route, destination and reason for journey. Gertie held in reserve a letter from the Chinese Consul-General testifying to their family's good standing in the community, and the children's excellent character. The letter ended with a request that officials the children might encounter during their travels be generous in lending assistance if required.

'Listen now. You better behave or I will *sommer* throw you out of my train. Do you hear? No noise and making dirty here – maybe you do that at home but this is different,' said the inspector as he handed back their permits.

'*Ja, meneer,*' said Gertie in clear Afrikaans. '*Ons luister goed en ons sal niks vuil of stukkend maak nie. Ons belowe u.*' As she spoke, Gertie hoped that this promise not to dirty or break anything would not be broken by some stroke of ill fortune. She kept calm and smiled up at the reddening face glowering over her. Gertie realised that the inspector had no more bluster in him. From experience, Gertie knew he would be on his way. Glaring at them once again, more for show than anything else, the inspector tugged open the door, stepped into the corridor, shut the door firmly and walked off.

The incident reminded Gertie of countless times she had travelled with her brothers and sisters – there were four boys and three girls – and had an unpleasant experience with officials. The inspector here had actually been quite restrained. Earlier in the year, on a local train, the inspector there had snarled at them, 'Why are there so many of you? Also, travelling without parents. Huh – I'm sure they are busy stealing my job.' It had been an attack from nowhere, for they had presented their tickets, not said a word to the man and contrived to smile despite his evident hostility. Then had come his outburst, and the part about stealing jobs had been impossible to understand.

Gertie had secretly pinched herself to avoid crying. She hoped that Vi'li would not burst into tears at the man's words, or that Philip, brave beyond his eleven years, did not do anything rash, like lash out at the inspector. As suddenly as it had begun, the onslaught was over. The inspector had turned on his heel, and strode down the passageway. Immediately, Vi'li had begun sobbing. Philip reached over to her, embraced her, and said to Gertie in a quiet, determined voice, 'One day, Gert, one day, I am going to show these bullies. Mark my words. No one calls us yellow and plays all lordly and grand as a white. No one. Just remember. I swear it to you now.'

'Yes, Philip. But don't go down to their level,' she had replied. 'And for now, let's just worry about Vi and the others – John looks as if he's about to cry too.'

It was a heavy responsibility for twelve-year-old Gertie, looking after her siblings. But Gertie was up to it, strengthened always by the trust that her father placed in her. She had soothed Vi, ruffled John's hair, and suggested that she tell them about the birth of Stone Monkey, the first part of the ancient legend of the Monkey King, told in the centuries-old novel, *Journey to the West*.

'All right,' said Gertie. 'Here is how it begins. Ages and ages ago, when the Creator P'an Ku first divided earth and sky, the world was made up of four continents. In one of those there was the land of Ao-lai, surrounded by an inland sea. Out of this sea rose the Mountain of Many Flowers, a peak famous far and wide. On top of the mountain was a magic rock that since the creation of the world had been blessed by the elements of heaven and the earth, the energy of the sun and the grace of the moon's light. One day this rock burst open and out of it fell a round stone egg. It was fertilised by the wind, and inside the egg a stone monkey began to grow. The egg hatched and out came Stone Monkey, with four limbs and five senses. He could see, hear, smell, taste and touch. Quickly he learned to climb and to run but even before that he bowed to the four quarters of the earth.'

Glancing round, Gertie saw that Vi'li and James were fighting sleep. The others seemed tired also and she herself was exhausted, the incident with the inspector having drained her of the energy that the excitement of beginning the journey had given her. '*Transvaakie* time – we are all sleepy,' she said. 'Come boys, over to the other side. We might as well try to rest before we reach Pretoria.'

Thinking now about that short journey, marked in a way that would long have an effect on the children, Gertie longed to have the whole gaggle around her. She and Andrew were the family's advance party and though they would be accompanied on the sea voyage by an older male cousin, Gertie already felt keenly the absence of her family.

As she and Andrew settled down on their bunks, the slow-moving train chugged on, the Transvaal highveld giving way to the plains of the Orange Free State, farmlands where the country's wheat and mealies were grown. Sleep did not come quickly to Gertie, who thought about the permits and why the Chinese had to endure such cruelty just for being different, for being what they could not help but be.

The next morning, another world presented itself through the now grimier window. Steaming for all it was worth, the train strained up and raced down hills, clung around the sumptuous curves of huge valleys and shot across the black iron of bridges spanning deep river gorges. The long familiar veld of the Transvaal, with its palette of gold, straw, russet and brown, edged here and there by low hills, was now contrasted with the green of Natal, framed by mighty hills and mountains. Enchanted by these new views, the children sat at the window for long stretches at a time. Every now and then they would break away and talk about the inspector, or of things they had heard about China.

Gertie asked Andrew if he remembered their journey to Pretoria with the other children and the encounter with the vicious inspector. Andrew said of course and reminded her how she had calmed the children by talking about Stone Monkey. Just then, his eyes gleamed and he suggested she tell the story of how Stone Monkey won the title of Monkey King by being the first monkey to jump through the Water Curtain Cave. 'Andrew, you know that one better than I do,' said Gertie, but, smiling, she did so and soon the two felt sleepiness creep up on them, quite the opposite of the energy shown by the famed monkey in his title-grabbing exploits.

As the sun rose on the new day, there was a clammy moisture in the air, a deliciously soothing liquid feel that made their dry skin feel smooth and even glowing. The air, too, smelt differently, with a dash of brine in the breeze that blew in at the window of the compartment. The sea was announcing its nearness, and the two of them began excitedly to look out for its line of blue on the horizon. As the train clung to the hillside and rounded another of the railway track's many bends, there it was, a dark blue curve rising to kiss the lighter blue of the sky. Closer up, the sea revealed itself to be green rather than blue. As the train drew up to the platform in Durban, they were relieved to see their welcoming party – a cluster of aunts, distant aunts many times removed but aunts nonetheless. The same day, taken down to the beach, they discovered that the green sea was warm. It was the Indian Ocean that greeted Gertie in Durban, and it was to be the foundation of her life for the next several weeks, as well as the repository of her hopes.

Two days later, and they were on the open seas, on the dependable liner, the *Daimaru*. They had been transferred from the ministrations of their aunts into the somewhat relaxed care of their cousin, Chok Kai. Gertie dimly understood that he was a ladies' man; in later years she was to call him a rake in recounting stories of the journey. Jauntily dressed in a white suit and panama-style hat, Chok Kai had greeted Andrew and Gertie in the Western way by shaking hands, and strode down the gang-plank ahead of them and their luggage. He was returning to China on a home visit after a rewarding time in South Africa, and it was clear that he regarded the voyage as a holiday, not a passage of endurance. He did not police the children, choosing instead to check on their whereabouts a few times per day and for the rest was more taken up by the earnest pursuit of several young women and the daily contest of *mah-jong* that developed in a corner of the lounge. All voyage long, this young man took on a trio of grizzled old ladies, sometimes from sunrise to midnight. Heedless of the changing seas and malleable skies, the fierce whip of the winds or the hush of a calm day, the four gamblers made their world of four chairs, a square table and the ivory tiles of the game. In consequence, shipboard life was an untrammelled adventure for Gertie and Andrew.

From Durban the ship had sailed eastwards to the island of Mauritius, their first stop. There, swaying palm trees, improbably shaped black peaks in the hinterland and the aromas of spices had been Gertie's most abiding impressions of Port Louis, the capital. The tang of curry had hung in the air, a presence that Gertie had also savoured in Durban, at the market run by its Indian merchants and traders. There had not been much time in Port Louis, just two nights and a day, but enough to take in the bursting colours of the fruits that vendors sold on the quay sides and the mix of islanders, Europeans, Indians and Chinese. After Mauritius, the next landfall was Singapore, a long haul during which Gertie and Andrew talked in circles about home, their new home and how comforting it would be when they were joined by Mother and Father and the others.

The ship was a white speck in the vast blue-green of the Indian Ocean as it sailed steadily north-east on its course to round Sumatra. Sometimes hours would pass without another ship in sight, and when another vessel appeared it looked small against the canvas of the sea, just as did the *Daimaru*, even though the children thought it enormous as they roamed its decks. On other days the sea lanes would be crowded with passenger liners and cargo vessels and the down-at-heel tramp steamers that captured Gertie's affections. When the waves were etched with craft, Andrew would rush from one side of the deck to the other, then towards the prow, and later make for the stern, his eyes agog at the many different types of ships. At such busy times, the *Daimaru* might be overtaken by swifter passenger liners, and occasionally by a merchantman at full steam. On three or four occasions, Andrew and the boys he had befriended had gaped and shouted at the sight of men-of-war, their dull grey, heavy steel hulls scything through the water. Most flew the Union Jack, but as the *Daimaru* moved further east, sightings of Japanese battleships, with their unmistakable flags of red globe on white, became more frequent. To Gertie it seemed that the *Daimaru* was neither awed by bigger or faster vessels, nor appeared to show any disdain to smaller craft. Through all the weeks of the voyage, her engines kept up their rhythmic regularity and she ploughed a beautiful line through the waves and sent out a glorious wake, which Gertie was fond of watching from the taffrail.

The cloudless days were dazzling in their definition, with sea and sky crisply divided at the point they met on the horizon, two distinct hues signifying the realms of air and water. When grey sheets of cloud covered every point of the compass, or when rain lashed down, Gertie, Andrew and the shipboard friends they had acquired lounged indoors, reading, talking or playing games. It was then that Gertie and Andrew most acutely longed for home and sought to recall the comfortingly familiar. Gertie spoke about their house in Vrededorp, with its small but carefully tended garden and stand of fruit trees. Sometimes such was the feeling in her words that the children believed they were listening to a story about an enchanted garden. Playing the role of comforter exhausted her, and at night she would walk up on deck and breathe in the air. Each clear night was a gift for her because the stars sparkled with a precise lustre that she had never before experienced. Out here on the ocean, which was undisturbed by the glow that cities gave off, and where there was only the occasional pinprick of light from a passing ship, Gertie had a sense of the heavens. The bowl of sea and sky formed a black canvas for the stars and she would lie on deck for hours gazing upwards, recognising shapes and catching the glorious burst of shooting stars.

At 90 degrees east, the ship crossed the equator, continued north-easterly and rounded the island of Sumatra. The night sky assumed a different aspect and Gertie saw a whole new starscape. Having nudged round the shoulder of the island, the ship bore south-east and coursed through the Straits of Malacca, with Sumatra to starboard and Malaya to port. At first almost hugging the Malayan peninsula, the *Daimaru* soon twitched east and there, rising over the prow, could be discerned the island of Singapore. Father had told them of the importance of Singapore, where trade routes to and from south-east Asia met at this free port, around which the city sprawled. It was built, he said, on hills that had been levelled and marshes that had been covered with earth. North of the equator by just one degree, it had a predictable climate of morning mists, afternoon thunderstorms and evening sea breezes.

In the port, a vast area that extended for miles in every direction, the children were fascinated by the cargoes of rubber, copra, lumber and spices. They marvelled at the number of Chinese – it looked as if three in every four people were of their race, a novelty in their short lives and one that made them feel curiously at home. They were not stared at in the streets, no one threw insults at them and they appeared almost to be invisible in that no special notice was taken of them. It was a freeing feeling, and as they gambolled along with their cousin, the children talked excitedly of how China would be, for there they would in all likelihood be entirely among *T'ong yan*, with no Malays, Indians or Europeans in sight, as so many were in Singapore. They noted that virtually all the trading and small business here were run by Chinese, while policemen and fishermen were invariably Malay. The Malays, Andrew whispered to Gertie, looked a little like the Coloureds in Namfeechow, but they had a different skin hue and more angular features. 'Father told me,' replied Gertie, 'that the Malays were taken from this part of the world by the Dutch, who ruled here, and used as slaves in the new Dutch settlement at the Cape. That's why these people seem so familiar.'

Their little group stopped at a coconut vendor. Cousin Chok Kai bought them each a cup of coconut milk, cool and frothy and uneven in texture but deliciously soothing in the accumulating heat of early afternoon. Andrew watched, more intently than the others, as the vendor swirled a long blade, then brought it down on a coconut, bisecting it and exposing its white flesh. Shards of nut flew up from the wooden chopping board, which, to judge by its roundness and stoutness, had once been the trunk of a tree. The man then sliced delicately at the fruit, dropping the thin strips into a bowl and offering them for sale.

A little way down the avenue, they came to the Botanical Gardens, of whose wonders the old ladies had told them during a rare break in their shipboard *mah-jong* sessions. 'There is a wild jungle there, with monkeys. Different monkeys, not as those you may have seen in Namfeechow,' an elder aunt had said. And she was right. Andrew saw it first, at the very end of the afternoon, when the cloying heat had drained them of all energy and any desire to see more. Thunderclouds had been building up, filling the sky with the promise of a cooling storm, and they were making their way through the primate enclosure. Very near where they had entered, at the base of the high trees at the far reaches, Andrew saw a reddish-brown swirl, a bright splash and blur against the green foliage and grey and brown barks of the trees.

'Look, look, what is that?' he shouted.

'Ayy – sshh, ssh,' said Chok Kai. '*Hai, hai,* it is something. It is an orang-utan. See, see. Not like the apes in South Africa. Their name means "man of the woods" in Malay.'

For the briefest time, perhaps a minute, the three humans had a view of the magnificent animal straight on, and then of it swinging from branch to branch, its remarkably long arms conquering the voids between trees. The boys in particular were in awe of such strength, suppleness and ease. Gertie, in whom there was even at this young age a streak of melancholy, found herself upset by the orang-utan's captivity and fancied that she had caught in its eye a look of infinite sadness just before it had turned from watching them and begun its progress higher and higher into the trees.

Days later, looking out over the wake of the ship as it raced towards Canton, Gertie thought again of the orang-utan and about the differences between it and the baboons that she had seen back home. Since she had glimpsed the reddish-brown man of the woods, Gertie had been unable to shake the idea that this ape had an air of mystery about it. It seemed shuttered away, living in its aerial canopy of trees – an elderly man on board, overhearing their conversation, had told them that orang-utans built sleeping platforms in trees, anywhere from 20 to 80 feet above the ground. Nor was the great orange ape vocal, unlike the barking baboon of home.

The day after they had seen the orang-utan had brought an adventure of a different nature. It was the last day in port and Cousin Chok Kai had told Gertie and Andrew that he had business in the town. He said that they should not leave the ship until he returned, in the late morning. The two had idled away the hours after an early breakfast and were reading on the deck when two Chinese men came up to them. 'Good morning, cousins from Kum Saan,' said the older man while the younger nodded and smiled. Surprised, Gertie and Andrew nonetheless greeted them politely in Cantonese, obeying all the civilities.

'We are cousins of Chok Kai,' continued the older man. 'He is busier in town than he thought and so he asked us to fetch you and take you to him for lunch. Please, will you go with us now?'

Gertie and Andrew exchanged glances. Chok Kai had been explicit in his instructions: they were to remain on board until he came back. He had not mentioned any relatives. Then again, how could these men know that the two of them were from Johannesburg, and cousins of Chok Kai? Only he could have told the men and described Gertie and Andrew in detail so that they could be distinguished from the other youngsters. It sounded reasonable that Chok Kai should send family to collect them. And he had promised lunch in town after he returned.

Before Gertie could say anything, Andrew got up, closed his book and said, 'Good, we will go with you to Chok Kai. Come, Gertie.'

The men laughed, saying they were relieved that they had found the youngsters and that the restaurant Cousin Chok Kai was lunching at was a first-class establishment. Smiling and beckoning, they indicated that Andrew and Gertie should follow them. The four walked through the docks, the forest of ships' masts and funnels on their left, the warehouses and throng of labourers loading and unloading cargo on their right.

Gertie asked the men their names, how they were related to Chok Kai and how long they had lived in Singapore. '*Aii*, pardon me. My name is Chok Peng and this is Chok Sheng, my younger brother.' The latter nodded vigorously and smiled, but said nothing. Gertie wondered if he was able to speak at all and thought she would direct her next question to him.

Chok Peng said his father and Chok Kai's father were brothers, but from different mothers. 'So you are very close,' said Gertie to Chok Sheng. Again, he just nodded and grinned, turning a little to his sibling and quickening his stride.

'Come, we must hurry, because the sun is high in the sky. It is almost time to eat and the restaurant is still some way away,' said Chok Peng. He and Chok Sheng fell back a little, and then walked next to Andrew and Gertie, four abreast. They picked up their pace, and then increased it, so that the youngsters were struggling to keep up. Chok Sheng smiled at Gertie and nodded.

'And how long have you been here in Singapore?' asked Andrew of Chok Peng, repeating Gertie's question.

'A few years. Cousin Chok Kai and I left Kwangtung at the same time, but I got off the boat here, and he continued on,' said Chok Peng.

'Ah. And what village do you come from?' asked Gertie, addressing Chok Sheng on her right.

'Sha Kiu, Sha Kiu,' interrupted Chok Peng, laughing after he said the name of the village a second time. 'We are from Sha Kiu, not far from Canton.' In his usual way, Chok Sheng nodded, and grinned.

By this time Gertie had taken hold of Andrew's hand; that way it was easier to keep up with the half-walk, half-run that their guides had adopted. At this mention of Sha Kiu, however, she squeezed Andrew's hand and then looked at him, quickly. Something was very wrong. Cousin Chok Kai was not from any of the Namsoon villages near Canton at all, but from the market town of Lok Chung, at their centre. Despite her youth, Gertie had a presentiment of things, a quality that she neither sought nor cultivated. Her instincts about things had invariably been proven correct. And this morning, before Andrew had agreed to accompany these men, she had felt the stirring of unease. She had suppressed it then and chosen instead to trust the logic of the men's mission over her feelings. After the hasty answer from Chok Peng, Gertie knew that she must obey herself and abandon obedience to adult authority and social conventions.

Andrew squeezed Gertie's hand and the two exchanged another furtive glance. 'Look! Cousin Chok Kai!' shouted Gertie, pointing ahead. In that instant, she released Andrew's hand and turned on her heel and ran, followed by her brother. The two men, momentarily checked by the shout, stared ahead in search of Chok Kai, whom they would not in any case have been able to recognise. Realising the trick they had been played, they rushed after the two children, Chok Peng letting off a torrent of the vilest curses.

The few seconds Gertie had bought for her and Andrew were vital. So too were their youthful energy and panic. Weaving in and out of the stream of pedestrians, the youngsters ran, shouting for help. It was due to luck, or perhaps more likely the result of Gertie's vigilance on the way from the harbour, that they were able to retrace their course. Less agile than their prey, and less fit, the adult pursuers slipped further and further back. Their progress was definitely halted by an old woman, who, seeing the children running and shouting, and then espying their followers, put out a foot and tripped Chok Peng. His clumsy companion, Chok Sheng, fell headlong over him and, seemingly regaining the power of speech, let out a series of expletives that earned him for his pains a bashing about the head from the old woman. Very soon a throng surrounded the two men, but of them Gertie and Andrew were to know no more, other than what cousin Chok Kai told them later.

Racing up the gangplank and back on board, Gertie and Andrew rushed to their cabin, locked the door and threw themselves on the bed, sobbing. 'Gert, I am so sorry, so sorry,' gasped Andrew.

'It is all right, Andrew. We got away and we are safe,' said Gertie consolingly, adding: 'I wish Cousin Chok Kai was back from town.'

For a while they lay in silence, recovering their breath. 'Those men were bad, Andrew, they wanted to take us away. They knew nothing really about Chok Kai. But how did they know so much about us?'

At that moment, there was a knocking at the door. Gertie and Andrew shot up from the bed, looking anxiously at each other. 'Is this them?' asked Gertie.

'Who is it?' demanded Andrew of the other side of the door.

'Gertie, Andrew, it is Chok Kai. The mate just told me he saw you running on board and below deck. Are you all right? Where were you?'

Hearing the familiar voice, Andrew unlocked the cabin door, opened it and admitted Chok Kai. 'I told you not to leave the ship until I came back,' said their cousin. It was after he heard their story that, grimly, he said, 'You have had a very fortunate escape. Those men wanted to take you away and sell you, or hold you hostage. I have been fortunate too, for I was entrusted with your safekeeping and have failed, only to be saved by your alertness, Gertie. And your intuition. I am relieved, and grateful to you. I will let your parents know how quick-witted and resourceful you and Andrew are, and I will also confess my failing and my shame.'

Gertie could not bear to see Cousin Chok Kai so downcast. She did not want him to lose face in her father's eyes. Nor did Andrew. In a chorus, they blurted, 'No, cousin,' and then Andrew let Gertie continue. 'Do not tell our father. It is not necessary. We are safe and it was through no fault of yours.. How did those men know so much about us and you? It was our fault for not obeying your instruction. So please do not worry yourself or our father. It will make him worry until he sees us once more, and it will also make him angry that we were disobedient. To spare us a beating, please do not tell him.'

'You are too kind, Cousin Gertie,' said Chok Kai. 'But I know your father shall not beat you. Andrew, perhaps, for agreeing to go, may be punished. But you, you are your father's favourite. Thank you for sparing my feelings and trying to persuade me but I must honour the trust your father placed in me and tell him, by letter, that you are safe, with no thanks to me for that. I was told that these gangs operate between ship and shore, gathering information on passengers and using that to trick travellers into trusting them. But enough of this for now. Should we have some lunch? Are you feeling well enough to have something to eat?'

Gertie had not been sad to take leave of Singapore the following morning. The misadventure had clouded her images of the city and she wished only to be speedily in China. The trek across the Indian Ocean from Mauritius had worn down the vanguard spirit that Andrew and she had started off with. Their physical well-being was a different matter altogether. They had been comfortable, even pampered, sharing a cabin, taking three meals a day in the dining room and enjoying deck quoits outdoors and parlour games in the lounge. In contrast, Gertie often looked at the poor souls travelling steerage and wondered how they could survive the privations of such a passage.

Less than a day away now, Canton seemed to be summoning Gertie from across the water. She moved round to the port side of the ship, its landward side. The smudge that she could make out in the distance was not Malaya, or Sumatra, beautiful and mysterious as they had been, but China. Hovering at the horizon, it cast its spell on Gertie's imagination, the suggestion of greenness enough to set her mind racing in fanciful flight. She pictured exotically shaped towers of rock, festooned with huge mosses and strange trees, and below that oddly-coloured rivers flowing in wide loops. Just then there was a tug on her sleeve. It was Andrew, telling her to come down and change for dinner. 'This is our last evening on the ship, Gertie,' he said, 'and the aunties say we should dress up and look nice. Come, let's go.'

'Wait, Andrew. Think how our lives will change tomorrow, when we get off the ship and set foot in another country. It's what Father has always wanted, us back on the soil of the land where he was born and grew up. It's a new world, only a night away. Aren't you excited?'

'*Ja*, of course, Gertie. But I'm hungry too.'

'Oh, you and your tummy rumbles. All right, let's go below. Race you down to the cabin!'

Twelve hours later, the *Daimaru* was working its way slowly up the Pearl River. Ahead lay Canton, while around the ship cruised sampans and junks, their sails breathing in the day's slightest of breezes and then surging on, almost dancing on the water. Gertie and Andrew were dressed, ready to go on shore, their suitcases and hat boxes packed and stacked in two chimneys of luggage propped against the cabin walls. Up on deck, Gertie in a light blue cotton dress and Andrew in a suit of the same cloth, watched together as the land drew larger and nearer. 'Those hills far away are the White Cloud Hills,' said one of the wizened *mah-jong* women.

'Father often told us about them,' Gertie said excitedly, peering at the shapes in the distance. At the same time, in her memory there formed a picture of her father, dressed in coat and tails, smiling at her. It was April 1923 and Gertrude Martin, eldest daughter of Chok Foon Martin and Cornelia von Brandis, had arrived in her father's homeland.

S E A

Two
Hong Kong and on the Yamato Princess, *Indian Ocean, 1911*

Hong Kong was not China. It took a while for Ah Kwok to realise that. At first he had felt comfortable, surrounded by familiars: the sound of Cantonese, the smells of home-cooked food, the typical Chinese faces. But something was not quite right. There was an oppressive feeling, an invisible hand hovering over the island. He knew, of course, that it was a British colony, and the presence of the *bak gwai* – the white devils – was very apparent. Uniformed men with pale skins were everywhere, crisp and curt in their dealings with locals, chummy with their fellows. The foreigners tended to stare over the Chinese they commanded or addressed, not because the whites were taller, but as if to deny the existence of the colonised. This was an attitude of superiority with which Ah Kwok was not acquainted. The hierarchies of Chinese family and society he knew a little and could understand, but the British and their studied callousness perplexed him.

Langshi had tried to talk about these *gwai lo*, these foreign devils. He said their attitude had come about because the English had such immense military and naval power and exerted control in other parts of China and the world via the diplomacy of might. They had sent gunboats to destroy Chinese cities such as Canton, Chenhai, Ningpo and Shanghai in the Opium War of the 1840s. It was as a result of China's bitter defeat then that Hong Kong had been given to the British. Mind you, it was then a barren rock, Langshi conceded, peopled by only a few hundred fishermen, and the sheer weight of British presence had made it into what they saw today. For Ah Kwok, however, Langshi's monologue had too many words and ideas, and he had not really heard what his father had to say. It was enough for Ah Kwok to observe the demeanour of ordinary Chinese on the streets, their browbeaten beetling along and their nervousness as the swaggering

Gurkhas of the Hong Kong police force went about their beats. On the mainland, life under the Manchus was not a particularly joyous affair, but the people seemed less under the whip than here. What Ah Kwok felt was that the island was as separate in spirit from the homeland he had left a few days before as it was geographically cut off from the mainland.

On their last afternoon before setting sail, Ah Kwok's misgivings were made real, sweeping away his father's dutiful explanations about the British and putting a visceral full stop to their Hong Kong sojourn. A long day's strolling was ending, and to cool off Langshi headed toward a public park. Palisade fences surrounded this pretty area of trees and from within the grounds came the gurgling, enticing sound of running water and fountains. Foreigners strolled the little tree-lined paths, the men in linen suits, the women in long, full dresses, holding parasols more in affectation than to escape the early evening sun. Just as Langshi and Ah Kwok were about to enter the park, one of the turbaned Gurkhas standing as sentries on either side of the gate leapt into their path, brandishing his truncheon at them.

'*M'hai, m'hai, m'hai.* No! No! No! Out!' shouted the tall man.

'Why? We wish to walk in the park,' said Langshi.

'*M'hai, m'hai,*' repeated the Gurkha, a little more insistently, if that were possible, given the vehemence of his initial prohibition. It was clear to Langshi that the guard possessed, insultingly, only this little bit of Cantonese: No.

'Wait here,' said Langshi to Ah Kwok and then continued towards the entrance. The constable leaned forward, grabbed Langshi by the arm and dragged him through the gate. The irony of being within the park was not lost on Langshi, indeed it was what he had been trying to achieve, but before he could remark on it, the Gurkha swung his truncheon into a wooden signboard. Looking at it, Langshi saw first two lines of unintelligible shapes. Beneath those, however, was Chinese. He blanched, then reddened in the face, for what was written in Chinese was 'No Dogs or Chinese Permitted'. Before he could give voice to his reaction, he was bundled back through the gate. Lest this ejection should not be understood, the Gurkha advanced on Langshi and Ah Kwok, waving his heavy wooden stick.

'Come, my boy, we cannot walk here for some reason I cannot understand,' said Langshi.

'Father, what was written on the sign? Did you not read something on that notice explaining why we cannot enter?'

'Yes, you are correct. It said that Chinese were not allowed in the park. I suppose the grounds are reserved for the use of the *bak gwai*, who don't want to mix with us. It is their island, after all: here it is we who are guests and servants. This is not Canton. Let us go now, and forget this misunderstanding.'

Although he tried to smooth over the incident, Langshi knew Ah Kwok would probe and probe until, eventually, he would wring from his father the whole explanation. For now, though, he deemed it best that the boy did not know the truth. Some time on the voyage he would raise the matter, because they were travelling to a place where such discrimination against Chinese was practised, and Ah Kwok would have to learn how to accept and cope with that. It did not encourage Langshi that South Africa had been under British rule, which Hong Kong still was. If this outrageous equation of dogs with Chinese, and the manhandling at the park, were pointers to life in Namfeechow, then he might have to reconsider the judiciousness of this venture.

'Father, what sort of place is this that allows some people to walk here and there but not others?' asked Ah Kwok.

'What we need to remember is that wherever we are, we are Chinese, and we must always be proud of that.' So saying, Langshi led them down to the causeway that ran to the harbour and the Japanese vessel that would take them across the ocean to South Africa.

Two nights on deck while in port eased Langshi and Ah Kwok into steerage life. They realised that when the weather at sea was stormy, things might not be as comfortable, if indeed sleeping on solid wooden timbers could be thus described. Nonetheless, this would be a one-way test of endurance, promised Langhsi, for on the way back they would travel in a cabin. Ah Kwok should see this shipboard voyage as a once-in-a-lifetime experience, besides which, he was young and hale, and the rigours of a few weeks on the planks, with the stars for a roof, would be an adventure.

It was in that mood that Ah Kwok, leaning on the deck rail, watched the dock slip away as the *Yamato Princess* passed through the harbour and steamed out into the South China Sea. He was glad to put Hong Kong behind him. It floated off the mainland, so near but forever apart. And while its hills were alike in shape and stature to those across the water, they seemed to him mere suggestions of the grandeur of the hinterland.

Around Ah Kwok, there was a mill of strange tongues, sounds that made no sense to him, carried by voices that had no natural music to his ear. Some were Chinese speaking different dialects, Langshi explained: solid pockets of the Hakka of the Moiyeanese people, Swatonese, Shanghainese here, and there a smattering of Mandarin. Oddest of all for Ah Kwok were the unfamiliar sounds issuing from people who looked quite similar, but were subtly different on closer examination. Black haired, short, but with more angular faces, these fellow travellers were from Japan, Langshi had told him. At this, a frisson of anxiety, excitement and hostility ran through Ah Kwok's being. So these were people from Yat-poon, Asian brothers and bitter foes. Grandfather had told him much about what they had derived from the Chinese: woodworking, art, writing, music and dancing, to name but a few. The Japanese had developed those in their own way, but the Chinese influence was evident.

Laying aside the burden of what he had been told, Ah Kwok devoted himself to immediate impressions. He listened carefully to a group of youngsters talking animatedly and found that their mode of speech was quieter and more reserved than the Cantonese. Still, half-remembered bits of history came unsummoned to Ah Kwok's mind. There was the war between China and Japan over Korea in 1894, which had led to China's losing the island of Formosa to Japan. A Japanese army had helped the European powers besieged in Peking by the Boxer Rebellion in 1900. Manchuria, China's territory, had been divided between Japan and Russia just four years before, in 1907. Japan was not loved by China, and here Ah Kwok was, on a ship from that country, with many Japanese travellers, for a lengthy voyage. He felt galled, but took boyish satisfaction from the fact that Japan's very name had been given by the Chinese: the land east of China had been named 'Source of the Sun', Jih-pen, in the northern dialect, Mandarin.

SEA

Later, as the sun disappeared into the sea and a coolness began to shroud the deck, Ah Kwok asked his father about the Japanese on board. Should he avoid them or ignore them? Were they also bound for Namfeechow? How could he make himself understood, in case he had to – or chose to?

Langshi reminded Ah Kwok of the Hakka people, and of how they were not nearly so bad as many would have you believe. 'True, though, that Hakka are closer to us than Japanese. There is bad blood between Chung-kwok and Yat-poon, especially because of the events of recent years. But we should behave always towards the person as a person, not as a representative of another nation. Try not to be angry; remember that when one is angry it is almost always because one is feeling threatened, but that often the threat is of one's own making. You imagine others are thinking badly of you or are about to act aggressively towards you. In fact, you cannot know what is in their minds and you should allow that they will behave correctly towards you. Act only when you know and for the rest believe that people are of good will.'

Ah Kwok had heard these sentiments of his father's before. He had sat at the pond in the village and listened to his grandfather utter the same ideas. Although he could rehearse the substance of this approach to life, his youthful temperament had prevented him absorbing and applying it. Repetition had not made this philosophy vivid for Ah Kwok, but turgid. Impatient, he asked his father again if they would share the passage all the way to South Africa with these people with whom they could not really converse.

'No, I believe most will disembark before then. But it will be valuable for you to learn to accept and live with others, especially in these rather uncomfortable circumstances. The world is made of many peoples.'

Ah Kwok settled down for the night, markedly colder than when the *Yamato Princess* had been in port. It was as if the water seeped up the hull, slid on to deck and over his body, where it was icily liquid. Waking in the morning, Ah Kwok found a crust of icy shards covering his blanket and a certain stiffness in his body. His father was not around, but steerage was full of sleeping forms, twitching and moving bodies giving off sounds and smells. The three-month journey would be a test of endurance and patience, he thought to himself as he went off to wash up.

THREE
On the Yamato Princess, *Indian Ocean, 1911*

At the rudimentary ablution area, Ah Kwok was amazed to see an entire family washing together. He had been told of the communal tradition of the Japanese in which family members washed and rinsed themselves and then climbed into a wooden bath tub filled with hot water. What greeted his barely conscious eyes was the first part of that process, with no promise of the second: there were no baths for steerage passengers on the ship. In the flesh, such a sight was too candid and too much out of Ah Kwok's own experience for him to bear. There would be no respite for him in the cramped and steamy room, no moment when the relaxed pink bodies would slip beneath water and submerge his discomfort as well. Smiling nervously, trying not to look in the direction of this assured gaggle, Ah Kwok began heading for the door.

A boy called out behind him. Ah Kwok could not understand. He hurried on. Then came a chorus of laughter and what Ah Kwok took to be jeering remarks. His face burning, the heat of the room stifling, sweat and condensation running off his brow and down his back, he rushed out, and on to the deck, where the crispness of the morning brought coolness and began to dry him off. The sun had pushed above the eastern horizon and was beginning to warm the starboard side of the ship. Ah Kwok crossed over there, leaned against the rail and looked down the sheer sides of the *Yamato Princess* and into the sea. The novelties of the past week were vivid memories, but beginning to recede against the reality of the long voyage and the absence of his mother, grandparents and friends. It would have been very fine to have Mudan and Ah Wa alongside him now, gazing down at the sea and the line the hull drew in it. The three of them would have enjoyed watching the rituals of shipboard life, and playing in the open air. Ah Kwok supposed he should seek out some youngsters his age and stop being so gloomy. That last day in Hong Kong weighed heavily on his mind, and he hated to think of how his father had struggled to maintain his dignity when being manhandled by the policeman at the park. He wanted to know what the sign had said. He had been too far away, outside the park and too scared to rush in and help his father, so that he could not make out the Chinese characters underneath those lines of strange shapes.

'Son,' said Langshi, putting a hand on Ah Kwok's shoulder. 'Come along, let us have our morning meal. Where have you been?'

'I went to wash but I could not because a whole family was there, washing, naked in front of everybody. I will have to go later.'

'You should grow accustomed to such sights,' said Langshi, laughing, 'for there are many Japanese on board and they will not be shy to wash in public. Here, we have some rice, warm with soft, full grains, to which I will add some *naam yu* for flavour. There is also tea, but stronger than you are used to at home.'

Ah Kwok took up his bowl, wrapped his fingers around chopsticks and began to eat. The rice was good, and even though it was everyday food for him, Ah Kwok could always appreciate the simple pleasure of a bowl of properly cooked rice. Besides, he was hungry and there was also comfort in warming himself after the strange experience that had begun his day.

On the mornings that followed, Ah Kwok made a point of rising extra early and washing when it was still dark and the water not yet warm. That did not matter much, because there was a limited quantity of warm water for the dozens in steerage. After a while it ran out and was cold and then, not too long after, there was no water at all. Drinking water was more readily in supply, and Ah Kwok and Langshi made sure to drink sufficient quantities because it was easy to dry out during the day, when the sun beat on the deck and turned your vision into dazzling white, through which shapes and patterns gradually emerged and became coherent. Dehydration, sunstroke and fever – all were risks for the unwary or the cavalier living under the sun by day and the stars by night. At first Ah Kwok had seen many passengers succumb to sea sickness, but those bouts of unease stopped after a few days as the ship's movement became familiar. Ah Kwok thought now and then of what it would be like to be on land once more, with an unmoving surface beneath his feet, no rolling or pitching, no sudden tilts and adjustments in your relationship with the deck that formed the ground beneath your feet.

By the end of the first week, Ah Kwok had established friendly relations with a number of Cantonese children. Not all were travelling steerage. There was a pretty girl and her older brother, both always beautifully dressed, who were in first-class cabins. They and their parents were bound for Singapore, their home, after visiting Shanghai, from where their family came. Although they spoke Swatonese, the goodwill that children often have enabled them and Ah Kwok to get by with signs, laughs and giggles and, increasingly, the discovery that dissimilar-sounding words referred to the same thing.

Matters were different with the Japanese children, and particularly one boy of around Ah Kwok's age. Lively, always talkative, he struck Ah Kwok as the boy who had called out to him in the washing-up area, for he always made some remark when their paths crossed. Whatever he said seemed not unfriendly, but nor was it overtly welcoming. After about a fortnight at sea, that changed. His overtures ignored, the Japanese boy began teasing Ah Kwok, pointing to his own face and then Ah Kwok's. He had chosen the most sensitive of issues for his Chinese counterpart, for Ah Kwok had pock marks and scars from smallpox, a disease he had been most fortunate to escape from at the age of nine with only these lifelong reminders. Had it not been for these disfiguring marks, Ah Kwok would have been an unreservedly handsome boy; as it was, his strong features helped to diminish and here and there to accentuate the ravages of the pox. It was a cruel circumstance to fix on, and hurtfully candid. Reminded of his deathly experience, its pain and maddening itch, Ah Kwok felt his mental scars being flecked open. Worse still, it set him to thinking of his mother, Soi Sien, and of how she had cared for him, almost saved his life by love and sheer force of will.

Smallpox sufferers were quarantined from the village as a matter of course. It was a highly contagious disease, the survival rate was desperately low and there was no cure, only treatments offering temporary relief. Langshi and Soi Sien harboured no false hopes, but they acted calmly, determined to give their boy a chance of living. Langshi built a reed shelter far off in the forest, a place where Ah Kwok would be cooler and so perhaps find some solace when his fever peaked, and the red spots that were becoming visible on his face and arms raised and then swelled to blisters filled with pus. For two weeks Ah Kwok would have to endure them growing bigger and becoming more painful. After that, if indeed he survived, the blisters would dry up and his fever would abate. Scabs would form where the globules of pus had been, and eventually those too would drop off.

Inside the crude hut, Langshi put Ah Kwok's pallet, a large vessel for drinking water and a cup. Then he brought his son up from the village, carrying him as if he were a baby, and thinking along the way of Ah Kwok when he was newly born. Soi Sien followed, carrying water and the pouch of ointments that Langshi had prepared. They laid Ah Kwok down, filled the pitcher with water and covered it with a cloth, and then set to work on his face and arms. Langshi had prepared a liniment made of numerous medicinal ingredients ground to fine powder and mixed with unguent. They applied this gently to Ah Kwok's spots. Later, Langshi knew, they would have to tend the inflamed body, and for the worst eruptions, he would make up a poultice of a stronger mixture.

'*Tsai*, when your spots become itchy, you must not scratch,' said Soi Sien. 'If you scratch, you will feel relief only for that moment. It will not help to take away these blisters, it will make them worse. When you scratch, you make certain that there will be marks left on that spot always. Long after the burning and the fever and the itch have gone, you will be left with a mark, a little pit-shape, in that spot. So do not touch, and especially do not scratch your face, hard though that will seem.'

Ah Kwok was on fire. He heard his mother's advice and urging, but he was too weak to respond other than to give a scarcely perceptible nod. His father had told him exactly this about the horrible effects of wanting to tear the pox from one's flesh, of wanting to rub off these flaming bubbles and have peace of body once again. He had resolved to try to heed the warnings but the burning and the itching were almost intolerable.

'I will visit you thrice a day,' said Soi Sien. 'Your father will not come, as he will then not be able to go about his work.'

'I am sorry, *tsai*,' said Langshi. 'Already as it is I am worried that I might pass on the smallpox to others. But Mother will bring you water and food and balms. We herbalists believe that smallpox is made up of ten illnesses all coming together and invading the body. You must be strong, you must want to live. I expect to see you back home in the village in two or three weeks, *tsai*. Rest and remember – do not scratch.'

Langshi looked at Soi Sien, nodded and turned away, walking through the shady green of the forest back to the village. Kneeling near the pallet, Ah Kwok's mother hummed a song, as much to herself as her son, and rocked gently back and forward. She would stay a little longer and then she, too, must go. She watched as Ah Kwok seemed to fall into an uncertain, troubled sleep, but his being out of consciousness at least lessened his terrible awareness of discomfort. Now Soi Sien was praying, tears running down her cheeks and despair clutching her heart. She would gladly sleep apart from Langshi to lessen the possibility of passing on the disease, but she wished that her absence there could be made up for by her presence here, in the whispering reeds of the makeshift hut, in the shadows of the stands of swaying bamboo. She and Langshi had deliberately concentrated on the cosmetic effects of the disease, scarcely dwelling on its fatal nature, in talking to their son. It was not that they denied the dangers, but they wished to lessen the boy's burden and make his time alone lighter to bear. By urging Ah Kwok to preserve his features against the effects of the pox, they hoped he would begin to think of life beyond the disease, and so in some way begin to vouchsafe his own survival. Whether it would work, Soi Sien now had no idea. Shaking her head, brushing away tears and righting herself, she rose quietly, looked at her son, and departed.

Ah Kwok did not wish to die but the torments of the blisters and their excruciating swelling from time to time made him think that any cessation of his irritation would do, even death. In the days and nights that imprisoned him, turning his life into a solitary confinement relieved only by his mother's visits, he thought of the small things that gave him pleasure: playing with his friends, scooping out the fish ponds during their annual cleaning, and watching the old ladies bring offerings of food and drink to the temple. Sometimes, he reflected with remorse, he and Ah Wa had sneaked up to the altar after the women had left and snaffled the tastier morsels. Perhaps that was why he was punished with this disease, he felt, looking at the red-scored palms of his hands and feeling the painful soles of his feet, tenderly brushing up one foot against the other. That was it: he was being punished for stealing the offerings to the ancestors and the gods, his hands being made into blazing emblems of his crimes, and his feet marked as the means that had taken him padding silently up to the altar and then quickly out of the temple. If he recovered, if this red and heat and itch ever subsided, he would vow never to offend the ancestors and the gods by such pilfering. What would happen if he were to die? Would he sink into some dark nothingness, or would Hell be as his grandfather had told him: ten levels, ruled over by the Kings of the Law Courts? Arriving souls would be brought before Yanluo Wang, the senior king, who would examine their past lives and then dispatch them to one of his eight fellow regents who each punished particular transgressions. The tenth and last monarch paired souls with bodies in preparation for their reincarnation.

Ah Kwok was all too familiar with the fearsome face and powerful body of Yanluo Wang, from a ceramic in Tian's house. The god seemed almost alive, not a piece of moulded clay: the locks of his hair stood like a coil of snakes ready to strike; his eyes bulged menacingly and seemed all-seeing; wicked molars showed at the edges of his mouth; and the elongated ears suggested that nothing that had ever been said escaped the god's hearing. From his grandfather, Ah Kwok had also learnt of the terrible punishments and tortures meted out to the worst offenders: death by being thrown into a cauldron of boiling oil, crushing by huge stones, and being sawn in half at the waist. A twinkle in his eye, Tian had remarked to Ah Kwok that it was very interesting that these were the self-same means of execution as the early emperors used for acts of treason or – and here the old man smiled quickly – to do away with loyal officials who were nonetheless too smart for the emperor's own good. These terrible fates did not await Ah Kwok in his earthly life, but he knew that he could avoid Hell only by living a blameless life and making regular offerings to Kuan Yin, the goddess of mercy. And it was precisely from the altar on the centre of which the goddess stood, that he and Ah Wa had made off with those delicious mouthfuls. Thinking of those moments, Ah

73

Kwok felt himself breaking out into a sweat that covered his already per-spiration-ridden body. He was hot in a way that he had never experi-enced, even during the fiercest, harshest summer that he had endured.

If the burning was everywhere on his body, so too were the marks of the pox: in his ears and nose, on his fingers and toes. His skin itched and though he struggled to obey his father's injunction not to, Ah Kwok scratched. His mother chided him each day, the red marks scored by agi-tated fingernails still all too clearly visible on his face, arms, body and legs. Sometimes there were trails of the broken sacs of pus, and she would grow angry. Always she begged him not to scratch his face.

'You are a good-looking boy,' she would say, 'and you don't want to put blemishes on your looks. You will always be handsome, but why carry shadows on your face for the sake of the lack of a little patience?'

Ah Kwok would nod and promise to heed her pleas. But in the long hours that he lay awake and alone, fevered despite gulping down some of the cool water at his side, burning in spite of the cool breezes that played in the forest, he would begin to touch the worst spots, then to rub and pick at them and finally to scratch.

Soi Sien was anguished and exasperated when she saw the horrible effects of Ah Kwok's torment, but that did not stop her gently applying the special powder that Langshi had made up. She did so three times a day, on each of her visits, while singing and talking to her son, and encouraging him not to give up the fight against the heat and the itchi-ness. To apply the powder she used a goose feather, lifting a quantity of the fine, dusty substance on to its tip and shaking it gently over the angry areas on Ah Kwok's body. It would fall in the softest drizzle, a miniature snowfall of beneficence that soothed mightily despite, or perhaps precise-ly because of, its lightness.

Although Soi Sien and Langshi were very worried by Ah Kwok's scratching – and even then it had to be admitted the boy had exercised restraint, given the way his body was covered in blisters – they took com-fort in what seemed to be a lessening of his fever. Two weeks after his confinement began, there were signs that some of the blisters were dry-ing up. It was at the very point that Ah Kwok had begun to lose confi-dence in his mother's assurances that the smallpox was reaching its height and would soon begin to subside. A few days after that, his body attained its normal heat. To Ah Kwok it felt suddenly unnatural not to be blazingly hot. Swiftly, the blisters dried and were replaced by scabs.

One morning, when she was certain the disease had run its course, Soi Sien said, 'Ah Kwok, you are fine, you have lived, my son,' and the young boy saw a large tear spill from each eye and roll down her cheeks. Two days later, Langshi came to the shelter with Soi Sien to take Ah Kwok back home. Before they went, Langshi tore down the hut, carefully piled the reeds, the bedding and even Ah Kwok's pallet, and set them alight. When the pyre had burnt down, Langshi threw sand over the guttering embers and raked over the clearing in the forest.

'*Tsai*, this is a very happy day for your mother and me, and for you,' said Langshi. 'We two could have been burying you today, had you not fought the disease and had not your mother cared for you each day. Life begins anew today for you and I am sure that you will appreciate it the more, even its small inconveniences.'

Ah Kwok, who had already thanked his mother frequently in the days of his convalescence, thanked her once more and said to Langshi, 'Yes, *foo ts'an*, even being bored is a sign that you are alive. Sometimes when I had bad dreams, I would waken and welcome the stillness and being alone and having nothing to do, because I knew I was not dead, as I had been in my dreams.'

'Come, come, *Kongkong* and *Bobo* wish to see their healthy grandson. And there are certain friends in the village who wish to see him too,' said Soi Sien, and the three of them began a joyous walk back home.

It was such memories that the Japanese boy's taunting brought to Ah Kwok's mind. They reminded him also of his sadness at parting from his mother, and of how keenly he now felt her absence. Most of all, the Japanese boy's gestures raised the spectre of how cruelly Ah Kwok had been teased in the village by the youngsters there, and how he had to live with the nickname Do Pi Kwok – 'Pock-faced Kwok'. This mass of memory, longing and resentment formed a compact of tinder-dry emotions awaiting a spark. Unfortunately for Ah Kwok's tormentor, one facial comparison too many was to prove the match that set Ah Kwok on fire.

It happened before dawn, in the ablution room. Ah Kwok, as had become his wont, had risen while it was still deep dark and made his way to the dank washing-up area. He enjoyed these quiet, private moments and had just finished running water through his thick, short black hair when he heard someone come in. Unperturbed, he carried on washing. A minute later, out of the side of his eye, Ah Kwok glimpsed the Japanese boy brushing his teeth. The boy had a very firm grip on the wooden handle of his toothbrush and was scrubbing away with surprising vigour. He sensed, or maybe he had invited, Ah Kwok's sideways glance and turned to face him. Quickly he took the brush out of his mouth, waved it at Ah Kwok in greeting and then, misguidedly, pointed to his smooth cheeks. Perhaps what Ah Kwok took to be a reference to the boy's unspoilt complexion was merely the progress of the brush back to the boy's mouth. In the moment, however, Ah Kwok's suppressed and complex feelings erupted and he leapt at the Japanese, grabbing the hand that held the toothbrush. In a blind fury, Ah Kwok rammed the brush further into the boy's mouth and then revolved it vigorously in that small space, as he held the boy's mouth closed with his other hand. The momentum of Ah Kwok's lunge had sent the boy sprawling and left Ah Kwok astride his chest. Stunned by the attack, his head ringing from connecting with the wooden floor and winded by the fall and the Chinese boy's weight, the Japanese boy at first was unable to react or resist. The white-hot pain in his gums soon animated him, and he brought both his hands up around Ah Kwok's neck and squeezed. Surprised in turn, Ah Kwok released his grip on the brush and the boy's mouth and grabbed the hands at his neck, yanking them away and down and leaping off the boy and back, taking up a standard *wu shu* stance, right hand extended, left arm drawn back against his chest, his feet planted firmly parallel with his hands. The Japanese boy remained prone, gingerly feeling his mouth. His hands came away bloody from the pink flesh of his gums and he looked up at Ah Kwok and shook his head.

'Yanagi, Yanagi?' came a voice from the doorway. 'Yanagi!' A woman rushed towards the boy, scooping him up from the floor and looking at his mouth. Ah Kwok was fixed to the spot, frozen in his pugilistic position and feeling ridiculous and a little remorseful. The boy's eyes flickered over towards Ah Kwok. His mother's darted up and saw the young Chinese boy. She shook her head. Then, in perfect Cantonese, she said to Ah Kwok, 'I am Chinese. I come from Canton. My husband is Japanese. So my son is half Chinese and half Japanese. You know that they say that "All men are brothers". Certainly we people from the East should always stand together, not against one another.'

Looking quickly at her son, she continued, 'It brings shame to both of you, yes, both of you, to fight like this. I wish you to make peace. You do not have to be friends but nor do you have to be foes.'

While she spoke, Ah Kwok had dropped his fists, and bowed his head. He felt a burning shame engulf him, more fiery than any of the fevers that had consumed him during the smallpox. The woman's words struck to his core. It was as if his own mother were reprimanding him. Hot, salty tears squeezed from his eyes and ran down his cheeks. He clenched his fists, not in resistance or anger, but because he did not wish to be so clearly reminded of his mother and her gentleness.

'My son, whose name is Yanagi, cannot speak Cantonese. That is my fault. I am going to tell him in Japanese what I have just told you and after that I hope that at least the two of you will not fight. In any event, we will be getting off the ship in Singapore, on the day after tomorrow. But remember, please, that if I could have married a Japanese man, then friendship between our races is possible.'

Quickly, she spoke to Yanagi in Japanese. He nodded in agreement, even though the evidence being uncovered by his hands, as they tentatively explored his gouged mouth, made disagreement the more likely response. When his mother had finished, he looked up at Ah Kwok and smiled. Then he pointed to his cheek and shook his head, maintaining all the while a conciliatory smile.

Ah Kwok bowed to the boy and his mother. He said to the woman, 'I am ashamed of what I have done. I did not mean to hurt your son and I hope that he will be better soon. Your words are true and remind me of things my mother told me, so I am doubly shamed for forgetting her advice. I will try to remember always what you have said.'

'Good, good,' said the woman. 'I am going to wash Yanagi's mouth, so excuse us. Do not worry that I intend to tell your father. What you say to him, if you choose to tell him of this fight, I leave to you.' With that, she turned to her son, asking him to open his mouth.

Ah Kwok slipped out of the room and made his way to the side of the deck. He would tell his father and he would try to heed the woman's words. It had been a painful lesson, more for him even than Yanagi, whose gums were bleeding and sore.

Ah Kwok did tell his father, who appreciated Yanagi's mother's subtle way of dealing with the incident. The two adults spoke for a while on the following day and Ah Kwok and Yanagi even spent some time spinning tops and working out the differences between the Chinese and Japanese versions. There was not enough time for the boys to become friends, but it was an improvement on their previous fraught dealings. When the *Yamato Princess* docked in Singapore, Yanagi thrust his top into Ah Kwok's hand. Ah Kwok took his from a pocket and gave it to Yanagi. Later, they waved to each other as Yanagi's Chinese-Japanese family disembarked, and continued waving until, at last, Yanagi and his family turned a corner and were lost to sight.

Towards nightfall of that day, Yanagi's mother returned to the ship, with a basket of Chinese foods. 'It is not much,' she said to Langshi, 'but I trust that it will help you on the rest of your journey.'

'*Toh tse*,' said Langshi. Overcome by the woman's generosity, he remarked, 'Truly, we are sister and brother.'

'*M'shai*,' she said, inclining her head to Langshi. Then she turned to Ah Kwok and said, 'Yanagi was not able to come because he is at his grand-parents' house. He sends you greetings.'

Addressing both Langshi and Ah Kwok, she said, 'Again, I wish you well on the voyage and in Kum Saan. May you make your wealth there for a long and happy life back home in Kwangtung.'

FOUR
On the Johannesburg to Durban train, 1923

The ticket inspector could scarcely believe his eyes. A White woman in the Non-European first-class carriage. And she had children with her. She must have made a mistake. Worse yet, what was she doing sitting next to a Chinaman?

Albertus van Wyk had been doing this job of ticket inspection for too long. He had been forced out of the gold mines because of a rock fall that had maimed his left foot, and even back then he had been worried by the prospect of cheaper labour, in the form of Non-Whites. Years before the accident, there had even been Chinese miners on the Witwatersrand's mines, though that had been before his time. Forced to seek less physical work, Van Wyk had joined the railways but quickly grown to the hate the sameness of his job. He hated the first-class passengers who were so smart and stuffy that they pretended he was not there when he asked for, examined, clipped and returned their tickets. He hated the second-class passengers for treating him as an equal. He hated the third-class passengers for resenting him, or cowering when he came into their crowded, smelly compartments to do his job. But most of all he hated these people in the Non-European first-class carriage, stuck there between the last Europeans Only first-class carriage and the first Non-Europeans Only second-class carriage. Only a while back he had even had these two Chinese children travelling on their own – in a first-class carriage! He had made sure they knew how to behave, and he had checked to see if they had travel permits allowing them to pass from the borders of the Transvaal through the Orange Free State and to that homeland of the *rooinekke*, the damned English, the province of Natal. Now there were more of these yellow people, surrounding this unfortunate White woman. He would soon sort matters out.

Opening the compartment door, Van Wyk bellowed '*Kaartjies!*' and then, in a polite voice, asked the white woman, 'Madam, what are you doing here? This is the wrong first-class carriage. May I help you to move?'

Looking up, Cornelia Martin smiled at the inspector. 'It is quite all right, sir. I am where I belong, here with my family. This is my husband.'

The inspector stepped back as if she had slapped him in the face. A tide of red, starting at his chin and moving rapidly upwards, rose to engulf his face. He stammered out, 'Madam, this is the coach for Non-Europeans. As far as I can see, you are European. Please move to one of the European first-class carriages.'

'I assure you, Mr Van Wyk,' said Cornelia, reading the name tag on the right pocket of his uniform, 'I am very comfortable here and would not be able to leave my family in any event. Here are our tickets.'

'Prove that you are this woman's husband,' said Van Wyk to the slim man at her side. 'Papers, I want papers. You people cannot mess around with me like this. Permits as well, travel permits – after I have seen proof that you are married.' Strange, these half-breed children – assuming these were the parents – did not look half Chinese, thought Van Wyk. They did not have even half-flat noses and half-slitty eyes, their hair was a sort of auburn-black and their skin – well, there was not much yellow in the mix.

The Chinese man drew from the inside of his jacket a slim leather folder, embossed with the letters CFM in gold. From this he produced a certificate, certified a true copy, of the marriage between Chok Foon Martin and Cornelia von Brandis, on 30 September 1907 in Kimberley in the Cape Colony. Next, he handed the inspector his passport, followed by seven travel permits, two for the parents and five for their children. As Martin looked up at the inspector, he thought about the two children who had gone ahead, Andrew and Gertie, the two first-born. They had been in China for six months, and judging from the two letters he had received, were enjoying themselves, if missing their brothers and sisters, and parents. Martin himself especially missed Gertie but found consolation in the knowledge that she drew nearer each day.

The inspector, having churned through the various official papers presented him, thrust them back at Martin with a sneer. '*Jussus* but you people breed like flies. All from one family. No wonder this country is going to the dogs with all these yellow children, getting ready to grow up and take the White man's jobs.'

Cornelia rose from her seat, glared at the inspector, and said, 'You ought to be ashamed of yourself, speaking like that in front of innocent children. If my children earn the right to work it will be because they are able to do those jobs, not just because they are white, like you. I do not know if they are yellow, as you say, but they are not like you, a walking disgrace to white men and women. Go! Get out of this carriage! I will complain about your conduct, yes, as a white woman I will complain about your disgraceful remarks.'

Van Wyk was shocked by the vigour of the woman's onslaught, confused by the evident circumstance of her having borne the children of this little Chinaman, who sat all neat and silent in his dark suit, and most of all dazed that a White woman would act and behave in this manner. Flustered, outraged, but unable to speak, he stepped out of the compartment and slammed its door.

'Thank you, Cornelia,' said Martin. 'Thank you, my dear.'

'It is the price for our happiness and children, a price I am prepared to go on paying,' she answered him.

The five children, while not quite veterans of such altercations, were getting on with their interrupted games and conversations. It was not the first time that they had seen their parents arguing with official-looking persons, and they had learnt that such matters were everyday aspects of their life. Sometimes, such rows were better than the silent stares, or the whispered venom that accompanied the family on the streets, or in shops.

Cornelia was a redoubtable woman. She had come positively to relish opportunities to confront the bigots who tormented her, her husband and family. Far better to have it out in the open, be able to retaliate, than to burn under the insinuated hatred of the snigger, or imagine replies to unheard but intuitively felt insults. She loved Chok Foon Martin, and had devastated her family beyond repair and recovery when she had married him. It was bad enough that she was an eligible, young white woman throwing away her future. It was worse that the family was of the Von Brandis clan, from the same Prussian stock as Carl von Brandis, the Transvaal's first

Commissioner of Mines, who declared a 'public diggings' on the Witwatersrand in 1886. The familial disgrace was unbearable, but not for Cornelia. For her, it was her family's manoeuvres that brought most distress.

Sinking back into the carriage seat next to Martin, Cornelia let out a small sigh and looked at the children. Elizabeth, Violet, John, Philip and James sat next to and across from her. Soon they would be a whole family again, after the train trip to Durban and the voyage to Canton. Cornelia mused about what life in her husband's village would prove to be, and reflected philosophically that any prejudice in China would be directed against her, a *bak gwai* – and a devil married to a Chinese to boot. She had meant every word she had said to her husband about protecting the family, and being willing to pay for it, but it was enervating and she knew that it was something of a life sentence wherever they decided to see out their days, South Africa or China or yet another place.

Martin had begun telling the children one of their favourite stories, about the Monkey King being made the groom of the Celestial Stables, and so Cornelia drifted off into thinking of things past. She saw, in her reverie, that moment when she had first set eyes on Chok Foon Martin, in the Chinese trading store in Ferreirastown, sometimes called in those days the Cantonese quarter. She and a male cousin had ventured to the western edges of the old Ferreira's Camp, the oldest part of the city of gold, for a glimpse of the Chinese and their mysterious ways. The two young Von Brandises knew a fair amount about the Chinese in history and culture, but virtually nothing in person. Of the local Chinese in Johannesburg, they had only newspaper reports of the day, which generally depicted the Chinese immigrants in a bad light, with tales of gambling predominating. Cornelia was fascinated by accounts of Chinese being arrested for playing *fan-tan*, a game that involved betting on numbers of beans. For a Lutheran girl, this sort of devil-may-care activity held a certain undeniable appeal. It was for a wider view of Oriental culture that she wished to go, however, and the occasional use in the papers of 'Sons of the Celestial Empire' to describe these foreigners further provoked her interest to see them in the flesh.

At first light Frederik and Cornelia set off in a family buggy, a two-wheeled, open vehicle, with Cornelia taking over the reins as soon as they were out of sight of the house. The restrictions of her family's correctness fell away and she felt free to take in the day. Ash-blonde hair showed beneath her bonnet, her sea-green eyes glistered in the golden light of early morning and she and Frederik talked animatedly about what they hoped to find. He was a handsome boy, blond and very light skinned, and staying in the sun too long without a hat invariably produced a reddishness in his face. Already, Frederik was beginning to loosen the clothing that he had been obliged to put on by the family's sense of decorum and position in society, and with satisfaction he eased his tie and loosened the topmost button of his white shirt.

'You look like a dissolute, a rake readying himself for action, and this with the sun barely up in the sky,' teased Cornelia.

'I wish I were,' laughed Frederik.

She nodded her head, understanding the appeal of careless freedom, geed up the chestnut mare and laughed up at the heavens. They were leaving the smarter eastern suburbs of the mining town and heading to where the first miners had made makeshift homes, way over on the west side. It had taken a great deal of persuasion to be allowed to borrow the buggy for the day, and neither set of parents believed that their offspring would dare do anything other than ride through the posher parts of town, as they had indicated. If they had the slightest notion of where Cornelia and Frederik were truly headed, their elders would have forbidden the excursion, for there had of late been newspaper reports of police raids on illegal games of chance in 'Chinamen's Dens' and of robberies of Chinese stores at gunpoint, or with accompanying threats of violence. Worst was the news about the Chinese mine workers, an experiment in temporary cheap labour that was proving disastrous. The miners had held protests and made demands about their crowded and insanitary living conditions, so far to little avail. Although these workers were more or less confined to mine compounds, and were not settlers, as were the Ferreirastown Cantonese, they had not lent lustre to the already poor reputation of the Chinese among whites in the city.

As the buggy made its way in a steady westward drift they moved deeper into the poorer parts of town. A brief section of what was the beginnings of a city main street, with some grand-looking buildings of dressed stone, topped with bronzed domes, gave way again to neglected areas. The sun warming their backs, finally they came to a place of corrugated tin shacks and rudimentary brick buildings, at its outskirts dotted here and there by the greying and frayed canvas of dilapidated tents that looked as if they had been there since the start of the gold rush some 20 years before. A change in the atmosphere suggested itself to them, and it was soon borne out by the bustle of Chinese speaking loudly and enthusiastically as they opened their various establishments for business. General dealers, laundries, market garden shops, tailors, butchers, restaurants, tea houses, and a fabric and gift shop met the eyes of the young visitors, each offering things alien and yet so enticing. Having traversed the length of this area, they turned down a short alley and peered into more shopfronts and windows. The same sorts of businesses were to be found here, but it was quieter off the main thoroughfare and shady as well, being a narrow strip hemmed in by buildings on either side. They stopped before what seemed to be a grocery store and spent some minutes looking in.

'We have to go in somewhere, sometime,' said Frederik. 'How does this establishment feel to you?'

'Let us have a brief look around and then I wish to visit the tailor in the big street, and perhaps stop in for tea at one of those small eating places,' replied Cornelia. 'Oh Frederik,' she continued, 'this is so very different.' The wholly new sights that greeted their eyes were one thing, but it was the bouquet of aromas that truly transported them, from the fresh, sweet steam of the laundries to the salty steam coming from the teahouses.

'Did you see that wonderful long gown – I think it is called a *ch'eung saam* – in the tailor's?' she asked.

'Yes, I did, or rather I noticed the gleam in your eye as you looked in. Do you think that you might want such a garment?'

Cornelia did not answer for already she was halfway through the door and looking round at the shelves and racks of the small grocery shop. To her, it seemed an emporium, for every little item was new to her, barring the rice, stacked in huge sacks in one corner. Next to those were barrels and wooden bins, promising surprises. On the shelves at the far left wall were glass containers filled with large and mottled brown-and-white objects of strange and contorted shape. She stepped closer, drawn by the fierce strangeness of these unknown items. Close up, she saw they were mushrooms of a kind, certainly some sort of fungal forest growth. Cornelia's mother had often told her of picking mushrooms in the forests of Prussia, expeditions that sounded to the young girl more like a hunt or a military campaign, such was the precision and care that Mother placed on every element of the venture. Particularly important, the matriarch had said in her clipped and stern voice, was establishing which mushrooms were poisonous and which edible. Cornelia, looking at the dried-out examples in the jar in front of her, felt as if all these were potentially fatal, such was the malignant quality of their gnarled features.

Frederik, less observant and more impatient, had already made a sweep of half the wares the shop had on offer. His tour was punctuated by an ejaculated 'Hmm' or a stifled 'Huh?'. His walking cane tapped insistently all the while, keeping beat to his progress. Neither he nor Cornelia had noticed any trace of a shopkeeper and she was about to remark on this curious absence when at her elbow a man materialised. 'Ohh! You startled me. Pardon,' she blushed at the sudden presence.

'I am sorry,' said the man in slow, deliberate English. Pulling at the sides of his apron, he coughed apologetically and made a note to himself not to approach customers in this silent way, which gave the appearance of stealing up on a prey.

At her sudden exclamation, Frederik, also surprised, had strode over and interposed himself between his cousin and this man of medium height, who wore beneath his apron a dark suit of good cut and a starched white shirt and tie. Frederik bowed, the man nodded and a smile suggested itself and then broke out over his somewhat flat features. His left hand twirled the left side of his moustache, and a little cough preceded his extending his right hand to Frederik. 'I am, sir, Chok Foon Martin, proprietor of this establishment. You are most welcome, as is your companion, whom I am most sorry to have surprised.'

'Oh, not at all,' interjected Cornelia, stepping forward and subtly nudging her cousin a little to the right. Cornelia shook Mr Martin's hand, saying, 'I am Cornelia von Brandis and this is my cousin Frederik von Brandis.'

'My pleasure,' said Martin in his courteous, grave way, shaking Frederik's outstretched hand also. 'May I be of particular assistance? Is there anything you require? Otherwise I shall be happy to be of general service in whatever enquiry you may have.' He smiled and drew back a little.

'These mushrooms, or what look like mushrooms,' said Cornelia. 'What are they really? And are they poisonous?'

'Ah, no. They are neither poisonous nor mushrooms. They are similar to mushrooms for they grow in the forests and in wet places on the mountains, but they are — how shall I say — a fungus that is delicious to eat. They are among the ingredients in a dish named monk's food, because the monks in remote monasteries gather what they can from nature and prepare it with soya bean curd in a vegetable dish that is, shall we say, heavenly to eat.'

Frederik could see that Cornelia's introduction to this world that she was so interested in from having read about it in books was going to constitute more than a single visit. Knowing and loving his cousin and her fancies and enthusiasms, he resigned himself already to accompanying her in future to this Cantonese quarter. He was certain that, in the way of many other of her interests, she would eventually tire of this delving into a new and exotic milieu.

For the moment, her keenness was at its fullest. The man was showing her various other dried foodstuffs, all of which, he said, were revitalised by soaking in water and, when filled out once more, used as ingredients in Chinese cooking. At the rate they were proceeding through the items in the glass jars on the many shelves, they could be here all day, delayed the more when custom began in earnest, thought Frederik. Summoning patience, he joined the elaboration by Martin that had his cousin so rapt.

'This is very special tea, and rare. It is an indulgence to stock, for there are not many Chinese here who can readily afford it,' said Martin. 'Still, this would be a poor quality establishment that would not serve the community well if it did not have some items of genuine quality.'

He opened the wooden cask and offered the contents for Cornelia's perusal. She looked in and before her eyes could focus on the leaves, she picked up the crisp scent of the tea.

'This is *Ti Kuan Ying*, Chinese oolong. What makes it a special kind of oolong is that it is picked by monkeys,' explained Martin.

'Monkeys?' chorused Cornelia and Frederik, in some alarm.

'Yes, monkeys,' replied Martin, smiling. 'You see, the bushes where this tea grows are on very high, very steep slopes, where it is difficult and dangerous for humans to work. The monkeys are trained to pick the leaves and bring them back down in small baskets strapped to their backs.'

Frederik shook his head, laughed and said, 'That is a very fine tale, but I do not believe it. Still, I am certain that the tea is very fine indeed.'

'Ah, Mr von Brandis, it is said that it has a "heavenly lingering crisp flavour" and so it does. I will prove that to you by making a pot so that you and Miss von Brandis may sample it for yourselves.'

'Oh, please, no, Mr Martin, that is unnecessary. I believe you about the taste of the tea and it would be rude to impose further on your hospitality. Already we have overstayed our welcome, I am sure,' said Cornelia. Throwing a fleeting scowl at Frederik, she added, 'I believe also your story of how this tea comes to have its name, whatever that cynical cousin of mine has to say on the matter.'

To this Frederik smiled and bowed ever so slightly, and quickly added, 'Mr Martin, I apologise if I have caused you offence. It seems so unlikely that monkeys could be trained to do such a task, and that succeeding generations of them should continue to labour away in this manner. Please accept my retraction. And now, indeed, we must go. Thank you for your patience and generosity toward us.'

'Please, please stay and have some *Ti Kuan Ying*. It will be my very great pleasure,' said Martin, hoping that these two young white people, who showed such an easy willingness to talk to a Chinese person, would accept his invitation. In the years since he had arrived in South Africa from Mauritius he had been granted very few sociable dealings with the white people of Johannesburg, in contrast to his time on the island where he had grown up. There he had been taught by French Catholic nuns, and his father's trading business had ensured a flow of heterogeneous clients: Chinese, Indians, Mauritians and Europeans. The young Martin had been able to engage in conversations with many of his father's merchant associates.

Cornelia and Frederik looked at each other. It seemed churlish to decline Mr Martin's invitation. Cornelia thought of suggesting they call around another day, but reckoned that it would sound as if they were fobbing off the courteous Chinese with a promise never to be kept.

'We gladly accept such a gracious invitation,' said Cornelia, and Frederik nodded his head in assent. Martin indicated that they should sit at the small round table in the right-hand corner of the shop, on sturdy wooden chairs with high, upright backs.

'Excuse me while I prepare the tea,' he said before disappearing behind a carved wooden screen to a room within. There was the soft sound of water being poured, the more robust noise of a match being struck and a Primus being lit, and then the clunk of tin upon metal, presumably a pot being placed on the Primus stove. A soft clink now reached Cornelia's and Frederik's ears, a series of such sounds, in fact, and a minute later Martin emerged, with a lacquered tray on which were placed three small green cups and three small plates, engraved with a beautiful geometric design. In the centre of the tray was a bowl of identical markings, in which were round biscuits that resembled shortbread in texture but had Chinese characters stamped on their faces and a square hole in their middle.

'These are almond biscuits, very tasty, please take for yourselves,' said Martin. 'I shall now bring the tea.' He went into the back room again, and soon there was a whistling sound and the suggestion of steam, the gurgle of boiling water being poured, and a satisfying plop, of a lid being dropped into its pot. All the while Cornelia and Frederik waited, their eyes roving over the shelves with their many and varied novelties, a cornucopia of strange and enticing shapes and colours, and intoxicatingly exotic fragrances as well.

Martin came back to the table, placing on it the tea pot, which matched the cups, bowl and small plates for the biscuits. 'We must wait a little for the tea to draw,' he said, and insisted they try a biscuit. Cornelia picked up one of the almond biscuits, put it on her plate and after looking closely at its face, raised it to her mouth and took a delicate bite. The taste of nut released itself as the biscuit melted and then, in its aftertaste, left a dryness that called for more biscuit to assuage it. She took a second, larger bite and noticed that Frederik had already almost finished his.

'These are *sehr gut*,' said Frederik, lapsing into a bit of German without thought. 'Excuse me, I mean very good. German is my mother tongue and I find it difficult to speak English without sometimes resorting to very common, very useful German words.'

'Ah, I know what you mean. I too have a struggle not to let Chinese words slip into my English when I speak. It is a little easier now than when I was a child and being taught French by the nuns. Then I used to speak as much Cantonese as French,' said Martin, who then allowed himself the luxury of a chortle that prolonged itself into a hearty laugh when Cornelia joined in his mirthful moment and Frederik, by now thoroughly at ease and prepared to believe that monkeys could fly, let loose his booming, Prussian laugh.

'If you do not think me impolite for asking, Mr Martin, please tell us about the nuns,' said Cornelia. And then, indulging curiosity and throwing decorum to the winds, she plunged in, keenly, asking, 'Did they teach you that in China? And your name, it sounds European rather than Chinese, could you explain it?'

'Cornelia, please, do not be so inquisitive. I am sure that Mr Martin has better things to do and more pressing business to attend to than answering these questions,' Frederik said in quick rebuke, accompanied by a swift frown at his cousin.

'Oh no, Mr von Brandis, it is quite all right,' said Martin, almost springing in between his visitors. 'Business is always quiet on a Monday, the weekend's eating and celebrating is over and people need some time to recover. The trade will pick up in an hour or so when people will come to purchase basics and then I may ask to be excused from your side, but for the moment it is an honour indeed to answer these questions and to be carrying on this entertaining conversation. Tea is ready and I shall pour before I begin.'

The dark brown tea poured smoothly from the pot, running unerringly into the cups. Cornelia, who was in search of just such a vessel that did not dribble down its spout or shower drops of tea everywhere, asked Martin where she could acquire one. Smiling, he suggested she wait till later, when he would direct her to the appropriate shop. 'Taste the tea, please,' he said, 'and tell me what you make of it.'

The two cousins lifted the cups, which they held in both hands because of the delicious warmth that the porcelain retained and emitted, and

brought them slowly up to their mouths. Before sipping at the rich liquid, which had the tawny dazzle of a fine single malt Scotch, thought
Frederik, both savoured the bouquet. Cornelia paused momentarily and
allowed the thought of monkey hygiene to distract her and then, mentally shaking her head at her silliness, drew down her first sip. Flavours and
hints of far-away places, halfway round the globe, prickled her tongue and
excited her imagination. She had an image of green hills sloping steeply
up to cliffs, with tea bushes clinging to the last rich soils just underneath
the overhanging rock faces. A platoon of monkeys was bounding up these
farthest reaches, wicker baskets on their backs. At the top line of tree
bushes, a larger ape seemed to call out and the monkeys each made for a
different bush and began the task of picking the best leaves. These were
no random choices they made: before a leaf was plucked, the monkeys
seemed to study it carefully, sometimes sniffing at it, and then removing
it with a care that was almost reverential.

'Ah, you do not like this tea, I can tell,' said Martin anxiously to
Cornelia, whose long silence and closed eyes he interpreted as a polite
way of deflecting his uncharacteristically direct question. He wished that
he had not been so rude to an honoured guest. What had taken hold of
him and possessed him with such intrusive candour, prompting him to
solicit an opinion from this charming and courteous young woman?

Before Martin could further entangle himself in the miseries of worried speculation, Cornelia opened her eyes and said, in a dreamy voice
that purred with enjoyment, 'This truly is heavenly tea. I have never tasted anything quite like it and now I am certain that I am forever spoilt for
I shall always remember it, when I am drinking the cruder type of tea to
which we are accustomed.'

'Hear, hear,' said Frederik. 'It is even better than the almond biscuit. It is
unique in my experience, limited though that experience is. I do not think
that I will ever forget this brew of oolong tea. Thank you, *Herr* Martin.'

Delighted by this turn of events, Martin nodded and smiled in an
embarrassed sort of way. He nodded again, then smiled, and finally said, 'I
am grateful that you appreciate this tea. I would have felt an unworthy
host if you did not find it had certain virtues. May I pour each of you
some more?'

Of course they agreed, though not without the usual preliminary protestations. The social niceties over, the three tea drinkers savoured their second cup and a comfortable silence. When the spell of the brew and the silence were broken, it was at exactly the right moment, with Martin taking up Cornelia's questions. 'I will begin with the matter of my name,' he said. 'This is always confusing because we Chinese place our names the other way round from Europeans. Whereas you have a Christian name and perhaps a middle name and of course definitely a surname, in that order, for us the individual is not as important as being able to identify immediately what clan, what family one comes from. So, take my name: Chok Foon Martin. My surname, so to say, is Chok. My first name is Martin, given by my parents because of a French Mauritian friend of theirs whom they first met in Canton. They hoped I would grow like him, and perhaps I have. I came to South Africa from Mauritius, stopping first at Mozambique. When I landed at Delagoa Bay in Lourenço Marques, I filled out the disembarkation forms in the Chinese style, with family name first. It was altogether a very difficult process, because Chinese is a pictorial language, not a phonetic one, and the official wanted to get the sound of my name and write that down. Naturally I said Chok Foon Martin, though I was aware of the differences in our customs. My surname was taken to be Martin and of course I could not change that in Durban, when I completed my immigration papers. So I have become Mr Martin, although I am always Martin to my family and friends.'

Cornelia and Frederik thought this reversal in the order of things entirely understandable; their world, after all, had been stood on its head by their experiences of this day. There was no right or wrong way to doing things, they felt – and were able to confirm to each other on the talkative ride back home – merely different ways of doing and seeing. And how enlarged their world had become, Cornelia remarked passionately to Frederik as they trotted home on the back of the buggy.

Martin had begun to tell them about his education at a Catholic school in Port Louis, the island capital. 'They were fierce – and I vouchsafe remain so to this day,' he declared, a fond and nostalgic lilt in his voice. 'They looked like giants to me. They were certainly taller than either my father or mother.

'Mother Patrice – many of the nuns took the names of Catholic male saints – was the head of the convent. She was a wonderful teacher, but a stern disciplinarian. The boys never got away with much when she was at the head of the class. Unusually, the convent had classes for boys and girls together, at least in the elementary years and in junior school. The girls hated the boys and perhaps it is not a good idea for them to be in the same classroom, because boys are so much younger in mind. Later, too, boys' minds seem to develop less quickly, but by that age I was in a boys-only school.'

Taking the last sip from his cup, Martin smiled again. 'So it is the nuns that I must thank for being able to speak French. For my English I have to honour my namesake, Martin Leconte, a tea and spice merchant who had spent much time dealing with the English in the tea trade in China, and also with them across the channel from France, before he went off to see the world.'

'Why did your parents go to Mauritius?' asked Frederik.

'South China, Kwangtung province, is very poor. I suppose most of China is very poor. For the people of this part of the country, the Cantonese, it is easier to go abroad. Not cheaper, but much easier to think of, and to arrange. Particularly for those living near the city of Canton, which is almost on the coast and is an old and busy port, it is possible not only to dream of making one's fortune abroad, but also to walk to the great city. That nearness brings the dream closer and prompts many to save for their passage on the seas to faraway lands: America, Australia and South Africa. And so you see me here,' he concluded, chuckling.

'And when did your parents go to Mauritius, and then when did you make your way here?' asked Cornelia. She felt that Mr Martin's life story was so much more interesting than hers, and his journey so much more romantic than that of her grandparents, from Europe.

'We went to the island in year 1885, from Peng Po,' answered Martin, 'one of the many villages in the vicinity of the local market town of Lok Chung, south of Canton. I was nine years old and did not really want to leave. When you are young you know nothing or very little of the bigger things that plague adults. We travelled on a steamer owned by the British India Steam Navigation Company, which made a huge northward loop to stop at Calcutta on the way to collect contract workers bound for

Mauritius. My parents became part of the sizable community of Chinese merchants and artisans on the island and made a reasonable living, and certainly a splendid one by the standards of home.'

Calculating Martin's age – he was 30 now – startled Cornelia, who could have sworn from his face and body that he was in his twenties. His demeanour and speech were grave, even old fashioned, but he had not seemed, in body at least, anywhere near to 30. Twenty herself, Cornelia regarded 30 as a lifetime away, a decade that spanned a yawning chasm from her present to some hazy future.

The door to the shop swung open and an elderly Chinese woman entered. She shuffled towards the shelves at the left, and with a quiet 'excuse me', Martin rose, left his Caucasian guests and went to attend the first customer of the day. A short, loud exchange followed and Cornelia wondered if the volume was because the old woman might be hard of hearing. The language was impenetrable but fascinating, rising and falling, seemingly filled with tones and inflections. Cornelia and Frederik listened as if they were able to comprehend the conversation, but eagerly awaited Martin's return to ask him what had been said. They saw that the woman bought some dried products, similar to those that had absorbed their attention when they first entered the shop, some hours – a surprisingly large number of hours – before.

As they were about to resume the conversation, the door opened once more, and admitted a group of customers. It was clear from the pitch of their talking that Cantonese was a well articulated, somewhat noisy language, but this mêlée of requests, questions and answers, as they seemed to Cornelia, only entranced her more. When Martin resorted to his abacus, whirring its beads along their rods at astonishing speed, she felt that she could have remained all day in the shop. She had read about this counting device, invented some 400 years before, but never seen one, let alone observed it in action. Frederik, of a mathematical bent, knew the principles and was most keen to ask Martin if he could do some calculations himself. For the moment, however, the cousins felt it polite to depart, given the evident increase in custom. They promised each other that they would return, soon, and waited for an appropriate moment to take their leave.

Finally, when Martin had served all those in the group, Cornelia and Frederik rose from the table and walked towards him, as he wrote something down, using a brush that he held at what appeared an odd angle, perpendicular to the paper and just below the heel of his palm. Fluid, elegant strokes covered the paper, rendered swiftly but leaving the impression of artistry rather than commerce or the mundane.

'My dear Mr Martin, most gracious and generous host, we regret that we must leave you,' began Cornelia.

'Oh, please stay, you have hardly arrived and my hospitality has been very poor indeed. You must be thirsty, and even hungrier still. Please allow me to make up for my lapse and offer you, first, more tea and then some food of greater substance than the paltry almond biscuits you have had to make do with.'

'It would be a great pleasure and honour for us to accept your generous offer, Mr Martin, but I fear that we need to make our way home,' said Cornelia. 'If it is not too presumptuous, however, may we take the opportunity of calling on you at some time soon in the future? This has been one of the most remarkable days of my life, and I thank you with all my being. Please allow us to call again, if only to reciprocate in some way for your generosity.'

'I have been unmindful of your comfort. I have neglected my guests. Please do visit again, so that I may put that to rights. I promise that next time you will be better looked after.'

Blushing, Cornelia and Frederik both, the cousins thanked Mr Martin yet again. Frederik asked if he could shake Mr Martin's hand, and when Cornelia extended hers, she was surprised, but even more pleased, that Martin took it gracefully and, in the French manner, bestowed the gentlest of kisses on it.

Touched, and with a strange feeling of empathy that she had never felt before, Cornelia inclined her head, smiled and said goodbye.

'Goodbye and thank you, Miss von Brandis and Mr von Brandis. I trust that I shall see you soon.'

'Goodbye and thank you, Mr Martin,' said the two cousins as, regretfully, they turned to leave the magical little shop.

That was how Cornelia and Martin had met, and as Cornelia thought back to that day in the shop, the train journey receded and she was absorbed entirely by the past. It was only when Martin leaned over and asked if she were all right that Cornelia brought herself back to the present. 'Yes, of course, dear Martin. I was daydreaming a little. Well, no, I was thinking of how we met, and how wonderful a beginning that was.'

Martin smiled and looked lovingly at Cornelia and then their brood. 'We have a new beginning before us,' he said, with quiet satisfaction in his voice. 'And I am going home at last.'

FIVE
On the Yamato Princess, *Indian Ocean, 1911*

Ah Kwok was itching to be on the ocean. So far, he felt, the *Yamato Princess* had been sailing in confined waters on its progress from Hong Kong. The fish bowl of the South China Sea had given way, after Singapore, to the Karamata Strait, the Java Sea and the Sunda Strait, only after all of which beckoned the Indian Ocean. It did not matter to Ah Kwok that they had been out of sight of land for much of the passage so far; he longed for that first taste of the boundless ocean. So, as the ship eased its way up the straits, he sat listlessly in steerage, feeling cooped up and impatient. Langshi wondered if it was the biting realities of shipboard life in the poorest class that were getting to his son, or perhaps he was regretting his fight with the Japanese boy. Langshi did not enquire directly, trusting that time would loosen Ah Kwok's tongue.

As matters turned out, it was an outside agency that restored the boy's good humour. At Singapore, the crew had been enlarged by a number of British sailors, one of whom found himself idling in Ah Kwok's vicinity on the third morning out of port. Ah Kwok was sitting cross-legged in the sun, eating his habitual and by now extremely dreary breakfast of *congee*, the rice gruel that feeds many economically but not always most deliciously. Observing the boy's lack of relish, the sailor asked, 'Wot ye got there, lad? Looks like horrid porridge ter me.' Ah Kwok looked up, not understanding anything the man had said, but catching in his ready smile and subsequent exaggerated grimace the drift of his words. The boy smiled, shrugged his shoulders and took another spoonful.

'My boy, I've got something better fer ye,' said the sailor, indicating with his hands that he would be back soon. He returned ten minutes later with thick slices of a hard bread with a black crust, cheese and butter on an enamel plate, and a mug of milk. With a flourish, the sailor sat down beside Ah Kwok and handed him the plate. 'Here, try these,' he said, making eating gestures with his right hand as he extended the plate with his left.

Ah Kwok looked down at the plate. He had never seen such food before. The yellowy-white slabs on the dark blocks, with a thinner yellow substance separating them, looked unappetising. Still, he could not refuse the man's generosity. Nodding his head, Ah Kwok took one of the portions from the plate, brought it up to his mouth and bit into the concoction. His teeth sank into the cheese, softer than it had looked, passed through the butter and into the bread. He chewed and swallowed. The sailor smiled and patted him on the back, then made a strange movement with his hand, raising his thumb. Ah Kwok smiled back at him, and continued conscientiously working his way through the food. One of the items dispatched, he sighed inwardly with relief and then, at the sailor's urging, took up the second. Suddenly, Ah Kwok felt very strange. His stomach had leapt into his mouth and he knew that he was about to be sick. Jumping to his feet, he ran for the deck rail, leaned over as far as he could, and retched. Langshi came striding across to see what was the matter, and the sailor, concerned, joined them.

'I'm sorry, sir,' said the sailor, pointing at Ah Kwok. 'Gave him some cheese sandwiches, I did, but I see he's not taken to them.'

Langshi nodded, smiling, at the man and asked Ah Kwok what was wrong. 'That food tastes very strange, Father. Never have I eaten anything like it. It is rich and feels odd, soft on top and then very chewy at the bottom.'

Walking back to the abandoned plate, Langshi cast a quick look at its contents and then returned to Ah Kwok, who was now leaning against the rail, feeling somewhat better.

'*Tsai*,' said Langshi. 'This is Western food that you will have to grow accustomed to. These yellow-coloured substances are made from cows' milk, so are entirely new to your body. Their novelty to your system accounts for your being ill.'

Turning to the sailor, Langshi thanked the man by inclining his head. The sailor smiled. 'Me name's Robert,' he said, pointing to himself as he did so. 'Ro-bert.'

'Langshi,' said Ah Kwok's father and then, pointing to his son, 'Ah Kwok.'

'Lungsee. Ah Cork,' responded Robert.

'*Hai*, Langshi,' said Ah Kwok's father and then, shaking his head, said, slowly, 'Ah Kwok. *M'hai* Ah Cork.'

'Ah Cork. Him he Ah Cork,' said Robert, with a hearty laugh that seemed to suggest that he thought he had mastered the young boy's name.

Langshi, realising the problem, decided to leave it at that for now and smiled back at Robert. '*Hai*, Rob-ert.'

'Well, good day, Langshi and Ah Cork. I must be off below now,' said Robert, waving.

Father and son returned the greeting and watched as Robert gathered up the enamel plate and its half-eaten contents, and picked up the mug. 'Don't suppose you'd fancy a sip of this, would ye?' he asked them. Politely, Langshi shook his head. 'Well, goodbye for now!' said Robert as he walked away.

'*Foo ts'an*, that man looks like the *bak gwai* in Hong Kong. Yet he is different from them, so very friendly. How is that so?'

'*Tsai*, as I have said to you before: always judge the person. Yes, he is a British man, and just as there are friendly *T'ong yan*, so too there are nice people from England. And just as there are unpleasant Chinese, so there are nasty British.'

Something alerted Langshi to the line Ah Kwok's questioning was taking. His parental anticipation prepared him for the next enquiry.

'*Foo ts'an*, what did that sign in the park say? Why could we not walk there that day?'

'My boy, it is correct that I tell you why. I did know the reason then but was too angry — and perhaps a little ashamed that Chinese should be treated in such a way — to be able to tell you that same afternoon. The sign said "No Dogs or Chinese Permitted".'

'They think we are dogs? How can they? I don't like these *Ying-Kwok yan*, truly they are devils,' Ah Kwok burst out. A few heads turned in the direction of the boy and his father. An old man gave a crackly laugh and turned to an old woman at his side and whispered in her ear. She chortled, turned to look at Ah Kwok and then continued on her painfully slow promenade of the cramped steerage deck area.

From behind Langshi and Ah Kwok, a voice said, 'Hai, these *bak gwai*. They fill China with opium, force trade on us and are all cosy with the Manchu in Peking. Mark my words, though: their time is coming to an end. First the Manchu will go, then the *gwai lo*.'

Langshi and Ah Kwok turned to see a man in his mid-thirties, tallish and with a debonair smile. He introduced himself as Lee Soon, bound for Mauritius. He and Langshi struck up an animated conversation about Hong Kong and the English arrogance there, while Ah Kwok gradually grew tired of the adults' conversation, with its talk of Sun Yat-sen and the United League and their chances of overthrowing the Manchu dynasty.

Settling into a corner of the deck shaded from the sun, Ah Kwok looked around at the passengers and noticed yet again how few women and children there were. He missed being with his family. It was unnatural for it to be just his father and him. His grandfather had been the last person of the family he had seen, on the road above the village, and he tried to conjure him up by closing his eyes and remembering very hard. Relieved, he held an image of the old man, hand held aloft, bidding him goodbye. In a way, it was fitting that this last clear image should be of his grandfather, who had been so pivotal a presence in his life. So many of his daily activities had centred on Tian's interests and way of living. The fish ponds, for one thing. Ah Kwok would help *Kongkong* clean the ponds, and had even graduated to cleaning on his own the pond of a great-aunt, the wife of one of his grandfather's younger brothers, since her husband and sons had gone to America. It was a job he enjoyed, even though it had almost got him into deep trouble the last time he did it. As usual, Ah Kwok had first opened the hole in the retaining mud wall and made sure that the water flowed into the furrows between the main pond and the temporary pond. When the latter held enough water, he began netting the fish and transferring them. Slowly the smaller pond filled with carp, mainly brown, but with the occasional more brightly coloured and larger fish, its hues indicating age and beginning to show beauty.

After the fish, Ah Kwok worked his way through the smaller, but no less important, pond life. These creatures were vital to the balance of the water, Tian had taught him, so very carefully Ah Kwok transferred the snails, water shrimps and worms. Whenever he could, he caught the swift and mobile frogs as well. The eels were even more elusive, but he caught sight of them more easily when the pond was almost empty, and then he managed to hold on to them despite their slipperiness and the sharp threat from their teeth. Still, he knew that many eels would have slithered into the mud and buried themselves beneath its sticky brownness. Getting them out would be fun, though nothing as exciting as hunting for snakes. The pond now empty of all but leaves and other debris that had drifted to the bottom, Ah Kwok set about the messy part of the ritual. Edging along, squeezing his feet into the mud, turning them this way and that and then advancing a little further, he would unearth a carp here, an eel there. Once a barbel's moustaches tickled his toes, alerting him to the presence of this mud-loving denizen and he lowered himself slowly towards what he guessed was the middle of its bulbous body, then shoved his hands quickly into the mud and came up with the fish.

But none of these discoveries pleased him. He was really hunting for that extra large carp that every pond seemed to have. For an hour or so, he trawled the mud with his feet. As the sun dried out the pond bottom, it was easier to see disguised forms, the fish-like bulge or fin that other-wise might have gone unnoticed. It seemed that all the fish had been cap-tured, and with disappointment Ah Kwok thought that the three medi-um to large, fairly brightly coloured carp were all the treasures the pond had to yield. It was odd, he could have sworn that the previous year there had been one much larger, beautifully coloured carp. Perhaps it had died, but then surely Tian or Langshi would have been told about it; such mat-ters were talked about for some days in the village.

Resigning himself to the less pleasant task of weeding the pond of grasses and other non-aquatic aliens that had insinuated themselves over the year, Ah Kwok turned and made a last diagonal walk across the pond. Perhaps his frustration and tiredness, for it was now half an hour past noon and very hot, made him dig his feet in more deeply and forcefully. Suddenly, he felt a wriggle. Drilling his feet into the harder mud beneath the surface, he felt a scaly presence against the big toe of his right foot. Tentatively, he dug in his left heel and then swivelled that foot towards his stationary right leg. His left foot came up against more scales. Trapped by the very effectiveness of its deep refuge, the carp could not escape. Its tail had begun to wriggle, but that movement would not propel it from its muddy fastness. This, thought Ah Kwok, must be the grandfather of the pond, the king of the *lei yu*, the carp.

Triumphantly but carefully, he reached down into the mud, tunnelled under the fish with his hands and then scooped up the prize with a whoop. The fish flailed around, almost slipped from his grasp, seemed to be glaring at him with baleful eyes. Rays of light, indeed almost a spectrum it seemed to Ah Kwok in that victorious moment, appeared to be streaming from the fish's dazzling and large, heavy scales. Ah Kwok had plans for this carp.

Just then the old woman came out of her hut. She had of course been alarmed by the yell from the pond. Reaching the embankment and peering over, she called, quickly, '*Lai, lai*. Come, come. It's the grandfather carp! *Lai*, Ah Kwok. Put it in the other pond.'

Ah Kwok had other plans. He got out of the pond, the carp still thrashing around, and made to walk towards the second pond. At the last instant, as he seemed to be about to throw the fish into the water, he turned and ran past the second pond and towards the hill leading back to the village, and home.

His great-aunt yelled after him, calling down the wrath of the gods on the little devil. She said she would tell his grandfather and father, just as soon as she reached their house. '*Aiee yah*, I am too old and slow to catch you, but one of your elders at least will beat you for this, you evil boy!' she called, long after Ah Kwok had dropped from sight over the top of the hill.

Ah Kwok knew that a *lei yu* of this size could stay alive out of the water for hours. But he knew that he could not arrive home with a living fish: his mother would reprimand him and send it straight back to the old woman, or keep it in water and have it returned later. Still, he wanted the fish to be as fresh as possible, and he already saw, smelt and tasted it as he walked home unhurriedly. He decided he'd keep it alive for as long as possible and then, just before he reckoned his mother would arrive home, he would kill it. He would leave it on a plate and then melt away to play with Ah Wa and Mudan, returning home around suppertime. Soi Sien might think that Tian had decided to celebrate the new season and the end of winter, or thought spontaneously to mark the coming departure of Langshi and Ah Kwok, by eating one of the old, prized fish. It would be enough that she did not at once suspect Ah Kwok. Certainly, she would not waste the food. Ah Kwok knew that when the truth came out, he would be in big trouble for this, and even anticipated the beating his father would probably give him, but he had been thinking of this carp for a year now, and of the wonderful meal it would make. And he would take some of the fish back to his great-aunt too.

Things turned out much as Ah Kwok had thought. His mother, seeing the fish, was startled that Tian would wish to part with so beautiful a specimen, and wondered why he had not left it alive. Nonetheless she quickly prepared it and looked forward to the evening meal. Langshi, arriving home before sunset, was as surprised by his father's largesse – and somewhat worried by the old man's exuberant gesture. When *Kongkong* and *Bobo* arrived, they were startled by the beautiful deep-fried carp that lay before them. 'Where did you buy so fine a fish, *tsai*?' asked Tian, at the same time smiling at Ah Kwok.

'*Foo ts'an*, we thought you had given it to us to make for dinner,' said Langshi in some alarm.

In an instant, Soi Sien and *Bobo* guessed. Women are always quicker at these things, and just as swiftly they concocted, unspoken, a plan of deflection. '*Hai, hai*, Tian, it was me,' said *Bobo*. 'I spoke to your sister-in-law, because Ah Kwok was going to be cleaning her pond today, and asked if we could buy the largest carp. You know she is always hard pressed and besides I thought Soi Sien is such a wonderful cook, and it is spring now, so we should celebrate the end of the hard winter we have had. A winter of talking, talking, talking about this Kum Saan. It was Namfeechow this and Namfeechow that. Now that the decision has been taken, let us relax and enjoy family, for we may not be all together for some years. *Sek faan*.'

Sek faan: literally, eat rice. And how they had eaten that night, though not before Ah Kwok had suggested to his mother that she put aside a piece of fish for his great-aunt. Throughout the dinner, neither his mother nor his grandmother gave an inkling that they knew the enormity of his mischief. Nor did they hint at the punishment that was to come. For that hour, the family enjoyed together the fat grandfather carp, a fish in its prime that Soi Sien had deep fried, and served smothered with sweet and sour turnips and sweet cucumber, dripping with a sauce made from rock sugar.

Later that evening, when the men had strolled across to visit the Li family, Soi Sien darted out a hand and grabbed Ah Kwok by the ear. 'Well, my fine boy, what did you do at great-aunt's? Stole her prize carp? If your father and grandfather hear about it, they will lather you, worse than a Manchu official punishing a Chinese. What were you thinking? How can you cheat great-aunt of something so valuable? Are you a thief and a coward? A liar?'

Ah Kwok said nothing. He had no defence, no pretence of innocence was possible, nor would he have wanted to adopt such a strategy. Before he had run off with the carp, there had been a moment of indecision, or rather an instant when he had weighed the consequences and had braced himself for the inevitable punishment. He had wanted the family to have a good meal, had wished for his mother to have something substantial on which to exercise her culinary skills. As he had run up the hill, away from the empty pond, he had also been preparing to meet his grandfather's shame and ire and his father's punishment. This berating from his mother, and the painful but by no means unendurable ear-pulling, were mild in comparison. There could, he thought, still be a beating to come, if his mother got angrier still.

'Soi Sien, Soi Sien,' his *Bobo* said from the corner of the room, 'the boy had good intentions. Leave him now. It is done. Tomorrow, early, I will walk up to my sister and make good. We will not breathe a word of this to Tian and Langshi. Besides, if she was so angry, do you not think she would have walked here this very afternoon? I think she thought better of the journey and I know she is fond of the boy. So, leave it to me. But you, young man, must come with me tomorrow to apologise. I never want you to do such a thing again. Do you hear?'

Ah Kwok nodded, and apologised to his mother and grandmother. Soi Sien, still a little angry, and red in the face, released his ear, which she had almost forgotten she was holding.

Next day, he and *Bobo* went to make amends, and after a blustery initial period his great-aunt calmed down and then, with a wicked gurgle, began to laugh. It helped that somehow *Bobo* had talked Tian into giving his sister-in-law a fine carp, with just the beginning traces of colour on its body, but Ah Kwok felt also that his great-aunt liked him anyway.

Ah Kwok was savouring that carp in his memory when a tap on his shoulder brought him back into shipboard life. As he adjusted quickly to the present, the last thought prompted by his recollection was a regret that the nose could not clearly recall what was so vivid to his eye, for he would dearly have loved to smell the aroma of the carp once more.

Next morning, even before Ah Kwok had picked up his bowl to fetch some *congee*, Robert the sailor was in steerage. He brought with him a plate on which wobbled two yellow blobs fringed by white, atop slices of the same hard, black-crusted bread of the day before, and a stack of strips that were pinky-brown and white in colour. Ah Kwok recognised the eggs but was unfamiliar with the accompanying meat. He pointed to it and raised an eyebrow.

'Aye, that's bacon — fatty meat from pigs,' said Robert. Langshi had come to join them, and looking down at the plate, smiled and said to Ah Kwok, 'Eleven years without sampling pork and now in a few weeks, *char siu* and bacon.' He nodded a thank-you to Robert.

'Oh, sir, I've brought some fruit as well. Helps keep the health up on these journeys. And also, for later, some chocolate for the lad.' With that, Robert handed over the fruit and a slab of a hard brown substance such as Ah Kwok had never seen. 'It's sweet and mighty fine, Ah Cork,' said Robert. 'But yer can't have it early in the day. Keep it for afternoon tea time, when yer feel like somethin' rich and sweet.'

Realising his words could not be understood, Robert made eating gestures with his right hand and mouth and then, with his left, pointed to the sky and described the passage of the sun from morning through noon to about four o'clock. 'Understand?' he asked anxiously of Langshi and Ah Kwok. They nodded and smiled, and Robert, hoping that he had made himself clear, waved goodbye to them.

Ah Kwok found the bacon strangely familiar, although entirely new to his palate. He guessed it was the *char siu* that had prepared him for this, although the bacon was salty compared to the sweetness of the Chinese pork. While he ate, Langshi turned the chocolate slab over in his hand. He smelt it but found no clues there as to its ingredients. Content to save tasting for later, he dropped the slab into a coat pocket and asked Ah Kwok how he had enjoyed his meal.

'This is strange food, but much better than yesterday. At least it did not make me sick.'

'Good, you must develop a strong stomach. And you will need to be strong for what I am about to tell you. Come, let us sit down out of the sun and I will explain to you how you will enter Namfeechow.'

The two found a sheltered spot. 'Tsai, you must listen carefully and not interrupt me or ask questions until I am done. Then I will answer anything you wish to ask.'

Ah Kwok looked earnestly at his father and waited for him to begin.

'You know that there are many official procedures and forms that we must complete when we reach Namfeechow in order to be allowed into the country. There are many laws there that stop us from entering, and make it difficult for us to do business. It is strange but true that Chinese cannot do in Kum Saan what they went there to do: prospect for gold. I speak here of free Chinese, not the contracted labourers who worked on the mines and have now been sent home. The *bak gwai* in Kum Saan refused to give *T'ong yan* permits, so instead of looking for gold, they became grocers and farmers and laundrymen.

'Since Namfeechow became united under the British, it is even more difficult for us to enter there. Because of that, you must learn a new name for the time we will be in Kum Saan. No, wait – I will answer your questions later.'

Langshi paused, both to give the boy respite and to prepare himself for the painfulness of what was to come. 'You see, I cannot bring you into the new country as my son. If I had been working there, and then gone home to visit and a child had been conceived during that time, it would be different. Then I would have been able to bring that child over at a later stage.

'Sometimes people who work in Namfeechow do not send for their children. Others report children who have not been born. Others yet lose their children. Many of these people give their papers to relatives or sell them. I bought your papers – *gee tsai* – from a couple who lost their son. That is why you cannot be known by your name, Fok Kwok Ying. You must remember that from now on, until we return to Sha Kiu, you are Ah Leong, not Ah Kwok.'

Ah Kwok took the surprise as a body blow. He did not wish to have another name. In the lengthening silence that followed what Langshi had to say, he wrestled with a dozen contradictory emotions. Finally, Ah Kwok said, 'But will I continue to be your son? And my grandfather's grandson?'

'Ah, but of course. You are my son and will be so always. You see, those who enter Namfeechow in this way are called "paper sons" because that is what they are – sons on paper only. In Kum Saan, you shall meet your "foster father", a happy, smiling man whom you will like.'

'And when shall I have my own name back? I do not wish to be this Ah Leong always.'

'When we are back home, so you will have to bear this new name for only a few years, and then everything will be as it always has been. I promise. Do not think that I, or your mother and grandparents, are happy with this arrangement, but we must use what means we have, for the time being. Now you and I must practise this new name of yours. I will call you Ah Leong and you will call me uncle, not father. And since we are starting on so many new things, let us try some of this brown-looking substance that Robert gave us.'

So saying, Langshi withdrew the slab from his pocket and broke off two pieces. 'Here, Ah Leong,' he said.

The boy took the gob of brown and placed it carefully in his mouth. Its texture and taste were strange, and far too sweet for his liking. Why did these foreigners enjoy this? He would rather have a Chinese pre-served plum, chilli olive or sweet lemon peel. The chocolate consumed, he turned to Langshi and said, '*Foo t'san*, we must ... ' before Langshi cut him off quickly.

'I do not know where your father is, Ah Leong. Perhaps he is elsewhere on deck. Remember, Ah Leong, who you are.'

'Yes, uncle. I thought we should give Robert some lemon peel or fig-roll, so that he may taste our food. I do not much care for this sweet brown food of his.'

'That is a good idea. I should have thought to do so before this. We shall do so when next we see him. Well, I too found the brown sweet very odd.'

When next they saw Robert, Langshi and Ah Leong pressed on him a number of Chinese preserves. Later he told them, in a mixture of sign language and vivid facial expressions, that he had enjoyed them very much – except, perhaps, for the lemon peel. Ah Leong laughed loud and long when Robert pulled a face and maintained an extended grimace as he held an imaginary piece of lemon peel and brought it towards his mouth, then moved it swiftly away with a violent tic of his arm. Remembering not to show any confusion when Robert addressed him as Ah Cork – the sailor never did get the name right – Ah Leong then followed him to the mess, from which Robert emerged with a plate of yet more foreign food.

'Moo, moo,' said Robert and then, when the boy nodded, handed over the plate and clapped him heartily on the shoulder. 'Off yer go, then, and enjoy.'

Walking back to steerage, Ah Leong considered the block of red-and-white meat. It seemed quite fatty, congealed even. When he and Langshi ate later, they were careful to keep it separate from their rice and though his father found it acceptable, Ah Leong thought it the weirdest of the foods that Robert had given him so far.

So it was that the days and weeks of the voyage passed. Ah Leong learnt some English from Robert, and the sailor a smattering of Cantonese from the boy. Langshi tried to get his tongue round the foreign words that his son was learning, but could not manage. It was as well, he thought, that Ah Kwok – Ah Leong, he reminded himself – was acquiring some words that would be very useful in Kum Saan.

The new world opening up to Ah Leong in these novel and intriguing sounds created an excitement in him for their destination. It lessened, too, the pain when he thought of his family back home, and, increasingly, of

Soi Sien. As the debate had gone back and forth over Kum Saan, she had spoken to him long and often of her hopes that he would marry Mudan one day. Soi Sien said that he must come back as soon as he could, as much for her sake as Mudan's.

On the evening before he and Langshi had left for Canton, Soi Sien and his *Bobo* had reminded him of his many escapades, and told again their favourite stories about his babyhood and childhood.

'Do not hunt for snakes in that new land,' *Bobo* had said. 'Those who have been there tell of dangerous adders and huge snakes that coil around one and squeeze the air and life out of your body. Beware!' And then *Bobo* had given that dry, harsh laugh of hers and had tugged, good naturedly, on his ear.

Soi Sien had said that he was to think of her kindly, and let her know through the letters that he and Langshi would send home, how he was faring. He was not to fall in love with anyone, she teased him, and above all he must not forget Mudan. When Soi Sien finished, she turned away and seemed to wipe away a tear, but when he asked her not to cry, she said firmly that something had lodged in her eye.

The next morning she had stood at the edge of the road, held him tightly and then daintily sniffed on either side of his face, in the way that Chinese have of expressing love and affection. '*Joi kien*,' she said and Ah Kwok returned the farewell, with its implicit promise of till we meet again. Then he and Langshi had taken their first steps on the journey to Kum Saan.

SIX
On the Indian Ocean, 1923

On the voyage from Durban to Mauritius, Martin had much time to prepare the children for what lay ahead. He told them of the island where he had spent his youth, of its wavy palm trees, rugged mountains and endless plantations of sugar cane. The children had marvelled at the greenness of the cane fields in Natal, but they were to find them, in retrospect, not half so impressive as those on the island. Cornelia listened almost as raptly, for in her husband's recounting she was transported back to the heady early days of their romance, when she would hang on every word of his as he spoke of Mauritius and, going further back, of China. That rekindling of magical places and times, together with the leisurely pace of life on board, with all workaday matters suspended, made the journey one of halcyon grace.

Afternoon tea invariably reminded Cornelia of that very first tea-taking with Martin, at the small table in the corner of his emporium of delights. That auspicious visit had been followed not long after by another. Frederik and Cornelia had contrived to persuade their elders that the two of them ought to enjoy the last weeks of summer as fully as possible, by riding out once more in the buggy for the day. When they entered Martin's shop, it was still early and, as they had calculated, business had not yet begun to pick up.

'Miss von Brandis and Mr von Brandis! I am honoured and delighted,' said Martin in warm and enthusiastic greeting.

Cornelia and Frederik were no less effusive in return and the three gravitated, almost as if it were habitual, to the little corner table. 'The last time you were here,' said Martin, 'well, more accurately that was the first time you were here, you remarked on the teapot and how smoothly it poured. If you will wait a while, I should like to take the matter up once more.' So saying, Martin darted to the back room. There was the sound of a cupboard being opened, and then the rustling of paper. Martin returned to Cornelia and Frederik with a small, box-shaped parcel, wrapped in red paper.

'Miss von Brandis, this is for you,' Martin said, simply.

'Oh, Mr Martin, I cannot accept such generosity,' Cornelia protested.

'Please accept this small token as recompense for my poor hospitality on your first visit,' Martin suggested.

'I will accept because of your graciousness, but not as amends for last time, because you were a most generous host and have nothing for which to make up,' replied Cornelia. A smile crept up her face and, accepting the brightly wrapped gift, she asked, 'May I open it now? I know that is very irregular, but I should so like to share this pleasure with you.'

After Martin assented, Cornelia carefully opened the present. Inside the box was a teapot of the type from which Martin had served them, but with a grander design of dragons and phoenixes in gold and red against a white background.

Cornelia's eyes sparkled. 'This is so very beautiful, Mr Martin, thank you,' she said and in that instant their eyes, and two worlds, met.

After that second meeting, the Von Brandis cousins visited several times more as the year relaxed into the crisp days of autumn, when the weather was gloriously mild, devoid of summer's baking heat or the dry, sharp clutch of winter. All three knew that in winter the excuse for these visits would fall away and it might be more difficult to meet and talk long and passionately, with Martin's range of teas providing refreshment and further stimulation. Indeed when winter came that year it seemed grinding, the wind more biting and the days longer, darker and drearier. Frederik and Cornelia managed to slip out and see Martin but twice in the months between May and August.

In the lengthy intervals between, Cornelia and Martin pondered the prudence of their burgeoning affection in a land beset with racial hatreds of so many kinds. Neither could have predicted such an attraction for the other, but in the stillness of long nights and the sharp, bracing clarity of cold days, the two began to understand why and how they were drawn to each other.

For Cornelia, Martin was everything her family, Frederik excepted, was not. An authoritarian father and unbending mother, both obsessed with the trappings of social status and ignorant of other worlds and other cultures, had served only to stimulate Cornelia's interest in peoples beyond her ken. The comfortably narrow purview her parents shared, in which Prussia was exalted and European culture and civilisation deemed the pure and sole path, was stifling and, to her young, expansive mind, ignorant. In his way, Martin was as single-minded as her parents, with China as his Pole star, but he knew far more of Western civilisation than her parents did of the East, and he was sufficiently flexible and humble to acknowledge the great thoughts and doings of other cultures. It was his humility and gentleness, a stark contrast to her father's arrogance and military demeanour, that most endeared Martin to Cornelia.

For his part, Martin found in this young woman a soul mate of the kind that he had never thought to meet. She had an inquiring mind, a lively intelligence and an active nature of the sort that he had not before encountered. In the time between precious meetings, Martin and Cornelia maintained a steady stream of letters, sent via Frederik and never bearing Martin's return address. As the correspondence grew in fullness and revelations, it was undeniable to the two that they had fallen in love. The letters served to fill in gaps left unanswered by the lively and wide-ranging conversations in the little corner of the shop. They also enabled the lovers to broach issues and answer questions that, perforce, could not be asked in Frederik's presence. As the sun rose earlier and the days grew warmer, Cornelia and Martin realised their snug idyll also was drawing to an end.

Cornelia and Martin knew that to take their love to its conclusion would strike at her family, his community and a score of taboos, not to mention the law. Martin was accustomed to the laws and regulations that everywhere hindered the Chinese in their daily lives. It had begun when he landed at Durban, where in order to be allowed entry to the country, he had to pass an education test in a European language. Never before had he been as grateful to the nuns for their severe lessons in English and French. Marriage posed almost as great a problem as immigration, but in the Cape it was still possible to have unions made such as the one between Cornelia and Martin. A slight difficulty would be Martin's travel permit to and from the Cape, but that was a trifle when set against the enormity of what the two young people intended. Not even Frederik, their steadfast go-between in the exchange of letters, was fully apprised of the speed at which their love had grown, nor did they reveal to him anything of their nuptial plans.

In late September, Cornelia and Martin boarded the train for Kimberley. As required by law, they sat in different carriages, and for the duration of the journey neither saw nor spoke to each other. When the train pulled up at the station in the city of diamonds, they proceeded together discreetly along the platform and then to the ranks of horse-drawn cabs outside the terminus. Hailing one, they made their way to a small church on the outskirts of the town. By dint of conscientious investigation and, she conceded, sheer good fortune, Cornelia had found a minister, newly arrived in the country, whose beliefs, idealism and youth enabled him to marry the pair. In a brief and simple ceremony they were married, and had for their honeymoon, the calm before the storm, the remainder of the day before taking the train back to Johannesburg that night.

'Our diamonds and gold are Kimberley and Johannesburg,' said Cornelia after they had left the minister and were on their way to see the Big Hole, site of the diamond diggings.

'True, my dear,' replied Martin, but as he said so he withdrew from his pocket a velvet-covered box, small enough to fit snugly in Cornelia's palm, and pressed it into her hand. 'Hitherto we have not been able to display our love, but now we can. It would delight me if you would wear this sign of our engagement next to the ring that you have had on for only this past half an hour.'

Now Cornelia had her gold wedding band and her diamond engagement ring, but neither was so pleasing to her as the man to whom she had pledged her troth, until death did them part. She drew comfort from the indissoluble nature of their vows, and especially from the part of the service in which the minister had intoned, solemnly, 'What God has joined together, let no man put asunder.' In the days ahead, she knew, those words would be her rock and comfort, her failsafe defence of the act that her family would brand a heinous crime.

'Black magic! Chinaman's wizardry! Can you not tell, child, what that evil dog has done to you?' Such was her father's instant response. Cornelia had matter-of-factly broken the news, which had provoked shock, anger – and tears from her mother. Puce and quivering, her father had demanded to know who the interloper was. Then had come the volcanic spewing of rage and hatred and vituperative racism, showering her with threats and the table with pounding fists. Throughout the rant, Cornelia remained calm, knowing that she was of age, if only barely, to have acted independently.

Menacing turned, finally, to compromising and then beseeching. Cornelia could have anything her heart desired, go wherever and for however long she wished, if only she would annul the union to the devil Chinaman. A court case was threatened. Witchcraft would be cited as the precipitating factor for this unnatural marriage. Cornelia remained unmoved. She had decided to remain at her parents' home for a week after her return from Kimberley and then to move to her new life, if necessary taking with her only the clothes she wore. She could tolerate the self-imposed seven-day sentence during which she would have to endure her parents' recriminations, attempted reconciliations and hypocritical blandishments.

Cousin Frederik was under an attack of similar vehemence from his and Cornelia's parents. He was cursed as a dissembler, the devilish agent at the satanic Chinaman's left hand who had helped bewitch an innocent and unsuspecting young woman. Traitor, black sheep, coward: Frederik suffered all these slurs and managed, somehow, to harbour no resentment towards Cornelia and Martin, even though he felt, at times, slightly betrayed not to have been taken into their full confidence.

When the purgatorial week had passed, Cornelia departed the Von Brandis household in a hired buggy, with some of her prized possessions and books and all her clothes, but without her parents' understanding. The farewell ran one way only, with Cornelia speaking of her gratitude and appreciation for what they had done for her, and assuring them of her lasting love. Neither Father nor Mother uttered a word; it was enough, Cornelia thought at the time, that her father managed to restrain any violent impulses and mastered himself to silence: perhaps that augured well for the future, when time might heal the current hurts. Frederik, the arch-conspirator in the family's eyes, drove with Cornelia from the plush environs of Belgravia and nearby Doornfontein, with its Randlord mining magnates' mansions, and headed west to Chinatown.

'Well, cuz,' said Frederik affectionately, 'this is appropriate.' Looking up at the summer sky, he continued, 'What did your Mama say? "The two rotten apples in a pod." English was never her strong point. Here we are, on our Journey to the West, just like the Monkey King.' He laughed and Cornelia shot back a smile at him, her blue-green eyes bright and shedding some of the cares that had clouded them.

The first thing they did when they reached Martin's shop was to have a pot of tea. At first the atmosphere was half sombre, half joyous, but soon the three had established the old rapport and ease and tea and conversation flowed.

'Another cup, Cornelia?' asked Martin. As Cornelia looked up, she realised with a start that she was on board the ship, not in the safe, cosy corner of the shop. Martin hovered at her elbow, a teapot in his right hand.

'Thank you, dear Martin,' she said and determinedly brought herself back to the present.

There was a stop of three days in Port Louis, during which the family regained their land legs. They went sightseeing in the Botanical Gardens, gasping at the giant water lilies in their large rectangular ponds. On an excursion outside the capital, along the north-western coastline, they were amazed by the exploits of locals who swam deep under the aquamarine surface and came up, after what seemed an endless breathless time, with beautiful pieces of coral and anemones, a trove they sold at some profit to tourists.

It was a source of sadness that Cornelia would not be able to meet Martin Leconte, but he had moved recently to Madagascar. Some years before that, the Choks had gone there, and Martin told Cornelia he felt that Leconte could not bear being away from his old friends. For their part, the Choks had found the influx of Hakka to Mauritius a nuisance. Martin's father had grumbled in letters sent to Kum Saan that he had left Canton to escape dealing with the Hakka, and now they had simply pursued him across the ocean to start up all the old rivalries and competition once more. Madagascar, still further to the west, appeared a refuge, and the Cantonese who had settled there assured him that they would be assiduous in keeping out the Hakka. The plaint was old, but Martin understood at once and never thought to question his father's decision, for Martin himself had left Mauritius for South Africa because of the encroachments on his business in Port Louis by Hakka merchants.

When news of her in-laws' move had come, Cornelia reflected ruefully that while the Martins and the Choks were in regular and delighted correspondence about the new generation in the family, they could not see one another, whereas the Martins and the Von Brandises, who by proximity were able to visit and talk to one another if they chose, did not. The latter situation was in the end scarcely surprising, given the bitterness and venom that had marked Cornelia's departure from the bosom of her clan. Foolishly, however, she had thought her parents' silence on the day she had left home was an implicit surrender and the first step in a gradual acceptance of her marriage. It was but the quiet preceding the battle, the pause before the fight was fully joined. After only one week of their wedded life had passed, she and Martin received a visit from a messenger of the court, serving them with papers indicating that the Von Brandises were instituting action to have the marriage annulled.

Cornelia was enraged. 'How dare they! How can they think they will succeed?' She clasped her hands together, their attenuated joints knotting in anxiety. 'What basis have they for this? I am of age and sound mind.'

'Shh, my dear. Let us examine these papers,' said Martin soothingly and calmly. As he perused them, Martin remained impassive, almost serene. Occasionally, an eyebrow would twitch upward, sometimes he would purse his lips and then his moustache would curl towards the corners of his mouth. Once or twice, his somewhat chubby fingers stroked his cheeks, and lengthened the moon-shaped face that Cornelia loved so much. She read alongside him, and could not fathom on what legal grounds her parents were bringing this vindictive action. Money enough they had to sustain a court battle, but that seemed to Cornelia her parents' only advantage.

'Well, my dear, it seems a very circumstantial affair. The plaintiffs – your parents, pardon me – allege that you were acting under diminished responsibility, being only six months into your majority. They say, further, that I drugged you with magic potions to win you and that your cousin Frederik, also, was taken in by this wizardry, and so failed in his duty to protect you. They intend calling him as a witness.'

'Imagine if Frederik owns up to that dangerous brew, picked by monkeys bewitched by their masters,' said Cornelia, now somewhat relieved on hearing the absurd substance and ridiculous nature of her parents' case.

'There are other arguments here,' continued Martin, 'mainly that since we are resident in the Transvaal, a marriage performed in the Cape has no validity. I do not think we have much to fear, for I went into all the legalities before we went to Kimberley. All we need fear is the pressure and the hatred from the white community, if this case should come to the attention of the newspapers. There is an excellent lawyer I know who will defend us, if need be.'

It was true that it was a criminal offence for a 'Coloured person' to marry a 'European' woman – Martin wryly reflected that no such injunctions applied to white men marrying women of other races – and that the term 'Coloured' applied to 'any of the native races of Asia'. That law, Law 3 of 1897 of the now defunct South African Republic, applied only in the Transvaal, however, and there was no law invalidating marriages recognised in other parts of the new Union of South Africa. Once Martin's lawyer came to grips with the case, he presented to the court a point-by-point rebuttal, though he hardly bothered to dignify with a response the charges of wizardry, black magic and the like. For a while, lawyers' letters went between the parties and the judge. Finally, ruling that there were no legal grounds to examine further, and dismissing the nebulous allegations of witchcraft, the judge threw out the Von Brandises' claims.

Cornelia and Martin were relieved, but not spared continuing contumely. Frequently, as they walked in the streets or shopped in the stores of the mining town now growing into a city, insults were hurled at them. Jibes were generally uttered loudly for the broad delectation of other passers-by, but it was the softly spoken, more extended and even sophisticated racial remarks that were most poisonous and hurtful. Hawking and spitting, timed for projection as Cornelia and Martin passed, were so commonplace that they barely noticed them after a while; it was only when a tall, bearded man spat down into Martin's face that the couple were shaken out of their cocoon of self-induced public calm and inscrutability. Exhausting as these incidents were, each one further armoured the Martins and they became, after some years, inured to word and deed.

What was more damaging than attacks on their persons was the arrangement of fate and choice that left the Martin children suffering most, since they were in a sense bereft of both sets of grandparents. Since the arrival of their first-born, Andrew, Cornelia and Martin had chafed at this isolation and worried about anything happening to either of them, for then the other would have no traditional family support on which to draw. That grim possibility was what had set Martin to thinking of going back to China. Moreover, business was brisk, and he was saving at a good rate and could put aside in a relatively short time, he calculated, what would be a fortune in Canton. Even as the family grew, often by the year, Martin carefully tended his nest egg. As return became increasingly feasible, Martin began to tell the children more about China. In the telling, his enthusiasm to be home became a yearning, and soon not even Cornelia could withstand the longing in her husband's voice and mood.

In any event, Cornelia had long ago crossed a divide – since the legal flurry there had been no dealings of any sort with her family – so there was little in the way of blood to hold her to Johannesburg. Of her kin, Frederik alone kept in touch and when he announced, one brown autumn day, that he was off to America the following spring, Cornelia felt that an uprooting of her own could do no great harm. Although she knew that in China she would be a *bak gwai*, the tolerable if grudging acceptance of the local community in Kum Saan gave her heart that in the end she and her children would be able to settle into life in Canton. That she was able to speak a passable Cantonese would help, and who could not but love the bouncing brood that she and Martin had made?

So it was that Cornelia and Martin had decided to make a new home in China. They and their younger children followed Andrew and Gertie across the Indian Ocean from Mauritius, but this crossing was to proceed less calmly than the first.

There had been signs of a storm brewing for some days, but none of that brooding malevolence, nor the stern warning from the captain, prepared Cornelia and Martin for the elemental fury that was unleashed on the ship. The gale, said Martin, must surely compare to the 'Divine Wind' that destroyed the Great Khan's fleet when it was set to invade Japan at the end of the twelfth century. As the ship pitched and rolled, bucked on the crest of giant waves and then hurtled towards their troughs, only to be sent shooting skywards moments later, Cornelia, Martin and the children huddled together and prayed for their safe deliverance. Too frightened to be ill, the children had shut their eyes and attached themselves to their parents. Time and again, the ship landed with a sickening thud that sent shock waves along the hull and intimations of disaster through the minds of passengers and crew. Every now and then, the children screamed and sobbed, and clutched more tightly to Cornelia and Martin.

'If we should not survive,' said Martin softly in Cornelia's ear, nuzzling aside strands of her ash-blonde hair, 'remember this: we have had a grand and wondrous love, for which I thank you. Thank you for the courage of marrying me, and of making these children. I love you and always will.'

Turning to look into his eyes, Cornelia smiled and nodded. 'I love you also. Nothing ill will befall us, Martin,' she said in a level but quiet voice. 'Thousands of vessels sail through seas as bad, if not worse, and one day we will all laugh about this storm. The children shall tell their grandchildren about it. It shall be part of the story of our passage, our journey from the West.'

They felt another sickening judder, as the ship reached the base of the triangle it had been describing through the waves. Cornelia and Martin looked clearly into each other's eyes and smiled. This storm, the exchange seemed to say, is as nothing to that which we rode out together in Kum Saan. Taking a tighter hold on the terrified pile of life that clung to them, Cornelia and Martin stared out of the porthole at the blackness of the night and of the enraged waves, and wished for morning and a calm, glass-like sea.

Towards dawn, the fury of wind and water began to abate. An hour after sunrise, there was scarcely a breeze playing about the deck. The ship had ceased its bucking and no tremors coursed through its framework, bringing in their wake nightmare visions of a rupture and a salty, liquid death. As the sun rose higher, a calm of relief and exhaustion seized the Martin family and they did what they had feared to do during the night: they fell asleep.

When they woke, it was late afternoon and the children were hungry, having slept through breakfast, lunch and two rounds of tea, morning and afternoon. 'For once you'll not complain about your supper,' said Martin. 'Up we get, time to change into fresh clothing, clean up and ready ourselves to dine. Come, hurry, all of you.'

An hour later, as the sun dipped towards the horizon, the children were washed and dressed. Passing their father's muster, they were sent out to play before dinner. Martin gave his arm to Cornelia for a stroll on deck, laughingly suggesting that it was, partly, to ascertain if they could walk properly. It was a fine evening, the calm a blessing after the battering of the previous night, and an apricot-coloured moon, almost full, began its climb in the heavens. Many couples were promenading on deck, appreciating the cool blues of sea and sky and the almost eerie quiet. Cornelia and Martin walked one circuit of the deck and then another.

'It will be marvellous to see Gertie again,' said Martin. 'I have no doubt that she and Andrew have settled down well at the village. Certainly, to judge from my aunt's letter, the children are enjoying the novelty of life there.'

'They will no doubt be up to some tricks as well. You spoil Gertie far too much, you know, Martin. She's too full of mischief for my liking. She ought to learn life is not all play and laughter.'

'You are far too hard on her, Cornelia. I have worked hard because I wanted the children to have light in their lives, and not fear hunger and the cold winters, as my parents and theirs before them did. It is true that Gertie is my favourite, but then you have yours too: Lil is the one you allow to do almost anything.'

They had reached the companionway leading below. Martin waited for Cornelia to grasp the railing with her left hand and then they proceeded down the stairs, arm in arm. It was as he took up the theme of the children once more that Martin missed his step and stumbled. At once, he freed Cornelia's arm to avoid dragging her down with him, and tried to steady himself. His right ankle turned under him, because the step was faintly wet, and Martin tumbled down the stairway, the sound of his body as he struck each step making a sickening metallic clang. Finally he rolled off the last step and landed squarely chest-down on the small level area before the next flight. 'Martin! Martin! Dear God, Martin!' Cornelia had screamed during his fall and now she was quickly at his side, but he brushed her off, saying only how very silly he felt.

'I am quite all right, my dear, merely somewhat shaken. It might have been worse. I could have broken something, but as it is, it is only my dignity that is battered.' Laughing at the mishap, Martin and Cornelia smoothed his dinner jacket and proceeded to the dining room and their first meal for a day.

It was only much later, deep into that night, that Cornelia realised all was not well. At first she thought she had been dreaming, but the jagged breathing was too close and too loud to be denied. She woke to find Martin sitting on the edge of the bed, clutching his midriff and rocking to and fro. His forehead and body were damp with sweat and his face had a sickly grey pallor. 'Martin, what is the matter? Why did you not wake me?'

Martin merely shook his head. A grimace of a smile crept up and then disappeared beneath the sheet of his face, which grew paler by the minute, it seemed to Cornelia. 'It is nothing,' he managed to stammer. 'Some bruising and discomfort from the fall, nothing more. I shall be fine in the morning.'

Cornelia saw and thought otherwise. 'Martin, you look very distressed. I am going to fetch the ship's doctor,' she said in a voice that brooked no opposition. First she cradled him softly in her arms, taking care not to give even the hint of a squeeze. Kissing him on the forehead, she rose and swiftly dressed.

'Mind the companionway stairs,' he wheezed, and then coughed. In that moment, Cornelia knew her husband had injured himself grievously, for a fleck of blood showed at his mouth. Wiping it before he could discern it, Cornelia left the cabin and made haste for the emergency room.

By the time one of the shipboard doctors had been summoned, a quarter of an hour had elapsed. When Cornelia and the doctor arrived, they found Martin slumped over on the edge of the bed, breathing with difficulty, and an ooze of blood and spittle collecting in the folds of the bed linen at his mouth. He could not speak. In response to her startled 'Martin?' his eyes flickered open and shut, open and shut.

Quickly and expertly the doctor moved Martin on to his back and began to examine his chest very delicately. The slightest pressure had the effect of electrifying Martin's limbs, sending his arms and legs extending as if in shock. Those sudden movements were accompanied by a low groan and Martin's face became a snarl of pain. The doctor signalled to Cornelia and they withdrew outside the cabin.

'I very much fear, Mrs Martin, that your husband has injured himself internally in the fall. He is haemorrhaging and it appears the process is accelerating. First I will try to make him as comfortable as possible and ease the pain. Then I must try to locate the damaged area and retard the bleeding. We do not have as sophisticated medical equipment on board as I would have wished.'

Cornelia had by now woken into a nightmare. Paler even than her husband, she nonetheless spoke to the doctor with characteristic directness. 'Tell me, doctor, how badly hurt my husband is.'

'Well, Mrs Martin, that depends on the extent of the injury and on our stopping the haemorrhaging. I cannot say for certain at this point. Things may be better than they appear. It is always difficult, if not impossible, to make a prognosis so soon.'

'But the fall, as I told you, was scarcely as serious as to warrant this. Surely he cannot be in danger of his life?'

'Do not agitate yourself needlessly. We cannot do anything about what has happened. I must concentrate solely on what is. Now, I shall require your help and will leave you instructions for your husband's care until I am able to send one of the nursing staff across to assist. I do not want to move him for the moment.'

Chok Foon Martin was not moved from the bed in the cabin. At least, not while he lived, which was for but half the day following that glorious apricot moon. He died as the ship's bell gave its solitary ring for half past noon, with his wife Cornelia and five of his seven children at his side.

Cornelia did not know which was worse: the swiftness or the silence of Martin's going. If only he had been able to speak to her and the children, but soon after the doctor's initial examination, Martin had slipped away into another realm, where her whispered words, her sobs, her pleas, her cajoling, her commanding were not heard. Perhaps, she thought later,

Martin had heard but been unable to respond. Then she cursed herself for burdening him, and obstructing the passing of his spirit, only soon thereafter to convince herself that it was good that she had spoken of her love and hopes, and it was certain that he would have listened and understood. In such circles, narrower and narrower, did Cornelia's mind run in the days and weeks after Martin's death. She allowed herself these thoughts when the children were asleep or being cared for by others who had declared their sympathies for the widow and her plight and offered to take a hand, now and then, in looking after the children.

Worries encircled Cornelia as the ocean did the ship. She was a 37-year-old widow with seven children, bound for a country that she had never seen, in which she knew no one, and whose language she could speak with only moderate fluency. And what would she tell Gertie and Andrew? God knew, Gertie would be inconsolable. For her there would not even be the dubious consolation of watching as Martin's body was sent to its rest under the waves. Cornelia had begged the captain to allow that rite of passage to be held on land, in China. Affected though he was by her pleas and her mention of the two children for whom such a farewell would be at least some comfort, the captain had remained firm. Carefully, he had set out the reasons for his decision: there were weeks still before Canton would be reached; there was no place suitable to store the body; the inevitable decomposition of the corpse would be a health risk for all on board. All that he could promise was as dignified a burial at sea as was possible, given the size of the ship and the distance Martin's body would have to descend from deck to water.

Dressed in coat and tails, and wrapped in stout canvas, Martin's corpse had been lowered gently and slowly on ropes from deck pulleys and deposited on the water with only the faintest of splashes. Cornelia and the children looked down, and a makeshift choir, all of fine voice, sang Psalm 23. At the captain's whispered command, the ropes were cut. They lashed into the water and within seconds, Chok Foon Martin began to drift away and aft of the ship. His family watched as the shrouded figure grew smaller and smaller until the white speck of the winding-sheet, and the beloved man it carried, disappeared from sight.

EARTH

Each country has its laws:
each family has its regulations

Chinese proverb

EARTH

ONE
Kwangtung province, China, 1923

The village was in uproar. Old women groaned in anguish, their husbands attempting to comfort them without success. Young people mingled excitably, throwing questions at each other in loud voices, oblivious to the shushing of older siblings, parents and grandparents. Neglected toddlers bawled and children firmer on their feet, but not old enough to join the gaggle of youth, played riotously and unchecked. Such a commotion was exceptional, and this was perhaps the most unusual hubbub in Peng Po for a score of years. A little way from the throng, community elders stood in a huddle, conferring in lowered voices and looking uneasily at the temple and ancestors' hall. Terrible misfortune had struck. The Earth God and the Rain Spirit had swopped places on the altar of the temple.

It had been three of the oldest women in the village who had raised the alarm. Their daily ritual took them to the temple at first light. There, they paid respects to the gods and the ancestors, and thanked them for watching over their families and the fortunes of the village. To ensure the continued beneficence of the various gods to whom the village was particularly attached, the women took offerings of food with them in bowls, and small cups of wine and tea.

Dressed in blue pants and black blouses with high-topped mandarin collars, the three women had shuffled into the temple, their black slippers sending up little puffs of dust as they moved towards the altar. Red and gold lanterns, many faded with age, hung from the wooden rafters of the ceiling. Each lantern bore a family name, but the characters on the oldest lanterns were indistinct. Recesses in the walls displayed plaques of red and yellow, the former for living husbands and wives, the latter for a relative who had gone to join the ancestors.

Stooped by their years and the relentless toil of rural life, with its regimen of endless bending, the women did not raise their gaze from the wooden floor until they were almost at the altar in the centre of the temple. The three bent, grey-black heads were dressed in two plaits and one bun, and gleamed with a liquid lacquer applied to keep the hair in place. Slowly, as the terminus of their devotions neared, the heads lifted in unison, the three pairs of gnarled and arthritic hands began to ready the food and drink for offering.

'*Aiee y*a! Where is the Earth God?' shouted the eldest woman.

Her companions looked at where the deity always stood, at the far right of the altar. In the god's place was the Rain Spirit, the early nature god invoked during times of drought and never forgotten in the village, even in times of plentiful rainfall. Since living memory the Rain Spirit had been placed on the extreme left. Unmoved, Kuan Yin, the Goddess of Mercy, serenely occupied her position in a tableau of figures in the centre, flanked by Shouxing, the Taoist god of long life, and Shen Nung, the ancient deity of medicine, health, farming and forestry.

Three pairs of eyes swivelled to the left, to be met by the sight of the Earth God, clutching his twisted wooden staff and tael of gold. As before, his long white beard and moustache flowed down to his lap, the thick white eyebrows stood guardian still over his gentle dark eyes. The Earth God, the local territorial deity so beloved of villagers throughout the land, appeared unharmed. But why had he moved? What had prompted this tutelary god of the village, the protector of the well-being of country and city dwellers, to exchange places with the Rain Spirit?

Shocked, then filled with awe and finally frightened, the three women turned round, still clutching their offerings, and walked as quickly as they could to the house of the village elder. They went in silence, their tongues devoted not to speech but to a circling of their dry mouths. Disaster could befall the village if its chief patron were dissatisfied, the women believed. And who could argue with that conclusion, given the many intercessions of the god? Although the Earth God was not regarded as fearsome, the range of successful appeals that people made to him attested to his power. In the village's worst times, the god's statue had been taken from the temple in a procession, to show the deity the roots of the problems that he was being asked to resolve. Always, during drought, it was the Earth God – rather than the Rain Spirit – who was shown the empty dams, the dying carp, the trickle where streams and small rivers used to flow. One year, locusts had devastated the crops, and the god and an entourage of priests, elders and supplicants had proceeded through the pillaged fields. A terrible frost in spring only three years ago had been the last occasion the celestial deity had been moved, to see the damage wrought by the unseasonal cold.

At the elder's house, the women broke out in a burst of talking and wailing. Disturbed, the man had sent his sons to gather the various holy men in the village, who between them represented followers of Confucius, Lao-tsu and Buddha. To verify the panicked talk of the women, the village elder had sent his first-born son to the temple. When the boy returned, he was as wide-eyed as the old women, who were now keening so loudly that containing the bad news was impossible.

A small crowd had begun gathering outside. As one by one the sundry religious men of the settlement arrived and hurried in, speculation and chatter spread from house to house until even the old recluse, whose ramshackle, stand-to excuse for an abode stood at the edge of the village, heard that something was amiss. Within the hour, most of the village was congregated in the smallish clearing in front of the elder's home. In this press of people, two somewhat different-looking youngsters stood out, though the villagers had long become used to their fairer skins and auburn-to-black hair and on this particular morning paid the erstwhile strangers scant notice.

'Gertie,' whispered Andrew. 'Everyone seems very upset. What can be happening?'

'Perhaps someone has died or is ill. Maybe there is bad news about the crops. I would ask Auntie but she has gone to market this morning. Let us wait and see.'

Gertie turned to a girl about her age and asked why the people were gathered together in this way, but the girl shrugged and said she wished she knew what all the fuss was about. A while later, a few words began doing the rounds of the crowd. Gertie picked up 'gods', 'angry', 'temple violated', 'desecration of the altar'.

'Something has happened at the temple, it seems,' she told Andrew. 'They say that the gods are angry, that the temple and altar have been damaged in some or other way.'

'I don't suppose it could have anything to do with the statues?' asked Andrew.

'Well, there's been no mention of them.'

Andrew smiled weakly at his sister and resumed his anxious watch of the elder's house. Everything would turn out all right in the end, he was sure, but the uncertainty and worry around him were most unpleasant. He must remember what Father always told him about a silent tongue in a wise head. That way, no one could guess.

'What did you mean when you said statues, Andrew?' Turning quickly to face her brother, and looking up at him, Gertie threw him a puzzled glance, her eyebrows almost knitting together and her brows furrowing. 'What statues?' Suddenly, her face assumed a horrified aspect. 'Oh, Andrew! Surely ... tell me ... you didn't.'

'Shhh, quiet, Gertie! They may not be able to understand us but we mustn't act suspiciously. I am sure they'll think it was us. And then what happens? This all seems much too serious for a little changing of the altar.'

Refusing to be shushed, Gertie glared at Andrew. 'How could you? Didn't Auntie tell you how important the ancestral hall and the temple are? Imagine going in to the Lutheran Church back home, or the Presbyterian, and moving things around. You wouldn't dare, because Mother would beat you and Father would not be too happy either. And we are guests here, this is Father's village and he would expect us to respect its customs.'

'I was only having a little fun. I didn't move the Kuan Yin, of course. Auntie told me that although that old geezer the Earth God is a favourite of the peasants, the Goddess of Mercy and Compassion is something altogether different. I wouldn't have dared move her. Her two companions on the altar, Shouxing and Shen Nung, they're more important too in the big scheme of things. I mean to say, Uncle told us that the Earth God is the lowest ranking official in the bureaucracy of the celestial pantheon.'

What the boy said was true. In a short time, half a year, he and his sister had learnt a good deal about their father's homeland and their own

One Day when we were young.

The Martin family (left to right): Gertie, John, Chok Foon, Cornelia, Violet, Andrew and Lil (Philip and James not yet born).

Ah Leong rings up the first sale on his brand-new NCR electronic cash register, in the grocery shop at 27 Perth Road, Westdene. In the background is shop helper Frans.

Family elders Andong and Tian, flanked by their sixth and youngest son Ah Lun (second from right), his wife Ah Lie (second from left) and their three children. Ah Lun was Ah Leong's Lok Sok – Sixth Uncle.

Gertie in a portrait taken at the New York Studio, Johannesburg, in the early 1930s.

Giddy and Julie on the day of their Chinese wedding, 22 July 1956. Portrait taken by Mr A. De Witt at his studio in 63 Queen Street, Pretoria, just up the road from Ah Hing's shop.

Ah Hing, the redoubtable mother of Yen and Kit.

A studio portrait of Langshi, seated next to some of his medical textbooks, including the Encyclopaedia of Plants *and* The Yellow Emperor's Canon of Internal Medicine.

Fok Yu Teem, his first son Yen, wife Ah Hing and second son Kit, in a portrait taken just months before Fok Yu Teem's death.

Gertie and Ah Leong in the early days of their marriage.

Auntie Annie, Andrew, Gertie and Cornelia, with Lil on the little chair in front.

Kit with his treasured Selma saxophone.

roots. They had been amazed by the eclectic worship, in which Confucianism, Taoism and Buddhism co-existed happily with reverence for age-old gods such as Shen Nung, early nature deities of legend like the Rain Spirit, and dragons. It was with dragons that Andrew and Gertie were most taken, for here they were not always the enemy of humans that Western mythologies depicted. They were very different in appearance also, a curious and marvellous assemblage of beasts, sporting the horns of a deer, head of a camel, body of a snake, scales of a carp, claws of an eagle, feet of a tiger and ears of an ox. When the siblings had seen their first portrait of a Chinese dragon, they had gawped. That fascination had been deepened by the explanations that followed. Supreme in the mystical hierarchy of 360 creatures, dragons represented sunrise, spring and fertility. Their position in the cardinal point of the east stood in counterpoint to the white tiger of the west, the harbinger of death. For those following Taoism, dragons were benevolent spirits, touchstones of happiness and prosperity and ever kind to people. In folk religion, the Long Wang dragon kings were a harsher presence, having authority over life and death through their command of the rain. These gods of rivers, lakes and oceans embodied on the one hand wisdom, strength and goodness, and on the other anger, in the exercise of which they would unleash storms, fog and earthquakes. They were the vocational protector of ferrymen and water-carriers, but the latter could not always count on the Long Wang's good graces, for they were wont to punish anyone who wasted water. Offerings were made to the dragon kings in times of drought, but today they were far from the minds of the community elders, who were seeking to explain the extraordinary omen of the Earth God and Rain Spirit changing places on the altar of the temple.

'Andrew, perhaps you should own up to whatever it was you did,' said Gertie, eyeing the confusion and edginess of the throng, and sensing the rise of hysteria in some.

'Never! They would skin me alive,' he replied. 'Things will calm down, you'll see. They will realise someone was playing a prank.'

'That's just it, my foolish brother. They won't. No one who was born here and grew up in the village would ever, ever, tamper with such important things. But you, as an outsider, not familiar with the ways, you might be forgiven. You are half a *bak gwai*, anyway: maybe they will have been expecting such bad behaviour.'

'Honestly, Gertie, stop going on about it. These superstitions are ridiculous. Why should a little statue or two have any power over rain, or people's well-being?'

'Why does Mother pray to God? What's the difference between these gods and hers? I think you are being a coward, and you should confess and accept whatever punishment they give you.'

Andrew glared at Gertie when she threw the word coward at him, but said nothing.

'Perhaps I should not suggest this,' said Gertie, 'but it might be a way of making everyone a little happier. What if you said that you were cleaning the altar, as a tribute to our ancestors, and that you put the statues back the wrong way round? I know that means you will be lying, but that lie will set the whole village at rest, and I am sure you won't go to Hell for doing a good deed that helps so many people. Then they can't be so angry with you, even though I am sure you are not supposed to touch anything in the temple without permission.'

'I could never lie. It's against one of the Ten Commandments,' Andrew shot back quickly.

'And moving the statues is also against some rule or other. We are here as guests and we should respect the rules of our hosts as much as our own, don't you think?'

'Why do you always take their side? I wish Father and Mother were here, then I wouldn't have been so bored that I switched the statues around.' Sulking, Andrew turned his attention to the crowd. At its head was a smaller gathering of the religious notables of the area, including a few Taoist priests and some aged men who Andrew knew held to the very old gods. The elder, looking more fearful than ever, was waving his hands and, almost with rhythmic regularity, striking himself on the forehead. The Taoist holy men shook their heads and, entreating the village leader not to hit himself, succeeded in stopping his whirling arms.

Shocked by the consequences of his mischief, Andrew sank into gloomy thought. He felt like the Monkey King, who had drawn on himself the anger of all the gods by eating the peaches of immortality in the garden of the Queen Mother of the West, Hsi Wang-mu, the very fruits that the deities had placed in his care. That story, from *The Journey to the West*, was a favourite bed-time tale of Andrew and his siblings, whether told by their parents or by Gertie. And, remembered Andrew with some satisfaction, although Monkey was caught by Buddha, Kuan Yin intervened and secured not only his release but also his being appointed guide to the pious Buddhist monk Hsuan Tsang on that journey to the West to fetch the sacred Tripitaka scriptures. At the suggestion of the Emperor, the monk had adopted the name Tripitaka and had set off on his quest, to be joined en route by Monkey, Pigsy and the Sandy Priest. Comforted by this reverie, Andrew grew in the belief that if he remained silent, all would be well, and that he needed only to be patient to escape detection.

'Devils! There must be demons at work in the village,' cried an old woman. At the sound of the word devil, Andrew's ears had pricked up and he looked, furtively, at the assembly, feeling suddenly that everyone must have detected his guilt. Shifting uneasily on his feet, he recalled the little figure of the Rain Spirit, holding a vase of water and a dragon on a plate, and how it had seemed to fix him with a disapproving stare as he had carried it across to the other side of the altar. And had that been a slanting ray of disapproval coming off the high, large forehead of Shouxing's serene, bone-white face? Carrying the peach of eternal life in his left hand and a staff and a gourd holding the water of life in his other, the old man – Andrew could not think of him as a god – might equally have been directing his timeless gaze at the prank.

'Demons, they say there are demons loose.' The words rippled through the villagers, bringing with them a chill and a darkening of brows. As the rumour spread, Andrew knew that he should not evade responsibility. Perhaps his sister was correct: a small lie for a small misdeed, and everyone would be happier. Surely his uncle would not beat him too severely?

'Gertie, come with me. You're right. I am going to tell them your lie.'

'It's not my lie. It's my way of saving your bacon, you silly brother of mine,' replied Gertie, feeling vastly relieved. Squeezing his hand, she followed Andrew through the crowd, and up to the edge of the earnest meeting of elders.

'What is it, boy?' said the elder. 'Whatever it is, not now. There are evil things afoot in this village and I have no time to speak with you.'

'It concerns the Earth God,' said Andrew in faltering Cantonese.

The adults had already turned away from the Chok children, but mention of the deity had them swivelling around quickly.

'What is that you say?'

'Sir, I was cleaning the altar, as a show of reverence to my ancestors. It was a mistake.'

'It was. No one touches the temple or the ancestral hall ...'

'And I moved the statues when I was cleaning and I put them back in the wrong places, at least the Earth God and the Rain Spirit and I am very sorry and I hope that you and my uncle and aunt and the village will not punish me and that you will forgive me. I was only ...'

'What's that you say? You moved the statues?' The old man stared at Andrew, fixing him with the most baleful look that the boy had ever experienced. Sensing something, the villagers pressed closer and fell silent. In the awful quiet, Andrew wished that he and Gertie had never set foot in Peng Po. He yearned to be home, playing under the fruit trees. It seemed as if time was dragging to a halt as the old man and the astonished priests looked down at the boy.

'Ha ha,' cackled the village leader. 'Our very own devil, our *bak gwai*, the spawn of that scallywag Chok Foon.' In an instant, there was laughter everywhere. The priests and elders dispersed into the crowd, explaining what had happened. Angry though they and the village elders were, they were relieved and delighted that a very human cause lay at the root of the altar's disturbance. Nonetheless, the elder took Andrew aside and gave him a stern dressing-down, telling him that it was not amusing to play with people's beliefs. 'Your father,' said the old man, 'though fond of playing tricks when he was a boy here, would never have dared do such a thing. Please respect the sacred places of the village.'

Suitably repentant, the chastised boy was released. Then it was the turn of Andrew's uncle, shaking his head and looking stern. 'I will punish you, my boy,' he began. 'Your father would do the same,' he added, before dissolving into laughter and gently cuffing Andrew on the ear.

Andrew looked at Gertie, and said, 'Thanks, Gertie, for saving me yet again.'

She smiled back, but added in a determined voice, 'Since Ma is not here, I'll say it for her: "Don't ever do that again." ' Then she and Andrew were caught up in the celebratory swirl that seized the village, relieved now that there were no demons at work other than the mischievous boy from across the seas, the little half-white devil from Kum Saan.

That was not the only day on which Gertie and Andrew saw the village crowded and excited. When the travelling theatre arrived there was at least as much excitement. First the stage would be set up on bamboo scaffolding above the river, as a precaution against fire. As the makeshift structure grew, so did the number of villagers, jostling for good positions on the bank. Once the stage was ready, the players would swop work clothes for those of conjurers and actors, to perform feats of magic and a Chinese opera classic. Through the day and into the night the opera ran. People watched and listened and from time to time partook of the food they had brought with them. Richer patrons had their servants bring them hot food and caddies of tea.

Andrew and Gertie were enthralled by the rich costumes and larger-than-life heroes and villains with their extravagantly broad, thick and long beards, colourfully painted faces and vivid costumes. The children learnt the stock characters, with their typifying traits, from the colours daubing their faces: red stood for bravery and loyalty, black for integrity; a gold face betokened a god, a green visage the spirits. Of all the garments the actors wore, Gertie and Andrew loved best the bright yellow robes, indicating that the wearer was royalty. The sleeves of the cast's attire provided further fascination, since movements of the sleeve were not some sartorial adjustment, but a subtle means of conveying emotion.

Most of all, Gertie and Andrew were amazed by the noisiness of the performance, much of the music rendered on strange stringed instruments that, to their ears, wailed and pitched and screamed. Even more astonishing was the way the crowd threw themselves into the tale, so that players and watchers became one in a grand confusion of colour and sound, of action, words and music. Afterwards, what dwelt most with Gertie was the curious delicacy of the heroines, whose voices had pitched higher and higher until they seemed to disappear altogether into the blackness of the night.

But it was the magicians that most fascinated Gertie and Andrew. The two children wondered whether these men were great illusionists or real wizards, such was the astonishing nature of their acts. Nor would anyone in the village say anything other than commend their brilliance.

The first time Gertie witnessed the food 'trick', she could not believe her senses. Yet there was no denying that the bowls that had been empty were now filled with hot foods of many kinds. Minutes before, the magician had placed a white cloth on top of the assembled crockery and then proceeded to entertain the crowd with a tale about hungry travellers. At the conclusion of his story, he had leaned down and whipped off the cloth to reveal a banquet. When he asked the villagers to sample the results of his work, they expressed some reluctance, but the bolder - Andrew said the hungrier – among them soon relented, and confirmed that the food was both real and tasty.

Another item in the repertoire greatly disturbed Gertie. It purported to show a boy who had been miniaturised and imprisoned in a bottle. The tiny creature pounded piteously on the smooth, light green sides of his gaol, his mouth opening wide in what, the magician assured his audience, were wails. No need to worry, he continued: the boy would be released as soon as he had learnt his lesson, as he was a troublesome youngster. For the next few days, however, he would remain bottled up. Long enough, Andrew whispered in Gertie's ear, for the troupe to have left the village far behind.

Despite her brother's scepticism, Gertie could not bear the suffering of the tiny being, because it reminded her of the secret of the forbidden forest. Deliberately, she and Andrew had explored the woods that fringed the eastern edges of the village, in order to discover why they had been placed out of bounds. Further and further they delved under the green canopy, and it grew colder and darker. As they approached a small clearing, they heard a cat mewling. The familiar sound cheered them: they missed Carl, their large tabby in Johannesburg. Andrew stepped forward and then stopped. There was no cat. This was a graveyard for babies.

Gertie pushed past her brother and then looked around in bewilderment. A few of the little bundles were still alive, making feeble movements and whimpering. Father had said that in China girl babies were sometimes left to die, as were infants who were born with some defect or became ill. That was the way of things: girls and frailties could not be supported because the people were too poor. Crying softly, Gertie reached for the sack of water Andrew had slung over his shoulder. Going up to one of the babies, she poured some water into the palm of her hand and then wet its parched lips with a few drops. Carefully, she put more water into the mouth and then moved on to another infant, who was near death. Most of the abandoned figures were dead, those who had lain exposed longest being mere bones while others were in varying states of decomposition. The stench was awful, and Andrew, who had said not a word, had backed away into the forest. When Gertie had done her rounds, she wondered briefly if it would be a great sin to baptise the babies. She had no sanction to perform such an act, and so it would have no power, she decided. Instead, she prayed silently for each of the forms, dead and almost so, and then left the spot.

On the way back, she and Andrew remained silent. It was curious, she felt, that her Father loved her so, when she was a mere girl. Why would he want his three daughters – Gertie, Violet and Lil – to come to a country where girls were looked on as handicaps? As they trudged through the forest, Gertie thought of the little servant girl who had been sold to one of the families in the village. She was very cruelly treated by the wife, who would blame the child whenever anything went wrong. The girl had to carry buckets of water from the river to the house and that daily task had bent her body, almost crippling her right side. Gertie had befriended her, and helped with ferrying water when she could but knew that it was small solace in the girl's servitude.

The women of the house – the wife and mother-in-law – would also demand from their slave *dum quat*: that she massage them by walking on their backs and manipulating their bones with her feet. Often, the wife would accuse the girl of hurting her and she would scream at her and rake fingers across her face. It might have been better, Gertie considered gloomily, if the girl had been abandoned at birth rather than become a lifelong slave.

However odd the reasons for returning to China might be, Gertie was sure that such a fate would not befall her and her siblings. She and

Andrew had been attending the local school, and had polished up the basics of reading and writing Chinese to add to their already fluid Cantonese learnt at home. They would have mastered more characters but on many afternoons their teacher would fall asleep, to wake only hours later. A middle-aged woman, she kept two jobs, teaching in the day and working at night in the silk factory. Once Gertie had visited the teacher there, and been shocked by what hard work it was, all done by girls and women. There were those who separated the silk by placing the cocoon in hot water and then catching the main silk thread with a chopstick and rolling it on to a reel. Others had to tie the threads to form a single, long strand. Around the dyeing vats stood yet more, ready to colour the white harvest. Younger sisters would bring food to the workers during their shift, which they would eat while continuing to work because they feared the wrath of the overseer who roamed the factory floor, muttering about loafing and resting and time-wasting on the job. Gertie did not like the man but she reserved her anger for the factory's owners, who for all this dedicated work paid a pittance, the equivalent of sixpence a day in Johannesburg.

'Gertie, we must try to slip into the village quickly,' said Andrew, uttering his first words since seeing the baby graveyard.

Looking round, they made sure that no one was approaching and then made a dash for the clump of mulberry trees at the outskirts of the village. 'Not a word of this to anyone, Andrew,' warned Gertie as they turned for home.

All her life, Gertie remembered and prayed for the babies in the woods, just as she wondered and worried about the boy in the bottle.

TWO
Johannesburg, circa 1913

Ah Leong was weary. He had risen at five, as he had to each morning, to lay and start the fire and boil water so that Third Uncle and his family could wash when they rose. Water on the go, Ah Leong turned his attention to preparing *congee*. Gathering last night's leftovers of meat and vegetables, he added them to a pot of rice and topped up the whole with water, setting the concoction to cook gently. Satisfied, he glanced up at the clock to check the time. The black hands, one long and thin, the other short and stubby, covered each other and pointed to the large numeral five. It was twenty-five past five and he had 20 minutes to prepare the shop for the day's trading. Swopping apron for white overcoat, Ah Leong left the kitchen and headed towards the front of the long, narrow building. Instantly on leaving behind the warmth of the kitchen, with its comforting coal stove, bubbling water and aroma of *congee*, Ah Leong felt the sharp, piercing chill of winter.

First, he measured out sugar, beans, mealie meal, flour, tea and coffee into quarter-, half- and one-pound packets. He did the same with the tobaccos, for smoking and chewing. Scanning the shelves, he saw that they were low on preserved tomatoes, watermelon *konfyt*, coconut ice and peanut brittle, all of which he prepared on weekends. The *tomahlikee*, a special type of Chinese toffee, made mainly from sugar and very popular with the locals, also needed replenishing. Quickly, he went to the store room, filled a tray with new supplies and returned to the shop. Restocking completed, he turned his attention to filling bottles with paraffin, always a good seller – people in the area cooked largely on Primus stoves – and even more so in winter, when the quarter-pound packets of coffee would find their way into water-filled pots atop Primuses. Last, Ah Leong dusted the counters and swept the floors, and then walked back to the kitchen.

'*Tso shan*,' he said, bidding his uncle good morning. The man, plump and bald, nodded grumpily and continued splashing his face with hot water from an enamel basin. Ah Leong ladled *congee* into two bowls, put them down on the bare wooden table and then set a small kettle of water to boil. When steam began issuing from the spout, he poured the water over black tea leaves in a Chinese tea pot, undecorated but of a rather striking jade green colour, and then placed the pot in a lined wicker basket. Cooled somewhat by standing, the *congee* would not burn his lips, mouth or throat, and just as well, thought Ah Leong, noticing that it was just after ten to six. Opening time, the start of the twelve-hour day, was under ten minutes away. Spooning down the gruel, blowing on it to cool it further, and slurping in a way he knew his mother would not approve of, Ah Leong finished breakfast in a few minutes.

'I am going to open the shop, uncle. I shall see you later,' he said to the flabby face burrowing in the bowl opposite him.

'*Hai, hai*,' said his uncle distractedly between gulps. On good mornings, the man would pause in his eating and wave a hand dismissively. Shrugging, Ah Leong began the brief walk to his long day, a day that seemed without end. He had not been prepared for this service to the family that had helped arrange his papers. His so-called foster parents, whose dead son's papers Langshi had bought, were different from Third Uncle. They were warm and jovial, and as Langshi had said, Ah Leong's foster father was a round, happy man of good spirits with what seemed a permanent smile on his chubby face. What Langshi had not reckoned on was the price that Ah Leong's uncle would exact for his role in the paper son process.

Indeed, Langshi had not had any inkling that Fok Shiao Shek, his third brother, and hence his son's Third Uncle, was involved. It had been Ah Sin who had succeeded in tempting Langshi to Kum Saan, and not the presence there of two of his six brothers. For many years there had been no contact between Langshi and Tian in Sha Kiu and the brothers in Kum Saan. Years before there had been a slow-brewing disagreement over how to work the land and Tian's pond, which had matured into a bitter rift between Tian and his eldest, Langshi, on the one side, and Ah Shek and Ah Chow on the other. When their plans for change were finally rejected by Tian, the third and fourth brothers left for Namfeechow without bidding farewell to their parents and Langshi. Before that, the other three siblings had gone to America, their way prepared by their uncles, three of Tian's brothers.

It was a shock for Langshi to discover that Ah Shek had insinuated himself into his life. And he had done so with great cunning, giving the impression to all that he was helping Langshi, his brother, in getting his son into Kum Saan. How he had even discovered the delicate dealings over the papers was a mystery, but Langshi hazarded the guess that because the community was so small, Ah Shek had been able to ferret out the gist of things. When the brothers met in Kum Saan, at the Cantonese Club in Chinatown, it was a moment of triumph and revenge for Ah Shek. Even before the awful moment, a reunion he would have resented even under better circumstances, Langshi had known he was cornered.

'But the favour I did you, the real favour, was commending your character and that of Ah Kwok, as I called him then, to the foster parents,' began his brother. 'That is not something that can be made good by money, instant or otherwise,' had continued the unrelenting words that churned Langshi's stomach. 'The custom in the community here is for such favours to be redeemed by work. Your son – or should I say your nephew, as you are forced to? – must repay the favour by coming to live and work with us. When I deem that my intercession in this matter has been honoured in return by his labour, then I shall release him.'

Langshi accepted that this debt, or even the perception of such obligation by the community, would hang heavily over the future. Should he fail to honour it, it was probable that repercussions in his medical practice would follow. And were that to happen, far from being able to save money and return home, he and Ah Leong – his gloating brother's menacing reference forced Langshi even in his thoughts to use Ah Kwok's new name – might not be able to eke out an existence in this new land.

Nor could Langshi turn to Ah Sin for advice, for his cousin had succumbed to a heart attack, mere days before they were to see each other in Kum Saan. But knowing the crushing nature of such honour-bound servitude, to which he had never suspected he was subjecting his son, Langshi did not immediately assent to his brother's demand. Slowly, he pleaded different factors: the boy's youth; his already painful separation from much of his family; and even the plans for his future, as an administrator in China. Throughout, the man opposite nodded in agreement, praised Langshi's paternal qualities and stroked his jowls to display his serious consideration. Then he turned almost all of Langshi's arguments against him. The boy would grow up quickly in conditions where he would not have a parent to count on; in any event Langshi would be but a mile away; Ah Leong would learn much about commerce, become expert in the use of the abacus and would have some opportunity to put his reading and writing skills to use. It was Ah Shek's sinister reference to Ah Leong's fragile status on paper that weighed heaviest on Langshi. Surely his brother would not betray his very own nephew? Langshi had no desire to test if Ah Shek would convert this blackmailing sort of threat into action. Accepting that further argument was fruitless, he decided instead to apply himself to securing his son's release from this commitment sooner than his antagonist intended.

Ah Leong did not take easily to yet another surprise and upheaval in his life. First he had to accept abandoning his own name, and now he had to leave his father too, for an uncle who was, if not a sworn enemy, certainly not demonstrably avuncular.

'We shall be but a short walk from each other,' Langshi had said, in an attempt at cheerfulness. He felt that already, in the space of a few months, he had betrayed his son on a number of counts. The name change had been difficult, but this was bitter: the boy for whom he held so many hopes would be a servant, or at best subject to the capricious whims of a man revelling in revenge.

'Father, I do not know about Kum Saan,' Ah Leong replied. 'When we arrived and stayed with Uncle Tim – I do not think I shall ever forget the first roof under which I slept in Namfeechow – things seemed bright. But now I wish that I had never left mother, *Kongkong* and *Bobo*. I wish that we will be able to return home soon.'

That had been almost two years ago. Life had not been as easy as the late Ah Sin had made out in his letters. Langshi's practice had good custom, but many of his patients struggled with money and often he would treat them on credit, and sometimes free of charge altogether. Not having Ah Leong to help meant Langshi was able to put aside less than he had thought to, even though his son took his meals at his home of temporary adoption. What most distressed both father and son was that Ah Leong's reading and writing of Chinese had fallen behind, and what he learnt in that couple of years was, perhaps, only as much as he would have acquired in the same number of months studying back home.

Neither father nor son gave away any of this in their regular letters to Soi Sien and Tian. As their second year in Kum Saan drew to its close, however, they had to broach the subject that they most feared raising: their return. It would not be possible to go back to Sha Kiu at the end of this or, indeed, the following year, for they had not saved enough money, despite Langshi's frugality.

Soi Sien sent back a letter that gave full flow to how she longed to see them both, the dreariness and emptiness of her days, and the rapid ageing of Tian. 'You must return before your father weakens too much,' she wrote, 'before his pining for Ah Kwok kills him. Although he will not admit it, he misses the boy more than life itself and slowly he is beginning to neglect everything that previously gave him pleasure, such as the fruit trees and, especially, the carp.'

Letters between Sha Kiu and Kum Saan sometimes passed within a few nautical miles of each other but, like the ships that bore them, they moved in opposite directions. For each letter pleading a return, there was one stating the need for a longer sojourn. Langshi spent many words explaining why their planned homecoming was perforce delayed. He knew that the longer he and Ah Leong stayed in Kum Saan, the more he would have to resort to ending his letters with the refrain that soon, probably in only a further four or five months, they would be back in Sha Kiu.

As Ah Leong removed the heavy wooden shutters from the shopfront windows, he wondered how many more winters he would spend in the service of his uncle. True, he had acquired some useful skills, such as speedy adeptness with the abacus. In the main, though, what Ah Leong had learnt most about was the repetitive nature of shopkeeping. Even his daily two-hour respite from the drudgery of waiting and serving had become routine and monotonous. At around half past eight each morning, Ah Leong would walk half a mile to the Indian traders who sold fresh seasonal produce and spices in a street that ran at a curious diagonal to its neighbours. In the first few months Ah Leong had been amazed by the shape and colour of these novel foods, and was cheered each morning by the jumble of produce, big heads of lettuce pushed up against bright red tomatoes, onions nestling next to garlic, green and red apples highlighted against the yellow and bright green of different sorts of bananas. Nearer home — his uncle's, not his father's — there were Chinese greens and melons to be bought, but in this little slanting street of the new, there was a satisfying plenty for Ah Leong to feast his eyes on. The spice shops, which came as sudden, pungent punctuations in the long rows of vegetables and fruit, were a palette that ran from red through ochre and brown to mustard and yellow. He would pause at the first spicery he passed, and the last, inhaling the tang and the adventures that each distinct smell promised.

But as the months at his uncle's passed, each seeming to stretch time closer to breaking point before turning the calendar into the next, the daily produce expedition began to assume a staleness. Nor could the wholesale market, in a cavernous building with a semi-circular roof, refresh him. It was there that his daily duties took him, his basket already laden with fruit and vegetables, to select and purchase meat, fish and poultry.

On special days, when a particularly fine meal was being planned, Ah Leong would come straight to the market and buy live ducks or geese, carefully assessing the intended dish for youthfulness or plumpness, as advised by his uncle. At the start, such responsibility, as well as this new knowledge, excited Ah Leong, but he was to grow weary of these horizons too, circumscribed as they were.

The last shutter removed, Ah Leong prepared for the day's business. Seating himself on a stool behind the plain wooden counter, he thought about his mother's latest letter and wondered how his father would assure her, once again, that he and Ah Leong — even in letters, Langshi made no reference to Ah Kwok, but only to his nephew, Ah Leong — would soon be back in the village. It was while he was contemplating this increasingly difficult and, he had to admit, untruthful task, that Third Uncle joined him behind the counter.

'Today, boy, I do not want you to waste time by going to the fruit and vegetable sellers,' said Third Uncle. 'And no need to go to the big market either. I have other things for you to do, more important. From now on, you will work and live elsewhere. I am sending you away ...'

'But, uncle, you cannot. You must talk first with my father,' interrupted Ah Leong.

'Quiet, boy, I have spoken with him. And you will be able to talk of this with him too. You see, I am sending you home, back to your father.'

'Uncle, thank you,' blurted out Ah Leong, jumping from the stool, his eyes suddenly bright, his heart pounding and his mind racing.

'All right boy, calm down. You have served me well. But do not forget that as long as you are in Kum Saan, you owe me still. There will be favours that I will ask of you. Do not forget that, really, it was I that made it possible for you to be here.'

'No, uncle, I have not forgotten, and I will not either.'

'Now, boy, pack your things. Your father told me he would come himself to walk with you to his house that is now your house also. Go, quick, I am busy here.'

Stunned, Ah Leong nodded, thanked his Third Uncle once more and then raced down the narrow, and suddenly very short, passage to his living space in a corner of one of the storerooms at the back of the building. Quickly, he bundled together his clothes. Into another bag he placed, carefully, books and brushes, ink and paper. In a few minutes, for Ah Leong had not very many possessions, he was ready. He could not believe that, after two years, he was going home: not his real home in the village but a proper home, with his father, and a new life in this now not-so-new Kum Saan.

THREE
Kwangtung province, China, 1923

Cornelia saw Gertie and Andrew from some way off. She recognised her eldest children by their light blue cotton clothing. Then they were waving, and suddenly they broke into a run, gathering speed downhill and closing the gap between the parties.

Turning to Lil, Cornelia said, 'Wait here. Look after your brothers and sisters. I will go on ahead to tell Andrew and Gertie the news.'

Cornelia quickened her stride, fumbling with her sun hat. She had rehearsed this moment countless times since Martin had died. Every version had ended with Gertie and Andrew inconsolable and Cornelia helpless. She knew that in this headlong, rushing reality, nothing would be different. Gertie and Andrew were a dozen yards away, shouting their hellos.

'Gertie, Andrew, we've missed you so!' said Cornelia.

'Oh, Mother, it has seemed endless without you and Father. How was your voyage? We had calm seas,' said Gertie.

'Where is Father? We couldn't see him from the hilltop. Is he coming up with the luggage?' asked Andrew.

The moment had come and Cornelia could not bring herself to tarry. The truth was best, equivocations would not do, she had always told her children. 'I am sorry, Andrew and Gertie, but your father is dead.'

In Gertie's mind, the finality of that last word her mother uttered refused to ring home at first. Thinking that she had not heard properly, she asked, 'Delayed? Delayed where?'

'No, child, your father died on board the ship,' answered Cornelia. Then she swept Andrew and Gertie to her, holding them tightly to her bosom. 'He fell and injured himself internally. The doctor could not stop the bleeding, not even by packing ice around your father's body.'

There was a moment's silence and then, sobbing and howling, Gertie and Andrew clung to their mother, who turned her head and motioned Lil to bring the others to console them. In that weeping huddle, the Martin family stood for a long time, a time that seemed longer to Gertie than all the days and weeks she had waited for her father to arrive in the village of his birth. Even in the anguish of this moment, with her eyes squeezed shut against the brine of her tears, and feeling as if she were once again in the womb, so closely did she cling to the warmth of her mother's enfolding body, Gertie resolved to herself two things. First, she forswore sea fish, lest she should ever indirectly eat part of her father. Second, she decided never to look forward to anything, since it was obvious that in an instant the world could take away your most cherished expectations. No disappointment, Gertie knew, would ever rival the dashing of her hopes on this day, outside the village to which her father now would never return.

Cornelia was met by her in-laws at the clearing in front of the village. Their first sight of her shocked them, although they had been informed by her husband's many letters of what she looked like. It was a battery of factors that seemed almost to arrest their greeting: her height, her blonde hair that was a hue alien to these parts, the curve of her nose, and the strangely long fingers with their pronounced joints. The relatives in Peng Po, long and keenly awaiting the return of the Choks' son, had known the bad news in advance of Cornelia's arrival, from a letter she had sent shortly after the ship had docked in Canton. In it she had asked them not to tell Andrew and Gertie, because she wished to do so herself. Setting aside their unease at her appearance, they expressed their condolences, first to Cornelia and then to the children, as each was introduced in turn.

Then they indicated that Cornelia would have to cross over a fire that had been set before the Choks' old home.

'In crossing the fire, you will be leaving his spirit behind,' Cornelia was told. 'You cannot enter the house otherwise, and it is essential for your home and the village that you part with the spirit of your husband.'

Tired by the journey to the village, exhausted by the events of the last weeks, Cornelia nodded her assent and asked that she be taken at once to the house to perform the ritual. Hugging Gertie under one arm and holding Andrew with the other, she came to the house that was now their home. The fire was lit. Cornelia paused at its edge for a moment and then strode over it and on to the wooden platform that led to the front door.

Turning around, she said, 'Come, children, let us go inside and see where your dear father grew up.'

It had been clear to Cornelia from the moment that Martin's body had slid into the sea that she would very soon have to reverse the direction of the family's journey. She could not hope to remain in China as a single woman, with seven children and no clear means of support. True, Martin had substantial money set aside but how would she manage that without his nous? For better or worse, Johannesburg was familiar, even though her family had cut her off. Cornelia had received that message from an uncle, a curt verbal communication informing her that she was no longer considered a Von Brandis and was never to bother her parents or any member of the extended family. In the years that followed, she and Martin had been happy, raising seven children and seeing his business grow steadily. Her father had died and when her mother remarried, Cornelia had acquired a stepsister who almost straight away introduced herself to the Martins. She was Anna Pienaar, known in the family as Annie or Auntie Annie, and she was to be a rock of strength to them, and especially to Gertie. Now, while Cornelia had no intention of acquainting her mother with the news of Martin's death and her changed circumstances, she looked forward to being able to confide in Anna. Yet, whenever she had such moments, she would chide her weakness, shaking her head angrily and vowing to be independent. And back in Johannesburg, she would be able to stand better on her own than in Peng Po, the poverty of which oppressed her.

The village was not at all as Martin had made it out to be. Cornelia had been shocked by the difference between his gilded vision of home and the reality. Life was simple, that was true, but in that simplicity there was a primitiveness that Cornelia found difficult to endure. Among many practices she found disturbing was the villagers using nightsoil to fertilise the greens, a process that seemed irredeemably unhygienic to her. Watching the buckets making their sloppy way down to the fields, carried on the brown-encrusted backs of the peasants, made Cornelia gag. She could not endure even the thought of eating the greens.

That was the worst of things, however, and Cornelia soon found a warmth and empathy from the people that banished such negative impressions as she had formed. Martin's family, and especially the elderly aunt with whom Gertie and Andrew had stayed, were kind and helpful to her while she made arrangements for the voyage back to Kum Saan. The old ladies of the village took a liking to her as well, though the strange brew that Cornelia made might have had something to do with their presence in the Martin house on many an evening. They would gather in the kitchen while Cornelia made coffee, enjoying the aroma as it permeated the air and then savouring the coffee in little cups, its darkness diluted by the addition of condensed milk. Gertie believed it was the sweetness of the milk that delighted the old ladies, as her father had told her that coffee was contrary to Chinese medicinal principles because it was *hit yee*: it heated the blood and so was not to be recommended. Gertie had always been very interested in things medical and wanted to be a nurse. Her aptitude for this was evident in the way she cared for her siblings when they were ill. Similarly, Andrew had expressed interest in becoming a doctor and the two had been looking forward to being boarders in Hong Kong, where Martin had planned that the boys should go to St John's College and the girls attend a convent school.

Travel visas and family rites seen to, Cornelia and the children left two months after her arrival in Peng Po. It was a very painful parting for Gertie, because of the close relationship with her aunt. The woman had begged Cornelia to allow Gertie, the now beloved girl she called by her Chinese name, Ah Laan, to remain behind, because she regarded her as a daughter, but Cornelia refused. She did not want to split her family and realised she would need the help of her two eldest children in seeing to the rest of the brood. Urging Ah Laan not to go, her aunt predicted that she would die of heartache on her niece's departure. On the day the Martins left, the old woman sat crouched behind a rock, put her head down and cried piteously. When she was back in Johannesburg, Gertie learnt that her aunt had indeed died some months later.

By then, other cares assailed Gertie. Her former life was gone forever: the old house with its fruit trees, the comfortingly familiar ball-and-claw furniture, the brass beds, the trap cart, the bicycles she and Andrew enjoyed so much. Most of all she missed the horses, her Ruby and Andrew's Jasper. The loss of all these had been difficult when they had set out for China, but easier to accept than now. Returned to Johannesburg, Gertie felt that these objects, animate and inanimate, were recoverable in some way. Their apparent proximity lay heavily on her at first, but she reminded herself that, the horses aside, they were merely material things and that, set against the greater changes in her life, they were inconsequential.

At first the family stayed in Ferreirastown, in quarters that Aunt Annie had taken upon herself to fit out with beds and kitchen basics. Soon, they moved to a house in Bree Street that they dubbed the Green House because its wooden window shutters and roof were painted green. Gertie delighted in this new home because it brought to mind their old, having peach, pear and plum trees.

Cornelia, as she came to grips with the gravity of her situation, began to rely more and more on Gertie and Andrew. Necessity, rather than premeditation, resulted in Gertie's being turned into a maid, housekeeper, nanny and general factotum. The children must grow up properly and at minimal expense, Cornelia thought, and whom better to entrust them to than the capable and responsible Gertie. Having no servants would mean more money for the many demands that would inevitably arise. Besides these considerations, Cornelia had always believed that Gertie had too easy a time as her father's darling. A little discipline would do the girl no harm.

Gertie was only slowly becoming used to daily chores that began before first light and ended deep into the night. Cooking, washing, scrubbing, dusting, cleaning, doing the laundry and ironing, tending to her younger brothers and sisters: such were Gertie's days. She would make sure the boys and girls were washed, dressed and fed for school, and then turn her attention to housework and shopping for daily provisions. As time went on, Gertie completed these chores more speedily and managed to do housework also for acquaintances of the family. She also mended clothing and tended children, contributing the few pence she earned from each task to the family income.

Only occasionally, on odd Sundays, was she able to snatch an hour or two for herself and read. It was her interrupted education that most affected Gertie. Sometimes it pained her almost as much as her father's death, but then she would upbraid herself for giving equivalence to the two. No matter how resigned she grew to the drudgery of her world, she preserved always the image of her father as he had stood on the platform at Johannesburg station on the night she and Andrew had begun their journey to China. His eyes had shone at her, his face had rounded into a smile that resembled the full moon and he had called to her, one last time, 'Have a grand time and take care. I love you, Yok Laan.'

FOUR
Pretoria, 1931

Kit Accone was born on 7 November 1931, six months before his father died. It has never been entirely clear what brought on Fok Yu Teem's heart attack, but one version goes that it was a fight over diamonds.

Ah Teem's third wife, Ah Hing, was more than 20 years his junior. That difference in age was due both to circumstances and choice, for his first wife had died and he had rejected his second when he discovered her infidelity. Calmly, Ah Teem had returned with the faithless woman and their young daughter to his home village of Ma Kiu in China, ostensibly on a visit to his in-laws. Once there, he had told them of the affair and then consigned their daughter and granddaughter to their care. He made arrangements for the care and education of the girl, committing himself to sending over money. Before he left again for South Africa, Ah Teem was captivated by Shue Pan Hing, a spirited young woman in her early twenties. The anger and bile of his recent betrayal melted in the face of the vivacious Ah Hing. He proposed marriage and some months later the two were living happily in Pretoria, his home from home.

Ah Hing had an acute eye for fine things, and it was the sparkle of a diamond necklace that is said to have caused the trouble. Perhaps it was the accumulation of expressed desires that broke Fok Yu Teem that day. His wife was expert at getting her way, hinting at this, appealing for that; invariably her wishes were granted, for Ah Teem was happy and satisfied in this third marriage. He had no fears about his new wife's faithfulness, and she had borne him two sons, something his beloved first wife had not managed to do. Indulged, pampered and much loved, Ah Hing was merely behaving in her usual way about the necklace. Accustomed as she was to having her wishes granted, perhaps she did not see the strain placed on her husband by this latest aspiration. When at first the piece of jewellery did not materialise, she began to make oblique references to it. Those seemed to have no effect, so she became more direct. When that, too, failed, she resorted to cajoling. Such flattery and deceit had often been deployed by Ah Teem's second wife, albeit in the service of more devious ends. Here the story descends into speculation. Some believe that the manner of Ah Hing's coaxing brought unwelcome reminders of her predecessor to Ah Teem's mind, provoking and building tension. In their gossipy way, the old ladies of the community maintained that the precipitate end came when, in discussing the wedding of friends in Kimberley, Ah Hing made a casual reference to it as the world's treasure-house of diamonds. It was then that Fok Yu Teem had risen, banged his fist on the table and begun to say something. Whatever it was, the words never emerged, for he clutched suddenly at his chest, gave a racking cough and collapsed. By the time Ah Hing reached his side, his eyes were staring vacantly at the ceiling.

His prevailing sense of contentment had made Fok Yu Teem complacent in certain matters, such as the drawing up of a will. Even as Ah Hing shut his eyes she began to grapple with the enormity of this intestate situation. Her concerns now were not for herself but for her two children, Fok Bak Yen and Fok Chong Kit, the first a few years old and the second an infant. Ah Hing knew that one family friend possessed the legal knowledge to salvage the situation, but he was at that very time on board the train from Pretoria to Lourenço Marques. It was a slim chance that had to be taken. Breaking the news hurriedly to another close friend, she outlined her plan and asked for help. The nature of the scheme dictated that the identities of these men be secret, and in family recollections they were referred to always only by means of pronouns, impersonal dubbings at odds with the personal service they rendered that night.

Within the hour, the first man was at the wheel of his car, embarked on a chase to overtake the train. Racing east of Pretoria, he passed through the small towns in that part of the Transvaal: Balmoral, Middelburg, Belfast, the train's schedule fixed in his mind. After Machadodorp and the twin sidings at Waterval Boven and Waterval Onder, on either side of a tunnel through a mountain, there would be only the station at Nelspruit and the brief stops at Kaapmuiden and Hectorspruit before the train slipped inexorably across the border at Komatipoort, where he could not follow for lack of the proper travel papers. Two miles out of Machadodorp, the car overtook the train. It gained time on the run into Waterval Boven and there he had a few minutes to compose himself before clouds of steam broke from the tunnel mouth and announced the train's advent.

Thank heavens, this one time, for segregated trains, he thought. He knew exactly which carriage to look for and before the target of his quest had time to protest, had bundled the man off the train and on to the platform. The two set off on the return journey, explanations being provided en route. Reaching Ah Hing's house in Queen Street, they hastened inside and there the second man drew up the will of Fok Yu Teem. Below the signature in Chinese characters that looked exactly like Ah Teem's easy, elegant hand, he stamped the personal seal of Fok Yu Teem, pressing the polished rectangular stone with its carved characters into a pot of red ink paste and then applying it to the page. The *chop* in place, he affixed the mark of the dead man's thumb in black ink. Then he washed off the ink from the thumb. Ah Hing and the children were safe, at least for the moment.

On the next day, Ah Hing bought a bolt of black cotton from an Indian fabric shop. She cut three dresses in a serviceable style. For the next few years, she wore and washed those in rotation. It was only at the funeral, where she dressed in white as dictated by custom, that she appeared in anything other than those plain garments.

In the shop that Ah Teem had run, Ah Hing now exercised floundering English rather than her previous refusal to engage with customers in anything but sign language. Her whimsicality was replaced by severity and practicality. It was as if in that instant of Ah Teem's death, she had changed her nature completely, partly to atone for what she deemed her culpability and partly to ensure her sons' well-being. The old ladies of the community, whispering over their tea, discussed the metamorphosis with disbelief and scepticism. It would not last, they said; perhaps Ah Hing would manage the public mourning, but in the long run, she would not bring up the two boys on her own.

To go with her black dresses, Ah Hing bought a dozen pairs of white takkies. Laboriously, she applied black polish to each pair. At the end of every month, she would consign a worn-out pair to the rubbish bin. It was no mystery how the takkies came to be used up so quickly. She was on her feet all day in the shop, and then afterwards also in the rooms at the back where the family lived.

Frugality and utility became her bywords, and she saved with an iron will to provide for the children's future. One day, she promised herself, she would have enough money to indulge her own tastes, and to dress finely once more.

FIVE
Johannesburg, circa 1919 to 1931

Ah Leong was going home. After several years in Kum Saan, he and Langshi had saved £300, a massive fortune to take to the family in Sha Kiu. Langshi's practice had gone well and Ah Leong had gradually established his own business after being released by Third Uncle. Not that Fok Shiao Shek had relented in making demands. Soon after sending the boy back to Langshi, Ah Shek suggested that Ah Leong work in a small bakery that he had just acquired. Needing to make money, Ah Leong accepted, and supplemented his earnings by selling dress materials and silk stockings to the women of the community in the evenings. When he had built up enough capital, Ah Leong opened a tiny general dealer, not far from Third Uncle, who continued to extract assistance from his nephew, this time in the form of stock for his shop. His wife demanded the privileges which would have been accorded to Soi Sien, something Ah Leong begrudged her, since he felt that if anyone in Kum Saan was worthy of such respect, it was his paper mother, not Third Aunt. Now, however, neither paper mothers nor imposed mothers mattered. He was going to see Mother, *Kongkong* and *Bobo*, his brothers and sisters, Mudan and his friends. He would be able personally to deliver the supplies of camphor ice and jerseys that he had formed the habit of sending his mother for winter.

A week before they were to take the train to Durban, Langshi, Ah Leong and his older cousin Ah Hoy met in the living room behind Langshi's practice in Malay Camp to discuss the homeward expedition they would be making together. Early in the conversation Ah Hoy reminded them that some travellers from Kum Saan had been diddled out of money by sharp operators en route.

'We must be vigilant,' agreed Langshi. 'This matter has worried me for some time. I think it best that we remain in each other's company as much as possible and that there should always be two of us together.'

'Indeed,' said Ah Hoy, 'and we might even consider you and me looking after all the money.' Turning to Ah Leong, he continued, 'These tricksters target younger travellers, thinking them more gullible and easily hoodwinked. My suggestion is not a slight on you, or a lack of confidence in you. But you are more likely to be approached, and more often as well, so it is only with your welfare and interests at heart that I say this.'

Langshi was about to reply when Ah Leong leapt to his feet. His face breaking into a rash of red mottles, he blurted out, 'No! I am old enough to make and save my money, why should I not be old enough to carry it safely with me? This money is going to our family, it is the fruits of our hard work here and so it goes without saying that I shall be extra careful in taking care of it.'

'*Tsai*, please hear what your cousin has to say,' interjected Langshi. 'He wishes to make your passage easier and safer by relieving you of the burden of being ever watchful over the money – your money.'

'*Foo ts'an*, I regard this as a matter of honour. If you insist on carrying my money, then I will abide by your decision. Know then that the money will go with you and Ah Hoy, but that I will not. I will remain here and one day, when I have made enough money to warrant going home, I will return bearing my money for my family.'

'I think it best that we do, indeed, carry the money,' said Langshi to his son. 'But it is quite unnecessary for you not to accompany us. Your mother and grandparents, not to mention the many others who await your homecoming, would be sorely disappointed.'

'*Foo ts'an* and cousin Ah Hoy, may my money be safe with you on your journey. I will remain here to make a beginning on the next voyage, when I will go alone, to show that I can be trusted.'

Before his father could speak again, Ah Leong turned and left the room. In the stillness that followed, the two older men looked at each other with sadness in their eyes. Clearing his throat, Ah Hoy ventured that perhaps Ah Leong would change his mind after he had considered things. Langshi nodded and undertook to speak to the boy in the morning.

When he set his mind to something, Ah Leong could not be diverted. Often this presented itself as hard-headed stubbornness rather than admirable determination, and Langshi hoped that reason and time would prevail over his son's intemperate outburst. On this matter, however, Ah Leong was not to be moved. Not even Langshi's appealing to the boy to make the visit for his mother's sake could win him over. Ah Leong said he was suspicious of the way that Langshi and Ah Hoy had agreed quickly that they ought to share the money-carrying. He said that showed some sort of prior agreement – which his father strenuously denied – and that he resented what he called their mistrust. Exasperated, Langshi finally said that Ah Leong's very reaction to the suggestion and subsequent behaviour showed that he was in some ways still immature. After this injudicious moment of his own, Langshi cursed himself for lacking restraint, and wished over and over that he had held his tongue. Still, this was to be a visit, not a return home. Langshi had determined to come back to Kum Saan and save more money before finally settling back in Sha Kiu.

While his father was away, Ah Leong threw himself into improving his shop. He had long abandoned any ideas of returning to China to enter the civil service, and contented himself instead with the dream that one day he would be wealthy enough to go home and take up the rural life practised by his grandparents, with perhaps the extreme indulgence of a boat to sail on the Pearl River. To ease the dry and windy August, with its bleached colours and pale skies, he bought bolts of fine and brightly coloured cloth to sell on his nightly rounds of the community. He felt heartened by the vivid sheen of the materials and was sure that his customers would be similarly cheered. The fabrics did sell well, and Ah Leong grew more venturesome in purchasing goods both for the shop and his second job of bicycle-borne pedlar.

On Langshi's return, Ah Leong endured the news of how saddened his mother had been by his absence. He vowed to visit home as soon as he could, and then plunged once more into his endeavours. Letters went between Kum Saan and Sha Kiu as before, and from these he learnt that his mother was pregnant and, later, that she had given birth to a fifth boy, Ah Horn, the ninth child in the family. Langshi could not afford to go and see his son, but consoled himself that it would be only a few years until he was home forever with the boy, Soi Sien and the rest of the family.

★

By the time he reached his late twenties, with almost seventeen years in Kum Saan behind him, Ah Leong was moderately well settled. His English was good, his Afrikaans passable, and he was acquiring more and more knowledge of Zulu, Tswana, Sotho and even Xhosa. He found the click sounds required especially in Zulu and Xhosa easier than some of the Rs in English and Afrikaans. Fondly, he looked back on his early days of shopping in the Indian fruit and vegetable markets, where he would use a cane to point out what he wished to buy. Such canes were also the means of commerce in Chinese shops where local languages were not understood, and even now Ah Leong affectionately kept in his general dealership the cane that had accompanied him on those early forays.

It was on a call to Mrs Martin, who had a house with green shutters and roof that offset its white walls, that Ah Leong became aware of a quiet young girl called both Ah Laan and Gertie. She was about sixteen or seventeen, with brown eyes that hinted at some deep sorrow. About once a month, his rounds would bring him to the Martin household. Whenever he visited, Ah Laan would be busy, darning clothing or attending to one of the younger children. Ah Leong was quick to notice that Mrs Martin favoured the other girls, among whom were Elizabeth or Ah Hoi, and Violet. The boys seemed to be well loved too, though the absence of a father in their lives was clear.

On Ah Leong's third or fourth visit, Philip asked whether he knew anything about Chinese martial arts. The young boy said that his older brother Andrew had told him of the peculiar kind of boxing and kicking that he had seen in China. Smiling, Ah Leong said that he knew a little and, with Mrs Martin's permission, would show the boys some basics. In truth, Ah Leong was rather better acquainted with the practice and subtleties of *wu shu*, the ancient Chinese martial arts, than he admitted. Tian, his grandfather, had trained him in the Southern style of kung fu from the age of six, so that by the time he had left Sha Kiu, he had been learning and practising for several years. Among the many reminders and practices of home, Ah Leong maintained his training. It was a way of holding on to the memory of his grandfather, even of bringing the old man closer. As Ah Leong stood in the backyard each morning, breathing in the coolness, he imagined himself in Sha Kiu, on the grassy verge above the pond, going through the various forms that made up the basic exercises while Tian watched and corrected him. In Kum Saan, he had not found a teacher, and was concerned that he might lose discipline or become stale. He feared rigidity too, born of the over-familiarity that can attend a small repertoire, no matter how complex that is. There was solace, though, in the notion that one could spend a lifetime practising and yet never attain anything near perfection; as his own experience had taught him, the more he learnt, the more he realised how little he knew. For some time Ah Leong had been wondering whether he should share that tiny trove with others. Philip's question was the answering intervention that confirmed his instincts and visits to the Green House became more frequent, both for *wu shu* and to become better acquainted with Ah Laan.

When the Martins moved to Hay Street in Ophirton, the weekly ritual continued. Ah Leong was imparting the style characteristic of the south of China, which uses the hands more than the feet. The legend goes that the fists came to predominate in the techniques south of the Yangtze River after a month-long contest held in the middle of the 17th century, at the beginning of the Ching Dynasty. Over a hundred Imperial Guards fought on the slopes beneath the monastery on Mount Chiu-lien, and in the river beds below, until one was triumphant: Tieh-chai, whose forte lay in fist skills. He was appointed chief instructor of the monastery and thenceforth Chiu-lien training attached greater importance to blows from the hands than from the feet. In turn, the folk warriors of the south drilled hand-work to a greater degree than before. The differences between the two schools, Ah Leong told his young charges, was captured in the old sayings 'Southern Fist and Northern Leg' and 'Northern Kicks and Southern Punches'.

There had been several times when Ah Leong had cause to be grateful for those southern skills. In each instance he had been unable to avoid a fight, which was the best way of defending oneself, his grandfather had drummed into him; only in dire circumstances should kung fu skills be deployed. Once, Ah Leong had been attacked in a shop by three Afrikaners. He disposed of two but the third, a tree of a man, blocked the way out. 'Now I've got you, you little Chinaman,' he bellowed, advancing on Ah Leong. It was time for the blow called *Ma lau tau tee*, a streetfighting manoeuvre used in cases of disproportionate odds. Charging the man, Ah Leong ducked nimbly between his legs and then reached up, like a monkey stealing peaches, excepting the target here was the scrotum. Grab, squeeze, twist and pluck, and Ah Leong was out the door.

Another brawl led to charges of assault and battery being brought against him. Five callow youths had tried to beat him up, but the resulting injuries had been sustained entirely by them: black eyes, a broken nose, twisted ears, sore ankles, missing teeth and bruised jaws. In court, the plaintiffs presented their case to the magistrate. Taken aback and disapproving, he asked the accused to rise and when Ah Leong did so, the magistrate said he 'refused to believe that this one small Chinaman could have done so much damage' and summarily dismissed the case.

While discouraging hot-headedness and inapt use of what he was teaching them, Ah Leong prepared the boys for threatening situations. He taught them basic blocks and punches, and after putting the brothers through their exercises, he would take tea in the house with them and thereafter see if Mrs Martin required anything. From time to time, with her consent, he would offer Ah Laan a piece of material or a pair of stockings. In turn, Gertie would seek Cornelia's approval, being mindful of the mores of the time under which casual acceptance could be misconstrued and result in scandal.

Gertie did not welcome Ah Leong's gradualist approach because there was someone else whom she admired, and even considered a soul mate, but she kept that to herself. At the same time, she had known Ah Leong distantly as a kind and pleasant member of the community since before her stay in China and, in any case, she longed to escape the service into which she had been pressed, yearned to educate herself somehow and wished to be independent in her own house. She would have to be patient, she decided. Time had made her father's death, as well as her changed circumstances, easier to bear. Perhaps in a few years, with the children off her hands, she might be able to entertain marriage to the man with whom she believed she would find fulfilment. By then Ah Leong would surely be able to accept rejection, though she resolved to be gracious in accepting his kindness.

Ah Leong did not manage to engage Ah Laan in anything more than pleasantries and short conversations. He found it frustrating that he could not discover more about this young woman, whose conscientiousness and care towards her siblings he much respected. He marvelled at the restraint Ah Laan showed in the face of her mother's attitude towards her, for it was as if Mrs Martin regarded her as the family servant. Ah Leong had overheard Ah Laan's mother refer to her as 'Blackie', a term which pained him. He gleaned from one of the boys that it stemmed from a belief their mother had that Gertie was darker than the others and that she might endanger their status in a country where skin colour was the chief determinant in life. This discovery enraged Ah Leong even more than when first he had heard the slighting, stinging nickname. The fact of the matter, clear to all who saw without jaundiced eyes, was that Gertie looked 'white', far more than any of her brothers and sisters except Ah Hoi. And, Ah Leong reflected ruefully, Ah Hoi's hue might be due partly to her seemingly weak heart, which had led to Mrs Martin's cosseting her and attempting to keep her indoors as much as possible.

Cornelia had done her best to obscure the Eurasian nature of her family. She had determined that it would be best for them to try to fit into white society, but the reality was that they were not accepted there. It was the same in the Chinese community. Regarded as half-breeds by both sides, they were stranded in an inescapable limbo. Only the government of the day was clear on their status, sending the children to the Coloured School in Bree Street, popularly called 'small school' as it was for Grades 1 and 2. Thereafter, it was off to the Newtown Coloured School, which went up to Junior Certificate.

There was some unexpected solace for Cornelia in Annie's marrying a Chinese, and in later years her daughter was to become one of Gertie's great friends. But the segregation laws of the day, and the pitiless racism of white and Chinese towards the Martins, resulted in Cornelia's thinking of ways to escape not only Johannesburg, but South Africa.

Ah Leong's visits to Hay Street caused consternation closer to home also. His father, aware of the mixed parentage of the Martin family, took to reminding his son of the importance of being pure Chinese. While Langshi never used that most pejorative of Cantonese terms for half-breeds, 'ox-head', his long digressions on the subject of miscegenation were almost as insulting. The more Langshi lectured, the greater grew Ah

Leong's determination to shield Ah Laan, at least from the prejudice of his own community. The possibility of marrying Mudan had lapsed some years before, for the Lis had made a good match for their daughter with Ah Sek, one of Ah Leong's childhood friends. When he had first read the news, in one of his mother's letters, Ah Leong had been disappointed and saddened, and then angry. After a while, though, he took comfort that at least Mudan had not been matched with the nervy, cowardly Ah Lai.

More swiftly than any of the parties could have imagined, Ah Leong's determined good intentions prompted him to act. Towards the end of February 1930, he asked Mrs Martin for Ah Laan's hand. While not wholly unforeseen by her mother, to Gertie the request seemed sudden, impulsive and irrational. True, Cornelia felt the offer somewhat premature compared with the customary way that such matters unfolded, but then, in a brief moment of empathy, she remembered her own marriage to Martin. That refulgent memory inclined her to accept the proposal. As she turned to Gertie to ask, 'Is that acceptable to you, dear?', Cornelia never for a moment doubted that her eldest daughter would assent.

Trapped by the desires and devices of others, Gertie sensed that she had little option. In the yawning moments before she acquiesced in her fate, she considered what it would mean for her. She scarcely knew Ah Leong, though there was no doubting that he was a hard-working and honourable person. Marrying him might be an escape from her servile existence but it would dash her belief that love was the most important factor in any union. She would have to relinquish the man she would have no qualms in accepting. What would Father have said? Gertie never answered the last question, for she knew that had Chok Foon Martin been alive her life would have proceeded very differently. But this was her life now, and to say no might mean years of desperation. A new way was opening and, for better or worse, Gertie accepted its challenge.

Ah Leong married Cornelia Catharina Chok Foon Martin on 30 April 1930 in the Magistrate's Office in Fox Street. When he saw her identity papers, which made no mention of Gertie or Gertrude, Ah Leong was surprised. He had not expected the documentation to bear her Chinese name, Yok Laan, but it puzzled him to find out that his wife's family called her by a name she had not been given. Wryly, he recalled that he, too, was in the registry office under a name that was not his. In the life ahead he would call her Ah Laan, of course, and perhaps Yok Laan when he was angry or needed to command her attention, and maybe Gertie sometimes, but not Catharina and never Cornelia.

The legalities over, the couple had a small tea party with a very few friends and family at Ah Leong's house in Mint Road, Fordsburg. There were not many gifts, but Cornelia had crocheted a splendid bed cover that vied as the most beautiful present with the embroidered Chinese tea cloth given by a friend.

A week later, Ah Leong posted a letter to Soi Sien, telling her of the marriage and enclosing a studio portrait of himself and his bride. He knew that his mother would be both happy and sad, but he regretted the conclusion that she would draw from the news: that his return to Sha Kiu would be postponed still further.

Six
Johannesburg, circa 1931 to 1938

A little over a year after they married, Ah Leong and Gertie had their first child, a girl Langshi named Hong Hgang, literally red apricot blossom. She was born on 28 May 1931 in one of the small living rooms behind Ah Leong's Mint Road shop. On hand was the German midwife who served the Chinese community at the time, there being no maternity homes or hospitals that would accept Chinese. At the beginning of labour, the woman had been what Gertie called 'Spartan' with her, but a few sharp words from Cornelia in their mutual native tongue smoothed the delivery.

Langshi, who had at best been reconciled to his son's marriage, began with the arrival of his granddaughter almost to approve of it. His presence at the wedding party had been subdued, though not sullen, and he had hardly warmed to Gertie in the first few months thereafter. When the news came that she was pregnant, however, the old man's attitude changed. His interest in her well-being sprang more from the personal than the professional, although he deployed all his knowledge in ensuring that she was strong and in good health during the nine months that they awaited the arrival of his grandchild.

In that time, the unease that had settled between Langshi and Ah Leong started to lift as well. Since the day Ah Leong had given up his visit home the two had never mentioned that matter, but it underlay all their doings. It was what made Ah Leong fear that his father would interfere in his dealings with Gertie. So, while Ah Leong had acknowledged his affections for her, he had never given his father an inkling of his plans to ask for her hand. After Hong Hgang's birth, father and son regained much of their earlier bonhomie. They realised also that the next time Langshi journeyed to Kwangtung he would not be intending to return to Kum

Saan, for by then he would have enough money saved to feel secure for life. Whether Ah Leong, with a family now, would follow soon was doubtful. When Hong Hgang was joined by Hong Lin, red lotus, on 10 January 1933, both men knew that it would be many years before Ah Leong could even consider going home.

Soi Sien was joyous at the news of her grandchildren. She read both precious letters from Kum Saan a number of times, and on each occasion went out to share the news with the Lis. When, she wondered, would she see Hong Hgang and Hong Lin? The day that Langshi, Ah Kwok – Soi Sien never thought of or called her son by his new name – and his family returned to the village would be one of inexpressible elation. It was a sadness that Ah Kwok's grandparents had not lived to hear the news of his progeny but Soi Sien told them nonetheless, on her daily visit to the ancestral hall. Soi Sien's life was busy and full, praying, caring for Ah Horn, and supervising the tending of the fish ponds, but it had a hollowness in the absence of Langshi. Still, she knew that he would be home soon, never to leave.

Soon after Hong Lin was born the family moved to Bevan Avenue in Newclare, an area for so-called Non-Europeans: Africans, Indians, Coloureds and Chinese lived and traded together in this dusty and insalubrious location. Houses and shops were cheaply built, with no amenities. There were no drainage systems, so that during the summer thunderstorms, the streets became muddy thoroughfares strewn with household detritus.

The poorest of Newclare's residents lived in mud hovels while the better-off converted the minute store rooms behind their shops into living quarters. A tiny bedroom where the whole family would sleep jostled against an adjacent kitchen area, with its coal stove. Out in the yard was the bucket-system toilet, which the night carts would attend to weekly, replacing used buckets with empty ones that smelt of Jeyes Fluid, the chief disinfectant of the time. At times, when Hong Hgang could not fall asleep, she would hear the rumble of the carts and smell the gaseous wake as they ferried away their noxious cargo, and she would worry that it was very late for her still to be awake.

By day, she and Hong Lin played in a space that Gertie made for them under the counters in the shop. It was there that they once smashed a gross of Price's Candles. One hundred and forty-four candles crumbled under the little pairs of hands, the soft waxy sticks cracking into bits and flakes and building into a snowy pile. Had it not been for Gertie, the children would have had a hiding from Ah Leong, who was furious at the waste. As it was, she reminded him that there was no garden for them to play in, only a back yard filled with wood and coal for their customers.

The holy trinity of everyday life in Newclare comprised wood, coal and candles. Only a few business premises had electricity, so residents used candles for lighting and improvised galleys for cooking and heating. Round or rectangular tins about eighteen inches high were turned into stoves and fireplaces by punching holes in them, filling them with paper, chips of wood and a layer of coal and then setting the pile alight. Such galleys were inexpensive and portable but very unsafe, and Gertie told her children of how often people would be suffocated in cramped sleeping quarters where they had been left burning.

Gertie did not like Newclare. The beer-brewing trade in its slumyards sometimes led to fighting and factional violence. While she did not begrudge the brewers, who were women, their income from beer sales, she could see the toll that alcohol took on the depressed, the unemployed and the unemployable. Newclare was no Rooiyard, the best known, or most notorious, of the Doornfontein slumyards in the east of the city, but it was not a fit place to raise her daughters. Gertie's favourite dog Billy would help her watch over the children, and tugging gently on their clothing, would bring the girls back into the shop when they had wandered outside. An ally, whom Gertie would often think of as an angel, came in the form of Ah Leong's landlord, Jack Cohen. On his visits to collect the rent, he would always bring some treats for Hong Hgang and Hong Lin, calling them by their western names, Jewel and Helen. He complied when, later, Helen insisted on being called Mickey, after seeing a Mickey Mouse cartoon at the cinema, and her adopted name stuck for life. It was Mr Cohen who broached the matter of the family's moving. As he was the owner of several properties in the western areas of Johannesburg, he suggested that they move to Westdene, where he was about to build business premises with reasonable living quarters at the back. These would be near to where Ah Leong was already trading in a second location, in a grocery shop in Perth Road East. Ah Leong and Gertie agreed, and while building was under way, they moved to Milner Street in Sophiatown, the suburb next to Westdene.

Just as Gertie was allowing herself to feel relief at their improving circumstances, Ah Leong's grocery shop ran into trouble. Westdene was a conservative Afrikaner heartland, where nationalist ideas such as '*Een Volk, Een Taal, Een Land*' – one people, one language, one land – were finding organisational coherence in various political and quasi-political groupings. Dr Malan's Purified National Party had broken with the National Party and set out on a path of even more extreme segregationist policies and ultranationalism. Commemorations of the Great Trek led to an ox-wagon cult and the formation of the *Ossewa Brandwag*, literally the ox-wagon sentinels. At first a cultural movement, it was to grow into a political movement characterised by intransigence, bullying and violent methods.

Stoked by such developments, the Afrikaners of Westdene, many of them members of the ox-wagon society, protested against having a Chinese trader in their area even though his shop was at the very edge of the suburb where, on the other side of Perth Road, lay Newclare and Coronationville, with their teeming numbers of non-whites. They began a campaign to get the *Chinkie* out. Ah Leong responded by putting up an explanation in his shop window of why he was there and what service he hoped to provide. Next to this, he placed a petition asking the locals to support him. No one had signed his or her name and, thought Ah Leong, probably not a single person had bothered to read his appeal. As business fell off and the prospect of running a larger concern in the new premises down the street seemed bleaker by the week, Johannes van der Walt walked in. Ah Leong saw only a giant tree trunk of a man, with massive branches for arms, who asked for a cool drink. In the outside world, Van der Walt was a wrestler whose exploits on the mat had made him a folk hero for Afrikaners and others alike, but of this Ah Leong knew nothing. While this customer stood slaking his thirst and looking round the shop, he noticed the handwritten sheets of paper in the window and asked Ah Leong about them. A short account of Ah Leong's troubles followed, with Van der Walt's curiosity slowly giving way to indignation and anger. Finally the huge man shook his head.

'This *Ossewa Brandwag* thing is no good,' he said to the shopkeeper. 'Never mind. Please give me a pen.' Deliberately, Van der Walt signed his name to the petition in favour of Ah Leong's remaining in Westdene. The sheet was blank no longer, and such was the respect and awe in which the wrestler was held that it required no further signatories for the campaign against the little Chinese grocer to be dropped. It was only later that Ah Leong and Gertie learnt that Van der Walt was an implacable opponent of the *Ossewa Brandwag*.

Sophiatown was an affront to the monolingual and mono-cultural ideals of such as the *Ossewa Brandwag*. A Babel of languages co-existed, spoken by people of diverse cultures and different colours. Africans, Coloureds, Indians and Chinese lived here, under very different conditions than elsewhere in the Transvaal, for many Africans were landowners in Sophiatown. They had bought their stands before the Urban Areas Act was passed in 1923, and by the time Ah Leong and Gertie made their sojourn, had turned a 'location' into a suburb.

Sophiatown, the long rectangle of Martindale tucked into its south-eastern flank, nearby Newclare and Western Native Township comprised the Western Areas, a place of social and cultural resistance to the separatist policies of the day. It was colour blind because its inhabitants mingled easily; it was inclusive of many classes because it embraced professionals, clerical workers, teachers, ministers of religion, traders, craftsmen and workers in industry. The Chinese formed the smallest minority in Western Areas, numbering between 300 and 400. Twice as many Indians lived in the area, and twice as many Coloureds, while there were almost 30 000 Africans.

When Ah Leong's family stayed in Milner Street, in the mid-1930s, the destruction of Sophiatown lay some 20 years in the future. Sophiatown was building up towards the flowering of the culture and music that were to make it legendary, but because the family were there only in passing, they did not encounter that rich vein of life. They did, however, become acquainted with an eminent Sophiatown resident, Dr Alfred B Xuma, the country's first African gynaecologist, who was to be president of the African National Congress from 1940 to 1949. For many years he and his black American wife would come to the Perth Road shop for supplies, and Mickey and Jewel were always fascinated by Mrs Xuma's accent.

Their time in the Sophiatown halfway-house brought two treasures: a car and a piano. Conceding the impracticality as family transport of his Harley Davidson plus side-car, Ah Leong arrived in Milner Street one morning with a Buick Roadmaster and a car salesman. Ah Leong hurried Gertie and the children from the house into the navy blue leviathan for a test drive. Curvaceous and muscular, the Buick had bumpers and door edgings of chrome, and a running board from which the children bounced into the leather interior. They smelt the car's newness and the hide seats, and looked at the array of gadgets: ashtrays, indoor lighting, hand straps over the back doors, and the radio recessed in the dashboard. Settling on either side of the armrest that divided the back seat, Jewel and Mickey waited for their father to start the car. Usually, they sat on their mother's lap in the side-car, cramped but filled with anticipation for the wind-blown and sound-filled journey, where they felt one with the world rushing and screeching around them.

A low rumble, followed by a burble, and the Buick sprang to life. The salesman waved at the girls from the pavement, Ah Leong eased the car into the road, and the family took their first such voyage together. The blue craft floated over the bad roads, absorbing bumps and gliding over corrugations. Ah Leong and Gertie spoke, at first loudly out of the conversational habits they had developed for journeys in the Harley, and then in a sort of muted wonder. The quiet and the sheltering atmosphere of the car were remarkable. There was no interfering noise from the engine or the wind, and both adults savoured the roof overhead, respite from the Highveld sun.

For Ah Leong, the Buick was the apex in his progression from pedestrian to cyclist to motorcyclist to motorist. Gertie could see the advantages of having the family safe and snug but she felt nonetheless that such a luxurious car was an extravagance. What was wrong, she asked, with the PUTCO buses or the municipal trams that most Chinese used? From behind the large smooth windows, the girls watched Sophiatown, Westdene and the Auckland Park Race Course go by while their parents argued, softly, in front. Ah Leong listened for a time, but then said, 'Yok Laan, it is my decision. I am buying this car. It is not as though we could spend the money on a house, because we cannot buy in the areas we might want to live. We cannot buy anywhere. Also the community is resisting being forced to settle in areas the government has demarcated for it. We need something larger and safer than the motorcycle for the four of us. Don't you remember when I was alone with Mickey and she crawled out on to the back of the side-car as I was going down Hurst Hill?' Perhaps it was this last incident that persuaded Gertie, or maybe she could see that there was no changing her husband's mind. His voice was beginning to take on that pitch and his face that demeanour of determination that she knew was fruitless to oppose. The Roadmaster came home within the week.

This motor car was to become more than a means of family transport. Ah Leong was invited to be the *wha que kong*, the driver of the wedding vehicle, at countless Chinese nuptials. It was felt he would bring luck, happiness and prosperity to the couple and, besides, his conscientiousness was well known. Ah Leong would do more than merely play taxi. He was charged with escorting the bride, her bridesmaids and other attendants, as well as taking care of the Apricot Woman, the go-between or matchmaker of the couple and their families. Seeing the bride through the volleys of fire-crackers that were ritually set off at various points in the day meant being a watchful fireman too, for many were the cases when the bride's dress caught flame from an errant spark. For his service, Ah Leong would receive the traditional red envelope, called *lysee*, filled with crisp new bank notes in thanks. Such customary acknowledgement aside, he was happy to discharge this important community duty, and Gertie and the children felt proud of him and the car.

Buoyed by Van der Walt's support, Ah Leong's business grew and he acquired not only the Roadmaster but also an electric stove, from Mackay Bros. Its arrival at Milner Street, however, had a far from positive effect on Gertie. She feared electrocution, or burning down the house. She was perfectly happy with the old coal stove from which all manner of delightful food could be made to issue. In truth, Gertie feared change and the new. Her father's death had made her wary of departures from the established way of things, and her caution embraced the spectrum from the everyday to the profound. Defeated in the matter of the car, Gertie had no intention of surrendering over the stove. Ah Leong was a very good cook himself — his time at Third Uncle had forced him to pick up culinary skills speedily — and he would have appreciated the convenience of electricity over continually ferrying scuttles of coal, but he relented. Gertie prepared most of the daily meals, while it was mainly on weekends and holidays that Ah Leong conjured up elegant and imaginative variations on the dishes he had first learned from *Mei Wei Kow Chun*, the cookery book his father had given him when he went off to live with Third Uncle. There, Ah Leong's cooking had lived up to the book's title, roughly translated as 'Tasty, Tasty Enough', and had begun in him a quiet passion for preparing fine food.

Although there was no refund for the stove, it could be exchanged for anything of equivalent value. Looking around Mackay's, Ah Leong saw in the far corner, on a platform, a number of upright pianos. Walking over, he raised one of the lids, touched the keys, and then closed the piano. He moved to another, made of dark wood that gleamed under the shop lights. Again, he opened the instrument, this time resting the lid against the bodywork. He ran his fingers over the keyboard, touching each of the keys. Those made of ivory were smooth and cooling to his fingers. Ah Leong smiled. This was no electrocution device, but in the instant of contact it had charged his body and soul. He had loved the sound of the piano ever since he had first heard it on board the ship from China, its delicate and sonorous notes unlike anything he had experienced at home. Ah Leong imagined the girls learning to play, and fancied himself at the keyboard also. That was how a Carl Ecke, made in Berlin, and costing £98, came into the lives of the Leong family.

Standing almost five foot high, the upright was an imposing presence in the Milner Street house. But before it had settled in, it was time for the move to Westdene. The Leongs, as officialdom had dubbed them, moved at last into their new premises at 27 and 27A Perth Road, next to the International Service Station that stood at the crossroads leading to four suburbs: Westdene, Rossmore, Hurst Hill and Newclare. Gertie and Ah Leong were delighted. The adjacent shops meant that they could run both a grocery and a fruit shop-cum-café. Best of all were the living quarters behind the fruit shop: two bedrooms, lounge, kitchen, dining room and long porch. Though all the rooms were small excepting for the porch, this was a place that could become a home. Outside, beyond the back door stairs, lay the outhouse with its bath and toilet – and a garden that the children thought a paradise.

In the garden and the outer yard, which the children called the Big Yard, they played in a way they had never been able to before. At first, Jewel and Mickey were joined by their cousins Marie, Patrick and Yvonne, the children of their Uncle Andrew and his wife Dolly. Andrew had lost his business in Newclare and Ah Leong had taken the family in for the time being. Games of princess and slaves and cowboys and crooks, and speed races on bicycles, filled the days. When the children were tired of playing, they watched the bantams and other inhabitants of the fowl run, or the ducks floating in their little domain, a pleasantly muddy pond in the Big Yard, or the comings and goings in the pigeon *hok*.

At night, the Leong children revelled in their own bedroom, of which they were very proud. They had their own beds, with coir mattresses, to which they became so accustomed that when Ah Leong bought them spring mattresses some years later, they could scarcely sleep because they felt suspended in air and missed the familiar hardness of the coir. The arrival of new mattresses was to the children the fulfilment of a wish to have something in vogue, but it betokened also another turnover, the steady rise in the fortunes of Ah Leong Family Grocers and Perth Road Fruit Shop.

Despite all the regulations and restrictions the government placed on Chinese traders, they were able to make a living by dint of selling the necessaries of daily life in small quantities, for a penny or a tickey, and often on credit. This was an ideal means of encouraging and maintaining custom, since the Chinese traded in working-class areas, many of the inhabitants of which were regularly unemployed. There was a bitter, and regular, element in the relationships between Ah Leong and Gertie and their customers, however. On Fridays, pay day for the men of the area, their wives would come to the shop begging for a loaf of bread, half a pound of butter, some cheese and milk on tick for the family at home. Their husbands were at the local bar, their wages washing down their throats. It was at these times that Ah Leong and Gertie were Mr and Mrs Leong, but on other days, whether they were in the street or on a tram, there would not be a word or even a look of recognition for the shop-keepers and no acknowledgement of their Friday afternoon kindnesses. The customers were the Europeans and the shopkeepers were the Non-Europeans and never would they meet in public.

Ah Leong and Gertie accepted this behaviour, perhaps because they had won a more important fight in their first year in Perth Road. It was the practice of the time that Indian, Chinese and Jewish shopkeepers were referred to generically by derogatory names. Indian men would be addressed as Sammy, Indian women as Mary, while Chinese would be called Charlie and Jews dubbed Ikey. When the burghers of Westdene addressed Ah Leong and Gertie as Charlie, they would immediately be told, firmly and politely, and in Afrikaans, 'My name is Mr Leong/Mrs Leong, and what is your name?' Some sniggered, walked out and laughed. Others, surprised or embarrassed, would apologise to Mr or Mrs Leong.

Woe betide the new customer, or someone who dropped in to the shop for a casual purchase, and began by saying '*Charlie, kan ek ...*' or 'Charlie, can I ...'. A lecture would follow, if the offender remained to hear out this cheeky Chinaman. In more instances than not, if the person was from the area, he or she would return as a customer and not repeat the mistake.

If the customers needed some working on, so did the children who would pass by. Invariably youngsters would chant 'Ikey, Mikey Moses/ King of the Jews/ Sold his wife for a pair of shoes' when the Aarons came to buy at the Leongs' shops. The same children would call out 'Ching Chong Chinaman' or 'Chongo Mo Le' as they walked past the shop, something the Leongs never worked out the meaning of. Worse still were the enthusiastic and unmelodious renderings of Jim Crow-like ditties. One went 'Ching Chong Chinaman/ Born in a bar/ All covered in shit/ Ha ha ha'. Others ran 'Ching Chong Chinaman/ Born in a bar/ Christened in a teapot/ Ha ha ha' and 'Chinkie Chinkie ring the bell/ Coolie Coolie/ Go to hell'.

This was something Ah Leong would not tolerate. Shortly after settling into the new Perth Road premises, he embarked on what he called a re-education campaign of the children. Seeing them making their way up the road, he would hide behind his shop door, listening. If a song went up, or a racist remark, Ah Leong would wait and then spring out and grab offenders by the scruff of the neck or by the ear, and give them a dressing-down. If something particularly odious had been said, Ah Leong would seize his Chinese duster, which had a handle of stout cane, and whack the culprit on the behind or across the back of the legs. In all cases, he sought to extract both an apology and a promise that such things would not be repeated.

The other side of Ah Leong and Gertie's shopkeeping had to do with avoiding infringing any of the numerous bylaws that had been set up, like an obstacle course, to trip up the careless trader. Squads of inspectors patrolled businesses, checking on minutiae, verifying weights and measuring up establishments in a score of other ways. No items of clothing could be draped or hung anywhere in a shop. If your coat was found on the premises, you were fined. Every item of merchandise had to be individually marked, as well as priced on the shelf. All shopkeepers had to wear aprons; later the dress code was amended to three-quarter-length khaki jackets.

There were inspectors for controlling weights and measures. First they checked the scales in the shop. Then they placed the randomly selected brown paper bags containing flour, chicken feed and sugar, on the scales. The four-ounce samples were correct. It was the turn of the eight-ounce bags. Next, the twelve-ounce packets, all the way up to the heavy-duty brown bags that could take a weight of twelve pounds.

There were inspectors for keeping the hours of business under observation. Ah Leong's grocery had to shut at 6 p.m. during the week and at noon on Saturdays. A minute over, and a hefty fine would be imposed, or perhaps even a licence revoked, sometimes by the very man who a short while before had been begging you to sell him some essential on credit. Ah Leong and Gertie never fell into these traps, though, for they complied with the trading regulations to the letter and, besides, Gertie had an unerring instinct for an inspector's trap. 'Bug, there is something fishy here,' she would whisper to Ah Leong, using the nickname the two had somehow devised for each other, and which they would resort to at all sorts of times, tense, happy, or sad.

It was remarkable that the Leongs could provide for their children, and make a home, given the slim profit margins: a penny on a loaf of bread, to take the staple item sold in Gertie's fruit shop and café. What was far more taxing was living on the tiniest of islands in the midst of a sea of hostility. Just to see the treatment meted out to those disliked by the locals was a salutary reminder of the fragility of the relationship between Chinese trader and local customer. Two families who were customers at 27 and 27A Perth Road were United Party supporters, and at each election they would be assaulted by supporters of the Purified National Party.

Wherever the Leongs went, they could be subjected to familiar and unwelcome indignities in song and verse. Jewel and Mickey would hit back sometimes with '*Jou wit vuilgoed*' ('You white rubbish'), but they knew it was ungracious and ineffectual. On a few occasions in the shop, tiring of words, the girls would grab over-ripe tomatoes and potatoes that Gertie put aside for customers who wanted to use them for seeding, and pelt their tormentors. Whether by accident or design, these salvoes happened on Saturdays, when the other children were dressed in their best, going-out clothes. Outraged parents would arrive to complain to Ah Leong and Gertie about what they believed were unprovoked attacks, only to be forced to listen to Jewel and Mickey explaining that their action was retaliation for immediate and accumulated slights. On hearing that, the aggrieved parties would often turn on their own children, chastising and whacking them for their rudeness. Slowly, the Leongs wore down the vocal, overtly hostile behaviour towards them and earned grudging respect from the community of customers.

Beyond the tiny world of Perth Road, things were less susceptible to amelioration. Travelling on the public trams was always fraught. Non-Whites were consigned to the 'monkey cage', the upper, open level of the trams, which was pleasant on warm, sunny days, but miserable in winter or when it rained. Summer afternoons were particularly forbidding, as bulbous white storm clouds gathered and grew in size. Two days in three, between four and six in the afternoon, the charged and leaden skies would open and drench the city with sheets of thunderous rain. Being atop the tram then was terrifying, as bolts of white lightning scarred the sky and emitted their cracking volleys.

Sometimes fellow travellers could be more violent than the thunderstorms. Merely trying to board the tram to and from school involved

Jewel and Mickey in a running battle of words, first with the conductor and then the passengers. The children had seen Chinese boys and men attacked and more than once thrown from moving trams. For protection, the girls carried small nail scissors on their person. A more effective defence was avoiding confrontation altogether, something their father often advised. Jewel and Mickey devised a tactic of disembarking at Hurst Hill, the stop before Perth Road, since it was at the latter that the harassing ruffians would gather. Throwing their cases out and rapidly pushing past the potential bullies at the exit, the girls would leap off just as the tram was resuming its downhill journey. Then they would take the long, back route home.

The sisters' morning journeys were easier when Mrs Daniels was on board with them. A customer and friend, she was a no-nonsense Coloured woman who carried in her bag an empty beer bottle of heavy brown glass. Rarely did she have recourse to using it, as her verbal tirades would often suffice as defence. At the hissed 'Chinkies, vok af van hier' ('Chinkies, fuck off from here') she would glare and shoot back 'Los die kinders uit, jou groot Boere bangbroek' ('Leave the children alone, you great big Boer coward').

If she found herself or one of the sisters being pushed or shoved, Mrs Daniels would reach into her bag, grab the bottle and pull the molester off the tram with her, if necessary delivering the coup de grâce of a blow to the head. The girls and their parents were ever grateful to Mrs Daniels. And they hated the way their protector had to stand with them outside the tram shelter, which was reserved for whites, in the rain or cold or under the relentless summer sun.

Watching Mrs Daniels waiting for the tram would remind Gertie of Soi Sien. When Gertie was in China, she had met Soi Sien very briefly. That chance encounter and the letters to and from Sha Kiu made up the picture that the young woman in Kum Saan had of her mother-in-law in Sha Kiu. Looking across the road now at the upright figure of Mrs Daniels, Gertie's mind wandered back fifteen years to a woman saying to her, 'Yok Laan, they tell me you know my son Ah Kwok, who goes by the name of Ah Leong.'

'Yes,' said Gertie to the woman, a small, neat figure in her forties, whose eyes seemed to show both hope and despair.

'Tell me, does he ever speak of me?'

This question was not as easily answered. Gertie had little of substance to say, for though her family had from time to time bought provisions from Ah Leong's shop, in reality there was little other than casual acquaintanceship between them. But there was something about the note in the woman's voice, the plaintive sense of her inquiry, that made Gertie pause before answering. She knew that Ah Leong had been in Johannesburg for some years. Whether he had been back home to see his mother she did not know. At best, he would have seen her a few times. Carefully, Gertie weighed the options: honesty that would be callous or an acquiescence in the woman's deepest yearnings.

'Yes, he often speaks of you and the village,' Gertie heard herself saying. 'He has missed being here.'

Even as the affirmative had been forming in the air, Soi Sien's eyes had begun to light up. When she heard the girl saying that her son acknowledged how he felt about his absence from Sha Kiu and his mother, Soi Sien's spirits lifted. She smiled. 'It is so many years since I have seen him – twelve years. Perhaps one day he will return home.'

As her image of the straight-backed Soi Sien receded, and Mrs Daniels came once more into view, Gertie pondered what quality the two women shared. It might have been a spirit of indomitability, or perhaps it was the solitariness of Mrs Daniels that recalled Soi Sien and how she had been forced to raise Ah Horn on her own. Soi Sien had been wrong about the return of her husband. Langhsi never saw Ah Horn. Halfway through 1934, he had begun to experience difficulties breathing. His lungs hurt and he struggled through each day, seemingly more ill than his patients. While Ah Leong reckoned that his father knew the nature of his ailment, Gertie insisted that Langshi seek another opinion, from a Western doctor. To satisfy his daughter-in-law, of whom he had grown very fond, and whose being half-Chinese he had entirely forgiven, Langshi agreed. The diagnosis was abscess on the lungs. It accorded with the old herbalist's own.

'Don't worry or try to do more,' Langshi told Ah Leong and Gertie on a midwinter's night, the sharp embrace of the Highveld cold fended off by the warmth of the coal stove they sat next to in the kitchen. 'Don't waste money on medicines for me. I know my time has come.'

184

Ah Leong and Gertie protested, but they knew in their hearts that the old man was right. He would know, better than anyone, of his imminent death. Langshi expressed delight that he had been able to see and name his grandchildren. He enjoined Ah Leong to send Soi Sien what little money there would be left over after the funeral, death duties and the winding up of his estate.

'I would have wanted to see Ah Horn, and visit again the place my parents are buried. No matter. When you go home to Sha Kiu, *tsai*, go to *Kongkong*'s and *Bobo*'s graves for me. And tell Ah Horn that, though I never saw him, I loved him as much as any of his brothers and sisters. Take care of your mother now, Ah Kwok, if you are able to, with useful gifts, and money when you can spare it.'

In those last months, Langshi prepared his patients for his death as carefully as he did himself. He grew weaker with the passing of time, paler and thinner. Whenever he was with the grandchildren, however, life fought in him and he seemed almost sanguine, colour somehow restored to his livid cheeks. But as the year drew to its close, Langshi weakened. He did not resist death, but in the last few weeks it appeared to Gertie that he struggled to die. On 4 December 1934, he passed away in Kum Saan, where he had spent all but three months of the last 23 years of his life. He left to Ah Leong his prized medical textbooks, the *Encyclopaedia of Plants*, compiled in 1590, and *The Yellow Emperor's Canon of Internal Medicine*, the centuries-old standard reference on acupuncture, energy circulation and treatment of diseases.

SEVEN
Pretoria, circa 1941 to 1947

A haze of heat clung to the horizon. Under the searching noonday sun, the enclosing hills were stripped of their mystery. Nothing moved on their rock-clad crests and steep sides. It was only down in the valley that there was any sign of life. A cloud of dust rose behind the wagons, and with it the sound of men and animals. Suddenly, from the bare hills that contained nothing, a score of tribesmen sprang up and, whooping fiercely, swept down on the party of pioneers. As arrows coursed through the air, there was a smell of burning. In an instant, the battle on the valley floor assumed a shrinking aspect, its edges blurred by a crinkling yellow-brown border that advanced towards the very centre of the action.

Someone shouted 'Fire!' The sounds of panic and the sharp, pungent smell of fear were unleashed. There was a clattering as seats smashed against backrests and the patrons of the bioscope rushed for the exit.

'It's only the film that's caught alight,' said Kit to Yen, stretching his arms and yawning. 'But I guess that's the end of the picture. We may as well go home.' The two brothers got up and made their way slowly to the door. From the projection room came the whiff of burnt celluloid and a clickety-clack as the film reel slowed to a stop.

'It doesn't matter. The next attraction is another cowboy flick, *Stagecoach*,' said Yen as they stepped on to the pavement and into the glare of a summer midday in Pretoria. The boys often went to the pictures during their school holidays, doing the rounds of the bioscopes and bughouses of the capital that they were allowed entry to. Most often they cycled west down Boom Street, away from the National Zoological Gardens, and towards Marabastad and Asiatic Bazaar, where there were three cinemas, the Royal, the Empire and the Orient. Here there were no whites in the audience, for this was the mixed side of town, far from the Europeans-Only cinemas near the city's central Church Square.

Between the Orient and the Royal, Kit and Yen would stop for cooldrinks at the Blue Lagoon Café, and then look into the windows of the bicycle shops before going to see a film. The sounds of *maskanda* poured out of Kalla's, the street's best music supplier, which stocked pennywhistles and harmonicas and records alongside bicycle tubes and pumps and puncture repair kits. Its quiet-voiced Indian proprietor would call the boys inside, and talk to them about bicycles and the latest films, of which he was an avid fan, relishing particularly those with cowboys and Red Indians, and cowboys and crooks.

Kit's fascination with cowboy adventures on screen led before long to his being in the saddle himself for regular horse rides at Blackwood Villa, a farm estate a few hundred yards from his home down Vermeulen Street. His mother Ah Hing's shop was at 275 Vermeulen, on the corner of Queen, a tiny lane off which you entered the living rooms that were attached to the business. The shop itself had a doorway a couple of paces from the intersection of the two streets, and with a view of the trees and fields of the villa. At least, thought Ah Hing, she knew when the rascal set off to go riding, but keeping an eye on him at other times was more difficult.

Kit had the passion and enthusiasm for horses that only the young tend to be able to conceive and sustain. When he came back from riding, he would pore over copies of the Arabian horse magazine that he subscribed to. It was an American publication which found the youngster's interest so unusual – he was likely the only South African subscriber – that it dispatched a letter asking him about his love of horses. Cowboys were part of the answer, those hired nomads who would have been nothing without their horses. Such was his Western fervour that for a few years, in the back of his homework books, Kit would sign a name full of homage and adventure: Buffalo Kit, Queen Street's answer to Buffalo Bill of the Wild West.

That was not the name used at school. There, everyone called him Giddy, a nickname that had been bestowed quite early on in his school life. Talkative and energetic, Kit had a maddening habit of jumping up and down in class, which made others giddy, so they said. Kit's excess of energy did not leave him giddy, though the moniker Giddy was to stick for the rest of his life, and later be elevated to Sinitic status when friends and business associates began calling him Ah Gid.

Between making his schoolmates dizzy, the bioscope, riding and playing with friends, Kit kept busy, though not out of trouble. He had not known his father, and Ah Hing's strictness and correctness were not fully a substitute for a paternal hand. Taking advantage of that, Kit often played truant from the Chinese school to visit the zoo, which was diagonally across Boom Street. Arriving early, he would watch the zoo-keepers and attendants on their rounds. His favourite sight was the baby hippos having their backs scrubbed with hard-bristled brooms, at a respectful distance.

'Why don't you go closer?' Kit asked the hippo man after watching this ritual three or four times.

'*Aikona*! This animal here is angrier than his big brother, the *makulu* hippo. This one, he is small but not so friendly. We must be careful, because also he is spending more time on the ground than in the water, not like the hippos there.' The man shook his head, laughing, and continued his animal ablutions.

Later the same attendant fed the real hippos, as Kit called them. He scooped from a massive pot a large ball of mealie *pap*, threw that on to a wheelbarrow and trundled over to a spot above the hippos. Accurately, he tipped the ball into the nearest mouth and then returned to the pot, repeating the procedure until all the bulky mammals had been fed.

Kit was happy that the hippos were served *pap*. He felt that what was good enough for him and Yen must be good enough for his friends. The boys were almost as used to *pap* as rice, for every morning Ah Hing took some maize meal from the bin in the shop storeroom and made a large pot of porridge. That was breakfast and sometimes lunch and a bite before dinner too, if the shop was busy and Ah Hing had no time to prepare a midday meal. Phineas, who helped Ah Hing in the shop, also kept an eye on the brothers and shared the *pap* from the blackened pot, the mute presence of which, squatting on the side of the stove, was somehow always a comfort.

For a young boy, the freedom of the zoo was exhilarating. Kit studied the buck, the primates, the big cats, the elephant, giraffe, rhinos, and animals from other continents, like the polar bear and the two-humped Bactrian camel. The zoo meant light and space, a relief from the compact and dim quarters of home, with its couple of bedrooms, minute kitchen and combined lounge and dining room. In the zoo his mind roamed wild, and he became both big game hunter and ranger. Sometimes he would be creeping through the jungle on the tracks of a Royal Bengal Tiger, at others he would be on the plains of east Africa, drawing a bead on a poacher who was snaking up on a trophy beast. The vistas in the Western movies that he saw leapt before his eyes when he stood at the bison enclosure, or watched the grey moose shaking its head and rattling its antlers.

Imagination got Kit through a long childhood and youth which, though not spent alone, was lonely nonetheless in the absence of his father. His mother had not remarried because she feared a stepfather would not treat the boys well. Kit's yearning for a father showed in the way he hung on the words of his classmates when they spoke about their fathers. Once, he eavesdropped on a boy and his father in the school grounds, lying on the other side of the hedge from where they were talking. Stretching himself out, he enjoyed their laughter and plans to build and fly a kite in the windy August that lay round the corner. Chin resting in cupped hands, propped up by his elbows, Kit pretended he was the boy. Enthralled, he gave no thought to his somewhat precarious position. His legs were stretched out behind him into the downhill bicycle path that the scholars took on their way home, but his limbs were not visible as he was lying just after the only corner on the steep descent to the main road. So engrossed was Kit in the conversation filtering through the hedge that he did not notice when a couple of schoolboys on bicycles rode over his legs and feet and cursed as they crashed into the hot cement behind him. Suddenly Kit became aware of the shouting at his back and the pain and pulled away from the objects of his attention.

There were other days when Kit was as rapt. At the end of the school week, classes would finish early and the pupils would gather in the hall to listen to the Chinese master relating the tale of Sin Yan Quai. This epic about the brave, strong hero who had many, many adventures with animals and humans, carried on for years. Explaining it in later life, Kit would say that it was like listening to Homer and the stories of Jason and the Argonauts, Sinbad and the Arabian Nights all rolled into one.

It was this weekly serial that Kit missed most when he finished primary education and transferred to the Pretoria Indian School, there being no Chinese High School in the area. Another option being exercised by the community around this time was not available to him because of religious belief. Some Chinese families were sending their children to private Catholic and Anglican schools. This was not legal, but certain principals and school boards ignored the rules on occasion. The limited number of places available, and the high cost of private schooling, meant in any case that there was no possibility of a huge influx of Chinese pupils. Religion also barred the way, because the tacit condition of acceptance was that pupils should be Christian. Ah Hing would have none of that. Her opposition stemmed from the fate of a family back in her home village Ma Kiu. Despite the prohibitions of the elders, this entire extended family had gone over to Christianity, and were attempting to persuade other villagers to join them. Terrible misfortunes befell the converts, all of whom died within a few years of the change in allegiance from Buddhism to Catholicism, and no one was left to carry the family name. Many in Ma Kiu also fell strangely ill during this time, but after the last convert's death, the villagers were restored to health. To Ah Hing this apparent retribution for faithlessness, and the operation of what seemed a curse, had left an abiding impression. It meant that not only did she not countenance educating her sons in Christian schools but also that she made Kit promise her never to forsake Buddhism.

Religious observance aside, Ah Hing was surprisingly accommodating of her sons. American fashions and fads were beginning to flood the country. Sharp hats and sharper shoes were the mark of white-collar professionals and working men alike. But it was jazz that the brothers fell for. Kit took up the saxophone, Yen the drums. After some time playing a Martin, Kit acquired a new instrument, a Selma, and a new ace teacher, Plato Michael. The sinuous sax replaced the Blackwood Villa steeds in Kit's afternoons. In his evenings too, he practised and practised, very nearly deranging his mother. Had it not been for the simultaneous counterpoint of Yen's drumming, Kit's attempts to draw smooth and articulate sound from his Selma might have been suffocated by his mother. As it was, Ah Hing went from one practising son to the other, lamenting the cacophony that now was her life, and waving her arms in frustration. The brothers chuckled, privately, that their mother looked like a caricature of some frenzied big band conductor, haplessly dividing attention and energy between two parts of an orchestra that were taking off in different directions.

As Kit's acquaintance with the sax grew, he shed puppy fat, and emerged into the late teens as an adventurous young man with a quick and impish sense of humour and a desire to become independent and get ahead as quickly as possible. Those ambitions brought sadness for Ah Hing, who had hoped that her sons would be interested in following the teaching tradition on her side of the family. Her brother in China was the latest teacher in the line and she herself was well read in Chinese, and knowledgeable about the history and culture of her homeland. Not that many would guess it, but Ah Hing was quite different beneath the curt, peremptory, utilitarian persona that she presented to the small corner of Pretoria in which she had established herself. It had been her sudden widowhood that forced her to become an adamantine businesswoman and a stern mother. The doe-eyed young wife and mother of early family photographs, such as the one taken three months after Kit's birth and three months before Fok Yu Teem's death, had given way to a hard-eyed, firm-jawed, middle-aged woman, sharp of tongue and quick of calculation.

She brought those qualities to bear in a conversation with Kit not long after his sixteenth birthday. They were standing in the shop during an afternoon lull in trading, with the only discernible movement being the window fan spreading cool air through the premises.

'The only letters I have behind my name and the only ones I want are B,S,C,' began Kit.

'What this BSC you talk about?'

'Behind shop counter. I've earned the right to be here after helping you over many years. I want to put that experience to use and turn this place into an even bigger success.'

'That so? That so?'

In some ways, Ah Hing was grateful. In the early days, she had begun to run *fah-fee* to supplement income from the grocery shop that had been left to her when her husband died. Business had been slow because of the general depression of the time and she had not wanted to be driven to asking anyone for loans, so she had immersed herself in the practice, lore and associations of *fah-fee*. In this numbers game the banker selects – 'pulls' in the argot of the game – one number from 34 available. Every draw excludes the two most recently pulled of the 36 numbers, the *Dodais* or impossible numbers, making the odds 34 to one for the punter. Players place money on numbers with runners who collect the bets and hand them to a head runner who passes everything on to the banker. The head runner receives in exchange the pulled number, ensuring no shenanigans on the part of the bank. Although *fah-fee* was illegal, the bankers behaved with unswerving correctness, paying punters' winnings immediately and, when they were due, the head runner's monthly wage and the other runners' fortnightly wages. It was a game of gamblers' honour and, for the players, it had the added frisson of being a small and relatively safe daily ritual that defied the constrictions of the country's laws.

As she became acquainted with *fah-fee*, Ah Hing learnt that it was no mere random numbers-selection game for either side. Each of the 36 numbers has a name, or association, and by tacit mutual consent the game is controlled by dreams. So, for example, if the banker dreams of a feast of good food and drink, he – or she, in the case of Ah Hing – will probably think about whether to pull 34, the number for backside, or excreta. For the bank, however, there are many other considerations, as Ah Hing soon discovered. How does one contend with the dreams of dozens of punters? The bank cannot guard against all of them, or anticipate them. But by a knowledge of the numbers linked to dreams, and a record of her punters' betting habits as she recorded them in a blocked, feint-and-margin school exercise book, Ah Hing was to become expert at minimising the risk of the bank's being broken and at maximising the bank's winnings.

In the beginning, she memorised what she called the glossary: 1 king; white man. 2 ape; monkey. 3 sea water; big water. 4 dead man. 5 tiger; also sometimes courage. 6 ox; blood. 7 *skelm*; rascal. 8 pig. 9 moon; stars. 10 eggs. 11 carriage; car. 12 dead woman. 13 big fish. 14 old woman. 15 bad woman. 16 pigeons; dove. 17 diamond lady; European woman. 18 small change; silver money. 19 little girl. 20 cat. 21 elephant. 22 ship; shoes. 23 horse. 24 mouth. 25 big house. 26 bees. 27 dog. 28 herring; small fish. 29 small water. 30 fowl; priest. 31 fire. 32 gold money; gold. 33 little boy. 34 backside; excreta. 35 *katpan* (woman's private parts). 36 'long one'; *nonkwayi* (man's private parts).

Next Ah Hing learned about the associations. Eight, pig, for example, would be played by those who had dreamt of food or stomach or a Chinaman; 24, mouth, by someone in whose dreams there had been kissing. People lying down meant a combination of four, dead man, and twelve, dead woman. Three and 29 had to be played together: big water and little water.

Then she mastered the partner numbers, a maze that was very important, as the runners also knew the combinations that sometimes provided a clue as to what the pulled number would be. Ah Hing forced her mind into familiarity with these curious patterns, such as one and 36 being partners, with the inherent danger that 35 is an attractive bet because it links the partners 36 and one.

Last Ah Hing picked up the superstitions and connections to real life that could play havoc with the pull. Players believed that there were certain impulses in the body – 'jumps' and 'springs' they called them – that gave clues to what the number would be. An itch or twitch in the ear portended 18; an irritation of the eye nine and one. A fatal accident might prompt a flutter on number four, dead man; one in which there was lots of blood, a whirl on number six. A mother-in-law's new shoes could encourage a punt on number 22.

All these arcana Ah Hing studied and absorbed. Confident of her mastery of the mysteries of the game, she set up a small bank, with a reliable head runner in Jack, a stolid and quick-witted Zulu. But the night before the first pull, Ah Hing scarcely slept. What would happen if she lost on every day of the first week? At two banks per day, she would be ruined by Wednesday. Would the community think it unseemly, even though she was a widow? Or precisely because she was? Most pressingly, what number would she choose for the first bank?

Thinking of how she might come to be regarded in the small, tightly-knit community, Ah Hing settled on 15, the number for 'bad woman', with some satisfaction. She did not regard herself as such, but if others wished to, then so be it. Feeding, clothing and educating her sons were the only priorities, and she would do whatever was required to fulfil them.

The first pull was small, as Ah Hing had expected. What she had not been able to predict, the success of her choice of number, turned out well enough: the bank registered a modest win. For the afternoon bank, she studied what the punters had backed in the earlier pull. There had been many bets on the number four, dead man; she reckoned that the players had been thinking of her late husband. Generally, the bank avoided a number backed heavily in the immediately preceding pull, but it seemed unlikely to Ah Hing that there would be as many bets on four this time round. That was what she played, and scored a satisfying win.

The *fah-fee* pull grew steadily over the years. At its height, it boasted a clientele of white, black, Coloured, Christian, Jew; the players were hawkers, lawyers, factory workers, doctors, maids, accountants, housewives, gardeners, teachers, street sweepers, firemen, manual labourers, nurses, soldiers and even policemen. Not many in the constabulary played, of course, and there were games of another, more earnest kind with the South African Police, with Jack almost always giving his pursuers the slip.

The end of the game was approaching, though, felt Ah Hing. The boys had finished school, the business was well established and she had saved money over the years. There was no need to court danger any longer, and she did not want Kit to run any risks, as he had recently. Riding on his motorcycle in Prinsloo Street, a few blocks from the shop, Kit had seen some policemen closing in on Jack, who appeared oblivious of the dragnet. The boy had pulled alongside the faithful old runner, indicated with a jerk of his head that he should climb up behind him and then ridden off, past the somewhat surprised cops. By the time the police flagged down Kit, he had safely deposited Jack in one of the city's alleyways. Kit got a dressing-down from an irritated sergeant, but nothing more: as the youngster said, what was the crime in giving an old man a ride?

Kit's wish to help run the shop meant that Ah Hing could allow herself to relax a little. Yen was running the farm shop near Kyalami, so she could contemplate travelling to Hong Kong, a voyage that she had always promised herself. Still, she hankered a little after the notion that her sons could do more with their education. She remembered, however, that astronomy and its earthbound obverse, astrology, had been Kit's favourite subjects at his Chinese primary school. What could one do with those in South Africa in 1947?

'So you want help run this shop. You want make it better,' said Ah Hing to Kit.

Gravely, he nodded. 'There is much more we can do. Turn it into ...'

'Okay, okay,' said Ah Hing, cutting him off. It was enough for now to agree, but changes would have to wait for another day.

EIGHT
Johannesburg, circa 1938 to 1948

'*Yum booi cha*, drink a cup of tea,' said Third Uncle to Ah Leong. Accepting a small cup steaming with dark brown brew, Ah Leong sat down opposite the older man to wait for Ah Wha, uncle's son, and the others in the letter-reading circle. Every Wednesday the men of the clan gathered at Ah Shek's to share letters sent from China. By law shops shut at noon on that day, making it an ideal time to meet and hear news from home. Now that China was unambiguously at war with Japan, the weekly sessions were even more important.

'Business is well?' asked Third Uncle.

'Business is quiet,' answered Ah Leong, giving the reply required whether you were making hundreds of pounds or tuppence. As he drained the hot tea, Ah Leong thought again of his mother and aunts. The invading Japanese armies were waging the war with terrible brutality. Wounded and captured Chinese soldiers were routinely massacred. Chinese civilians were the victims of atrocities that made the letters unbearable to read. Ah Shek would stop on such occasions and simply pass the letter on, unwilling to let his mouth utter the words he had just descried on the page. The horrors told by the ink-black characters were bloody red: villages razed, young men butchered, young women raped, tortured and killed, children and babies bayoneted. When young women were spared it was only to be used as prostitutes for the imperial Nipponese armies. Older, non-combatant Chinese men, many barely able-bodied, were used as forced labour. If the war should sweep into Sha Kiu, only his mother's age and uselessness to the invaders' cause would save her life, Ah Leong realised.

It was a bitter frustration that ever since Langshi's death, Ah Leong had tried to bring his mother out to Kum Saan. Money and connections with the right authorities in South Africa had seen a fair number of Chinese granted official entry, despite the legal strictures on such immigration. While Ah Leong could have raised the money, he lacked direct access to those who might bend the rules. Among the clan were those who had established such mutually beneficial ties, but Ah Leong's appeals for them to intercede fell on deaf ears.

Why that was, he had not worked out. Perhaps it was because he had married a half-Chinese. The community did not take readily to such doings, and treated such individuals cruelly, habitually disparaging them as 'ox-heads'. There had been unpleasant incidents at weddings and other social occasions, with him and Gertie hearing a deliberate murmur here, a viciously cast remark there. But it was their children who suffered most from this venomous discrimination. Ah Leong thought back with anger to the day he had taken Hong Hgang to enrol her at the Chinese 'small school'. She had been only a few months past her fifth birthday, a blameless child. The principal and board had declined to admit her because she was, they said, a half-caste.

Picking her up in his arms, Ah Leong had said to them, 'My shoulders are broad. I will carry my child.' Hong Hgang had gone to a Coloured school instead.

'Come, come, *tsai*,' said Third Uncle as his son arrived. Another five men entered the room with Ah Wha, exchanging greetings and asking one another about business. When the formalities and the tea-taking were over, the group took seats and the first letter was handed to Ah Shek. From its contents, they gathered that Sha Kiu remained untouched by the Japanese, but that the fall of Canton was imminent. Given the interval between the letter's dispatch and its arrival, Ah Leong calculated that the city must have been captured by now. As Ah Shek made his way steadily through the news in the other letters, Ah Leong let his mind wander back to the day 27 years ago when he and his father had sailed up the Pearl River and seen the White Cloud Hills for the first time. He had not thought then that he would spend so much time away from home. Or that he would never see his grandfather and grandmother again. And the unthinkable separation from Mudan and Ah Wa had become a banal reality of his life.

There was a mill of voices suddenly, Ah Wha shaking his head and a glistening of eyes around the room. Ah Leong forced himself to listen and caught the last part of the letter. 'Three of my friends were killed by the Japanese,' read Ah Shek. 'When the soldiers had gone, I crawled from my hiding place and tried to bury them. There were no spades or shovels, the enemy had taken everything and burnt the rest. So I had to dig the graves with my hands, and it took days before they were deep enough to lay my friends to rest, and even then I think that they will be uncovered by the summer rains, or perhaps eaten by some animal. But it was all I could do. Now I scarcely have nails on my fingers, but that is nothing as compared to the terrible fate of my friends. I pray that this will not be the last time I write to you, but I fear even as I write, that this letter may never reach you in Kum Saan. Pray for us. Your niece, Yunling.'

There was quiet in the room for a long time after Ah Shek stopped reading.

Not long after came the war in Europe, Gertie's brothers, Philip and James, enlisted. Many of the Leongs' customers, men and women, volunteered and 'went up North' and to other theatres of war. As children, many of them had mocked the Leongs, but they had grown into affable young men and women. They would come in to see Ah Leong and Gertie and talk about their posting, then bid farewell and say they hoped to meet again. When they returned home on furlough, they would rush down to 27A Perth Road to shake hands and exchange smiles with the Leong family.

The shop became a meeting place for the mothers who would come down each morning for Gertie to look up the column in the *Rand Daily Mail* where the soldiers were reported as wounded, taken prisoner, and the worst one, missing in action, presumed dead. It was a time for friendship, conciliation and compassion, with pot after pot of tea being brewed and served to the customers, and discussions about 'the boys', Hitler, Smuts, 'Monty' and the hardships being experienced by those at home. One of the blackest moments was the fall of Tobruk, when General Klopper surrendered to Rommel and nearly 10 000 South African troops were captured.

EARTH

There was rationing during the war, with every customer allowed only a certain quantity of sugar, butter, oil, meal, flour, cheese, jam, rice, condensed milk, floor polish and so on. White flour was not sold; flour was mixed with bran instead. Gertie paid her daughters sixpence each to sift the flour through a clean silk stocking to get cake flour, even though using a silk stocking was a luxury, as there was a shortage of silk garments because of the war.

Rationing led to a black market in all sorts of commodities. Some shopkeepers made fortunes from selling customers more than the quantities they were allowed, at a hefty surcharge. Ah Leong refused to profit. There were times he gave the family's rations to needy customers, and then 27A Perth Road ate yellow mealie rice in place of real white rice. Gertie would make jam from all the ripe fruit in her shop and so the workers she liked to call the Brickyard Boys had homemade jam on their two slices of morning bread for every day of the war. The war really brought the customers closer to Gertie and Ah Leong.

Despite the war, the adults tried to ensure that Jewel and Mickey enjoyed themselves. People were allowed to save petrol coupons, which were used for special occasions. Ah Leong and Lil accumulated coupons to have enough fuel to go on picnics at Muldersdrift, north-west of Johannesburg. There they would lie on blankets, eating sandwiches and drinking Suncrush orange cooldrink, ginger beer, lemonade or creme soda, and listening to music on the portable gramophone. The children would splash about in the river, blissfully unaware of bilharzia until a friend told them about the hazard.

It was Lil who constantly reminded Jewel and Mickey of how children in England, France and elsewhere had no sweets other than carrots dipped in syrup. Nonetheless, she spoilt Jewel and Mickey because she had lost two sons, both soon after they were born. The Leong children always found it very sad to go to their cousins' grave, which was so small even though two of them were buried there. There was a white marble angel over the headstone, and their names, Alexander and Ivan, were chiselled in beautiful letters that were etched in black.

During the war, Jewel went to Chinese school at last. There was a campaign by the Chinese Consul-General to attract those Chinese who attended other schools to the new, second Chinese school in the city. Despite what had happened before, Ah Leong said it was all right because he wanted his children to appreciate their culture. Jewel went to the Kuo Ting – 'Stability of the Nation' – School, which had blue blazers with silver stripes, those colours coming from the Chinese flag. The old school was the Overseas Chinese School, which had navy blue skirts and blazers with a sun insignia.

Going to the Chinese school was a mistake. Jewel and her family were denied complete acceptance because they were considered 'halves'. She was ridiculed and mentally tortured by fellow pupils. She made few new friends, because even though there were girls and boys who wanted to be friends, the peer pressure from the 'purists', those who did not tolerate half-Chinese, was too strong. It was not only the Eurasians who suffered this treatment, but Moiyeanese – Hakka – pupils as well.

Once a new girl came from Pietersburg to join the school after completing her primary education at a Coloured Government School. During break Jewel made overtures to her new classmate and they played happily, swearing to be friends forever.

The following morning Jewel ran to meet her friend but the girl turned away and made for the classroom. Jewel ran after her, stopped her and asked, 'Is something wrong?'

'No,' she said.

'Are you cross with me?'

'No.'

Jewel was puzzled. 'What have I done?'

'Nothing.'

'Can we play?'

'No, no more.'

'No more? Why?'

'They told me not to play with you because you are *sommer* a half.'

'Please,' Jewel said.

'I can't but I will talk to you whenever I can, when they can't see. I'll smile at you and you will know that I am your friend.'

Jewel stood there, looking at her.

The girl shrugged, and smiled.

'Must go,' she said and ran off.

Jewel stood alone in the middle of the quad, tears on her cheeks, anger and revenge in her heart. She had done nothing wrong.

Revenge took the form of her deciding that she would never speak her mother tongue again. If nobody was going to be her friend, what was the use of learning the language?

School carried on. Jewel did her work but would answer only in English. Neither her father's wrath nor her mother's pleading ever made her speak Chinese at school. She learnt but kept silent.

It became clear to Jewel also that to be white meant that one was always right. Once, not realising that Ah Leong was nearby, she shouted, 'I want to be white.' It was a cry from her soul to be free to go to any school, any film, to live anywhere. Ah Leong was furious. He grabbed Jewel by the ear and admonished her: 'You are Chinese. Nothing, nothing can ever change that. You are Chinese and be proud that you belong to the most civilised and cultured race on earth. Never, never wish to be anyone else again. They are the barbarians. You are *T'ong yan*. Remember.'

Had the letter-reading circle been able to partake of alcohol the day they heard Yunling's letter, they would most certainly have done so. But the laws of the Transvaal prohibited all 'Coloured persons' from buying or possessing any liquor, which was defined as spirits containing more than two percent alcohol. Chinese religious and social ceremonies, where numerous libations and toasts are made, were seriously affected by the legislation; the only way around it was to seek special dispensation to serve wine at these times.

For some years in the 1920s, the Chinese Consul-General had legally circumvented the restrictions using his diplomatic immunity. His status allowed him to purchase liquor and offer it to Chinese guests at functions he hosted. Nonetheless, the Consul had humiliatingly to obtain permission from the Criminal Investigation Department of the police and had to ensure that he was present when the liquor was delivered to the venue where the function was taking place.

In 1928, a new liquor law had come into effect whereby Japanese no longer fell into the legally restrictive 'Asiatic' category, freeing them to buy and keep alcoholic drinks. The Chinese objected to being regarded differently, and demanded equal treatment under the law. It was, wrote the Consul-General in a letter to the Secretary for Justice, a matter of national honour. The Commissioner of Police advised against granting Chinese the same rights, and in a letter to the selfsame Secretary, declared: 'Although the Chinese are members of an ancient civilisation, and at the present time struggling to re-gain some of their former prestige, they are not to be compared with the Japanese, who are to-day a recognised world power, and who are both from an educational and mode of living point of view superior to the Chinese.'

As the listeners in Ah Shek's house let the silence soak up their shock, Ah Leong thirsted as never before for strong drink. He could not bear thinking about the horrors the last letter described and implied. What chance did his mother have of surviving when the enemy was so heartless? Thinking back to his father's journey home, Ah Leong realised the folly of his impetuosity in not going back as well. Three newly arrived female relatives had once told him how his mother had anticipated his homecoming and prepared for it.

'Your mother rose early on the morning of your expected arrival, cleaned and prepared the home for you, cooked a little feast for welcome. Do you know how sad she was when you did not return? She was bitterly disappointed.'

From that moment, the conviction had grown in Ah Leong that parents could not depend on children. Constantly he revisited that fatal evening at his father's, and lived in inescapable remorse.

As the succeeding months brought worse and worse news about the Japanese occupation, the meetings at Ah Shek's grew more and more sombre. Slowly, almost infinitesimally, however, things began to change in the arena of the world war, tying down the far-flung Japanese armies in south-east Asia and somewhat easing the position in China.

Turning the station-finding button on the valve radio, and adjusting it in the kilocycle half of the dial, Ah Leong would tune in to the BBC. After the valves warmed up, the world poured into the small lounge of

27A Perth Road. First the Leongs heard the chimes of Big Ben preceding the evening bulletins, and then the crisp voices of BBC announcers bringing the latest news.

The Japanese attack on Pearl Harbor brings America into the war. Montgomery turns back Rommel at Alamein. The German thrust into the Soviet Union is halted at Stalingrad. North Africa falls to the Allies, who begin working their way up the boot of Italy. From the east, the Soviet juggernaut expels the Nazis from Russia. On 6 June 1944, Allied forces land on the beaches of Normandy. First France, then Paris is liberated. On 30 April 1945, the Red Army reaches the Reichstag building in Berlin. Hitler commits suicide on the same day. General Jodl signs Germany's surrender on 7 May. Churchill and Truman proclaim V-E Day on 8 May. After the twin terrors of the atomic bombs dropped on Hiroshima and Nagasaki on 6 and 9 August, Japan surrenders. V-J Day is declared on 15 August.

Actually, Jewel and Mickey heard the news of V-J Day at Damelin College, the privately run secondary education institution where they were now studying, having left the Chinese school. Joel Damelin had to shout for silence as the wireless prepared to yield up the news that the whole war was over. The students made bunting from toilet rolls, throwing the paper from the windows of Frasers Building, near the Johannesburg Public Library, and went home early. In Westdene, Ah Leong had heard the news, and did the unprecedented: he closed the shop for the day. The Leong family went to Chinatown, visiting in turn the Transvaal Chinese United Club, the Cantonese Club and the Reform Club, the last being the Chinese Freemasons, the Chee Kung Tong. Tea and cakes were being served everywhere, as Chinese shook hands and even slapped one another on the back in celebration of the news of the day.

Yet Ah Leong was not entirely satisfied. Japan had not yet surrendered to China. When that happened, on 9 September 1945, he poured himself a double whisky and sat alone for a while on the porch of 27A Perth Road. He was able to drink legally at home because by the Liquor Act of September 1943, Chinese had been removed from the Asiatic category. Fifteen years after they had sought equality on this score with the

Japanese, they had been granted it. But that was nothing set against the triumph that Ah Leong toasted quietly on this September day two years later. '*Yum seng*! To victory!' he whispered to himself, and then smiled as the toast brought vividly to mind the fisherman Ah Biu, who had taken him and Langshi up the Pearl River to Canton.

Casting his mind back over the past couple of years, Ah Leong recalled having a legal whisky in public after occasional games of billiards at the Cantonese Club. It was curious, he thought, how Chinese being on the same footing as Japanese in Kum Saan had somehow been a harbinger of change for the better in the war in China. Gone were the days of brewing *hoppan*, a ginger beer-type drink that acted as a substitute for alcohol, he thought wryly. Soon the Japanese would be gone from his homeland too, and he would be able once again to attempt bringing his mother to Kum Saan.

★

News from Soi Sien during the war was terrible, sometimes too terrible to hear. The Japanese garrison commandeered almost all the food and the villagers had to eat grass, leaves, insects and rats to survive. But there were some good letters, such as the one telling how the aged villagers managed to save some of Ah Leong's female cousins. The elders dug a hideout under the stove, and the girls would spend whole days at a time in the small, dark and almost airless refuge.

Other than the feeling of complete helplessness when Ah Leong received news from Sha Kiu and other parts of Kwangtung, things were easy in Westdene. Because Gertie and Andrew had worked so hard to feed, clothe and educate their siblings, Gertie had learned a lot about scrimping and saving and making food and even scraps of food go further on the plate and in the tummy. When she was still at her mother's, she used to bargain with the fishmonger for fish heads and use those to make a nice stew for the boys. All that thrift was probably due to her aunt in China, the old woman she left behind when the Martins came back to South Africa. Once Gertie spilt a cup of uncooked rice and was brushing the pile of grains back into the cup. She left a few on the ground, because they were scattered, and it seemed tedious to pick up each grain by hand. She thought she would just sweep them up and throw them away. Guessing the intent, her aunt raised her voice and said, 'No.' It was quite a shock to hear the old lady talk so loudly; it was the only time she scolded Gertie. 'Ah Laan,' she said, 'every grain is precious. We cannot waste even one.' And then her aunt had stooped down and picked up all the remaining grains.

Now that the war was over, and the girls were enjoying college more than the Chinese school, Gertie looked forward to having a little time to try and further her education. She knew that she would have to learn things by herself. She hoped that she would be able to understand the subjects she was interested in. Yoga, Eastern religions and the cultures of people of different races were what she wanted to read about. Maybe she would have to buy a bigger dictionary, because often she could not find words in her trusty old friend, the little *Collins Gem Dictionary*. The thought of buying books took her back to the day she used the meat money on two books at an auction, just round the corner from the Green House. Her mother had been furious. Gertie was shocked when she read one of the books, *By Reef and Storm* it was called, and found some terrible words like bloody, bosom and bastard.

All these years later, Gertie reflected, and Chinese still were not allowed to use the public library. Perhaps things would change for Jewel and Mickey. After this war, surely people would be kinder towards each other, she mused, and even things in this country could change: look at how we and our customers have grown closer.

But she and Ah Leong seemed even further apart than before from Cornelia and that side of the family. The Martins were more intent than ever on trying for White. Gertie wondered how Philip would take being demobbed and returning to civilian life. Before he volunteered, he had been appointed foreman in the furniture factory, only to be dismissed a week later when some of his fellow workers reported him to the boss as Eurasian. Philip was seething, though he had long ago given up his boyhood promise to Gertie that he would make sure that 'no one calls us yellow and plays all lordly and grand as a white'. Cornelia had said to Gertie, 'You see, this is why we can't be seen together in the street. People talk. They say the boys aren't white. We can't afford such things to happen, not after all the hard work we've all put in.'

It was difficult to keep Jewel and Mickey from being angry about this. They saw John visiting Lil every Saturday for grocery supplies and then coming round to Gertie and Ah Leong for dinner. When Ah Leong dropped John at home afterwards, it would be a few blocks from his house, just in case of nosy neighbours. Cornelia visited Lil very week too, when Gertie would sneak off for a quick chat, but Jewel and Mickey were not allowed to acknowledge their grandmother in public. The children said they understood the situation, and though hurt and saddened by this treatment, they had never been spiteful or jealous, never made the mistake of greeting their relatives even when paths crossed accidentally in town. James used to come to visit before the war and Jewel would stand at the door of the fruit shop and wave at him as the tram passed by, taking him home. Lil had to explain to her why she shouldn't do that.

How Gertie hated all this pretending and concealing and lying. She always had, except for that one big white lie that she persuaded Andrew to tell back in the village when he had moved the statues of the gods. It seemed as if all the lying might end soon, because Cornelia had been talking about going to settle in Australia, with that side of the family. She had even told Gertie that they were going to change their surname to Martini. Whispering to herself, Gertie said, 'Father, I am sure you do not like that; but I am a Martin: Cornelia Catharina Chok Foon Martin, better known as Gertie, sometimes as Bug, and always Yok Laan, your daughter.'

China was not yet free of war. United only by the fight against their common Japanese enemy, Communist and Nationalist forces now weighed each other up again. When the Generalissimo Chiang Kai-Shek had seized Peking in June 1928, the country had come under Nationalist rule. But it was due mainly to the Communists, led by Mao Tse-tung and Chou En-lai, that Japan had been defeated. The political capital and popular goodwill of that achievement meant that for a short time there was a ceasefire. When it broke, battle followed battle until, in April 1949, the Communists captured Nanking, where the Nationalists had established their capital. Six months later, on 1 October 1949, the People's Republic of China was declared and two months later Chiang and the Nationalists had retreated to Formosa, later known as Taiwan.

Ah Leong drew deep satisfaction from the Communist victory, as did Gertie. They felt that the poverty of the China they had known could be addressed by the Communists whereas Chiang had set in place a government based on the Fascist regimes of Germany and Italy. The 20 years of Chiang's military dictatorship were also an oligarchy and plutocracy, with the so-called four great families − Chiang, Soong, Chen and Kong − dominating. Ah Leong's opinions were not popular in the community, and he had to be even more cautious because in the meantime there had been political upheaval in Namfeechow as well.

It is the morning of 28 May 1948. A white woman, with curlers in her hair and a net cloth pulled tightly around her head, shuffles in to a shop and greets the Chinese woman behind the counter.

'Morning, Mrs Leong. May I have half a loaf of white bread on tick, please?'

'Hello, Mrs Botha. Certainly. Anything else?'

'No. We are too happy to need anything more this morning, you know.'

'Oh, yes. You must be very happy that the National Party has ousted General Smuts and the United Party.'

In an instant, the sedate Mrs Botha, generally a browbeaten and dishevelled figure, transforms into a whirling dervish. '*Ja! Ja!* We won!' she shouts exultantly, waving the freshly-cut half-loaf above her head as if it were a victory banner, and skipping around the shop floor. 'Now we are in charge. We will put all those *kaffirs* and *coolies*, those *klonkies* and *Chinkies* in their place. This is our country now!'

Mrs Leong lets the pejoratives and the irony of the half-loaf bought on credit hang in the air and dissolve. Always the embodiment of graciousness, she smiles at Mrs Botha and says, 'Oh, yes. I'm sure things will be much better for you now. You must enjoy the celebrations with the people from the other houses on the hill and we'll see you tomorrow, I'm sure, to talk more. Good morning!'

It is the advent of Apartheid and nobody's life will ever be the same again.

NINE

South Africa, circa 1948 to 1955

'Today South Africa belongs to us once more,' declared National Party leader Dr Daniel Francois Malan on Friday 28 May 1948. 'For the first time since Union, South Africa is our own. May God grant that it will always remain so.'

By 'us', the former Dutch Reformed Church *dominee* meant the Afrikaners. Malan had brought about his vision of the country ruled by one people and one language. To supporters of the *Herenigde* – Reunited – National Party, it seemed as if divine will, working through their *dominee* leader, was on their side. How else could their party have overturned the United Party's majority in Parliament? Before the election on 26 May, Jan Smuts and his UP had held 89 of the 153 seats, and their potential allies fifteen. The Nats had just 48. Thirty-six hours after the poll, Malan's party had 70 to the UP's 65. A right-wing parliamentary majority was ensured by the nine seats of the HNP's ally, the Afrikaner Party. It was cold comfort to Smuts, the UP and the other parties that they had received 624 500 votes to the 443 719 of the ultra-conservative alliance.

It was added delight for the Nats that the *rooinek*-loving devil, Smuts, had even lost his Standerton seat by 224 votes to Wentzel du Plessis, who had been booted out of the Public Service in 1945 for refusing to resign from the *Afrikaner Broederbond*, a secret fraternal society dedicated to Afrikaner advancement. How clever was *slim Jannie*, crafty Jannie Smuts, now? As the HNP supporters celebrated their seismic victory, they remembered also that the year before the election Smuts had the temerity to arrange a visit by the English royal family to South Africa. Afrikaners in particular had been repulsed by the visit. How dare Smuts devote the money and time of the State to entertaining these representatives of the nation that had killed *Boer* women and children in Kitchener's concentration camps? That had razed *Boer* farms to the ground? That had suppressed the Afrikaans language?

For the first time since 1931, 28 May was not cause for celebration in the Leong household. The day was Jewel's birthday, but this year a mood of dread prevailed. She and some fellow students were gathered at Aunt Lil's house, listening on the wireless to confirmation of the results. Later in the day, the South African Broadcasting Corporation relayed live Malan's victory speech, laying claim to the country. By nightfall, the streets of Westdene were lit by the torches of the *Ossewa Brandwag* and candles carried by Afrikaner youths and Malan voters. An ox-wagon rumbled along Perth Road, flying the *Vierkleur* flag of the Boer republics. Although the constituency was traditionally a Nat stronghold, for the local Nationalist faithful this night was unlike any other. Leading the parade was a senior National Party functionary who affected a Hitlerian hairstyle and cultivated a toothbrush moustache.

Stopping at the International Service Station, he turned to the crowd. 'Friends!' he called out in Afrikaans, raising a jubilant fist. 'Through the love of country and *volk* and with the help of the Almighty we have finally won! This is our land, a White land, an Afrikaner land! God has helped Dr Malan return to us what is ours, ours and no one else's. Let the English go home, let the Natives know their place. *Hoera* for Dr Malan!'

Moving with the speed of zealotry, the new Government introduced law after law based on racial classification. At their heart was the unholy trinity of the Prohibition of Mixed Marriages Act, No. 55 of 1949; the Population Registration Act, No. 30 of 1950; and the Group Areas Act, No. 41 of 1950.

Not without a certain wryness, Ah Leong and Gertie reflected on their marriage and that of her parents and how now neither would have been possible. But in reality there was no comfort for anyone who was not classified White. Lil's shop hand, Petrus Willemse, was reclassified from Coloured to black – 'Native' – under the Population Registration Act. Despite his birth certificate and other material evidence, the decision was made mainly on the basis of the humiliating and unscientific 'pencil test'.

At the end of his appearance before a classification board, Petrus had a pencil placed in his rather thick, curly hair. He was ordered to bend forward so that the top of his head faced the floor. '*Skud jou kop!* Shake your head, man!' barked the registration officer. Petrus did. The pencil did not fall out.

'Under the Act, you are classified as Native, Petrus Willemse,' said the officer, bringing his official stamp pounding down on the classification forms before him and thrusting one at Petrus. 'Next!'

Petrus was a broken man. It was not so much that he objected to being classed as Native, he explained to his employer; it was that under the new Government, Natives had far fewer opportunities and choices than Coloureds. Then bitterness and rage set in, and Petrus cursed his birth, his patrimony and the country.

Lil tried her best to assuage his grief, assuring him that his job in her shop was safe. How could she run the little odds and sods establishment without him? The Sun For Family Grocers kept household basics, make-up, crockery, haberdashery and select toys. It was down the road from Ah Leong and Gertie, at 23 Perth Road, comfortingly close for Lil to her sister Gertie and convenient also for her husband Ah Wha, who was Ah Leong's cousin. Jewel and Mickey enjoyed the proximity too, and they would go down to Aunt Lil whenever they had a disagreement with their mother, or when Gertie's strictness was too much to bear.

Lil's narrow and sunless shop had been a refuge to the girls in the year before the election, when Gertie and Ah Leong argued frequently about Cornelia and the Martins' attitude to the Leongs. The series of rows had been set off by an incident at the showgrounds in Milner Park, where John, James and Philip had pretended not to see Ah Leong and Gertie. Not an unexpected action, nonetheless it proved to be one slight too many for Ah Leong. If his groceries and food were good enough for the high-and-mighty Martins, he told Gertie, then he was good enough to warrant the glimmer of a greeting. How would strangers be able to interpret a smile or a vague nod as recognition of family ties? The quarrel quieted, then erupted once more, went into abeyance and then resurfaced. When Cornelia and five of her children had left for Adelaide in 1947, it was not too soon for Ah Leong, whose patience was at its end. And patience was what would be needed in the days of Grand Apartheid.

Of all the new laws, it was the Group Areas Act that was most worrying to Ah Leong and Gertie. On the one hand it stipulated that the Chinese must live in demarcated zones, and on the other it reclassified places where they currently resided and traded. The implications were enormously threatening. By aiming to settle Chinese in particular locations, the government would be forcibly removing them from the communities whom they had served as shopkeepers and artisans, and where they had lived. Reproclamation meant that the Chinese could not return to their previous environs to do business, as in the interim they would have been given to members of another group, probably 'Europeans'. An awful pincer, the Group Areas Act was intended to squeeze the wherewithal out of so-called Non-European communities, making it impossible for them to earn a decent living and relocating them in residential ghettoes outside the cities. In introducing the Group Areas Bill to Parliament, Malan had described it as 'the essence of Apartheid policy', and now this gargantuan piece of social engineering was about to be visited on the Western Areas, at the eastmost edge of which lay Westdene.

Mobilising nationally, the Chinese proposed that they be allowed to continue trading under a permit system. As a very small community, they argued, it was not economically viable to trade only among themselves. Consequently, they suggested that Group Areas apply to them only for residential purposes. Representations on these substantial matters did not address the host of other indignities visited by the Act on anyone not acknowledged as white. Hotels, sports facilities, public halls: all these were to be earmarked for use by different groups, vigorously reinforcing the separation of races so earnestly sought by the architects of Apartheid.

Closer to Ah Leong and Gertie, the Western Areas Chinese Association was established to look after the interests of the many Chinese traders in the locality. For over 20 years, the Johannesburg City Council had wanted to clear out what it regarded as the slums of Sophiatown and Martindale. Now the Government was about to do the council's dirty work, using greater force that would displace a large proportion of the city's Chinese population, together with thousands of Blacks, Indians and Coloureds.

Jewel could bring other perspectives to the gathering crisis. She had found a job. After finishing her Bachelor of Arts degree at the University of the Witwatersrand, she had spent six months looking for work. Early on, her great varsity friend, Rosemary Cohen, told her about a job at the South African Medical Research Institute. Rosemary was among the young students working in their laboratories monitoring chicken eggs for diseases. Jewel was granted an interview, but it was clear to her when she arrived that her prospective employers had not been expecting a Chinese face. 'It's not possible to employ you as the institute falls under the Government,' she was told in the first and last minute of the interview.

It was back to poring over the ads in the daily papers and walking up and down the streets of Johannesburg, on the lookout for job notices. When she was fortunate enough to secure an interview, it was always the same story: 'In spite of your admirable qualifications, it is not possible to employ you because you are Chinese.' One or two places had been prepared to risk taking her on, but when the staff were told, they threatened to walk out or to report their employers to the authorities.

By chance, Jewel met a varsity friend who was working in the library at Wits, their alma mater. Approach the Librarian, Miss Elizabeth Hartmann, she advised Jewel. There were no posts at Wits, Miss Hartmann told her, but she promised to let her know if anything suitable should turn up. After almost half a year of disappointments, the undertaking seemed to Jewel merely the most gracious rejection that she had received. But three weeks later, Miss Hartmann phoned with two options: a place at the Wits Library or a vacancy at the Institute of Race Relations, the research library of which was housed in the third basement of the Wits Library. When the two met to discuss the jobs, Miss Hartmann recommended that Jewel apply for the institute post as it was more challenging. She also offered the services of lecturers from the Wits Library so that Jewel would be able to take the SA Library Association examination.

Then came the interview, conducted by the institute's director, Quintin Whyte, and his assistant, Freddie van Wyk. Jewel had testimonials from her two favourite lecturers, Dr Jeffreys in Anthropology and Professor Haarhoff, Head of the Classics Department. In addition, in between searching for a job, she had taken courses in typing and shorthand. All went well, but the two men had one not inconsiderable misgiving: they felt that, at nineteen, Jewel was too young. They told her there was another short-listed candidate, reading for his Master's degree, and that they would make a decision soon. On a Friday afternoon, Mr van Wyk phoned to say that the institute had decided on her, though there would be a trial period of six months. Jewel could begin on the following Monday, if she liked.

A restless weekend preceded Jewel's first acquaintance with the institute library, situated next to the Logopaedics Department. Half an hour into her first day, the scope and challenge of the job struck home. The previous librarian, Mr Moche, had ruled over this domain for almost 20 years and in all that time had relied largely on his encyclopaedic memory and voluminous mental capacity; he had in fact catalogued hardly anything. He had gone away on home leave, taken ill and died. With the ordering of such a backlog and her probation very much in mind, Jewel set about examining the book stock, the press clippings, journals and government publications. Daily papers came from all over southern Africa. Periodicals covered South Africa, the race question and politics. There were stacks of *Hansard*, the *Government Gazette*, Blue Papers and White Papers. The books, journals and government documents had to be catalogued, and the press cuttings maintained. In this last area, Jewel could rely on Armstrong Mphahlele, who was responsible for reading, marking, cutting and pasting from the newspapers.

Beyond library work, Jewel produced the *Race Relations Library Bulletin*, which was issued to institute members, students and libraries. She also supplied institute staff with information on whatever subjects they requested. Queries would be sent from the institute, located in Auden House across the road from the university, to Jewel; books, cuttings and journals would flow in the opposite direction from the library. Bill Hecht, the publications officer, constantly required material for the monthly *Race Relation News*, among other things. But it was Muriel Horrell, the research officer who compiled annually *A Survey of Race Relations in South Africa*, who was the library's best customer. Requests would come in also from abroad, many focusing on a new subject, of which little was known: Apartheid.

After six weeks, Mr van Wyk had cancelled Jewel's probation and confirmed her appointment. Settled in, she loved and lived for her job, reflecting that she could easily remain there and die a contented old maid. Happily, she acknowledged the crucial role libraries had played in her life, beginning years before with her unexpected admission to the children's section of the Johannesburg Public Library. Chinese could not belong to public libraries, with the exception of pupils attending private schools. On Saturday mornings, Jewel and Mickey would meet their friends Esmond, Irene and Willie Song on the steps of the main library, bounded by Simmonds, Sauer, President and Market streets. Esmond and Willie, attending a Catholic school, would exchange their library books and then the five children would go off to the movies. One day, Jewel was on her own, waiting right outside the children's library for Esmond and Willie. She stood on tiptoe and gazed in through a window at this wonderful world of books. Row upon row and shelves and shelves of books met her eye. She crept up to the doorway and peeked in, first from one end and then the other.

Inside, at the front desk, a librarian noticed the small girl and the hungry and longing look on her face. From afar, Jewel heard a voice saying, 'Don't you want to come in?' She did not respond, certain that the invitation could not be addressed to her.

'Come in, come in,' the voice called.

Jewel looked up at the woman behind the counter, who was dressed in a blue smock. What was happening? She wondered if she had misbehaved somehow.

'Come, don't you want to join? Here is a membership application form for you.'

Dumbfounded, Jewel remained where she was. Esmond came to her rescue, walking across quickly and whispering urgently, 'Take it ... Come on, take it. It's a privilege.'

Jewel walked up to the counter, and held her out her hand for the card. She managed to stammer a thank-you and to smile.

'Have your principal sign and stamp the form,' said the librarian, 'and then bring it back to the library.' Smiling, the woman added, 'Then you will be able to take out books for yourself.'

Jewel had taken the form to Mr Wong, who expressed his surprise and delight. He lost no time in reminding her that it was an honour to belong to the library, and he urged her to obey its rules and respect the books. Then, with a flourish to his cursive, he signed his name in the Roman alphabet, after which he applied his personal seal in Chinese characters and last of all placed the stamp of the Kuo Ting School on the form.

When Jewel took the completed application back to the library the next Saturday, her benefactor was not there. Indeed, she never saw the woman in the blue smock again, but she thought always with gratitude of 'her magic librarian' who had opened wide the doors of reading and learning to her.

At the institute, Jewel became friends with Bill Hecht, whose sharp and witty tongue helped leaven the heavy days the country was living in. Bill's father had been one of Thomas Alva Edison's sound recordists, and Bill and his brother had in their possession the priceless collection of wax cylinder recordings laid down by their father. Jewel also spent many weekends with Quintin Whyte and his wife Mada at their house in Roseville, just over the way from Alexandra Township. Mada worked on literacy programmes and educating gold miners, using the 'Each One Teach One' system. One weekend, the Whytes invited Jewel and the Doeschers, an American couple compiling a report on the institute in order to raise international funding. Those in the house were aware of uninvited guests without: the security police, deliberately noting the car registration numbers and those visiting the Whytes.

In 1953, the institute published a pamphlet titled *The Western Areas Removal Scheme: Facts and Viewpoints*. It arose from the institute's conference on the issue at Wits University on 22 August 1953. Among the speakers was Dr Alfred Xuma, whom Jewel remembered from his buying supplies at her parents' shops. Dr Xuma had been ruthlessly discarded as president of the ANC in 1949, replaced by Dr James Moroka, who promised Congress Youth League leaders places on the movement's national executive in return for their votes. But Xuma had lost none of his oratorical powers, and in his address to the conference, republished in the institute's pamphlet, noted:

'In place of existing amenities, we are asked to accept assurances about Meadowlands, the area to which we are to be moved. We are assured that no one will be removed unless accommodation is provided, that transport will be available, that services will be provided. Do you wonder that we are not prepared to accept these assurances? We have been fed too long on assurances that were not carried out. It is not a sustaining diet. It gives rise to the disease of scepticism.'

Powerfully, he concluded: 'And not only the Africans of Johannesburg, but Africans throughout the Union have their eyes focused on the Western Areas. They know that the Minister regards this as a pilot scheme, that the present threat against one is the future threat against many. Africans regard this scheme as the acid test of municipal promises of a "square deal for the Natives" and of Ministerial assurances that it is "in the interest of the Natives". Their conviction that the present scheme cannot provide a square deal and that it is in the interest of the Europeans is deep and certain. The compulsory implementation of the scheme can only engender hatred and antagonism between white and black.'

Jewel's working at the institute enabled her to bring one of its former presidents, Dr Ellen Hellmann, to talk to the Chinese residents of Newclare and Sophiatown on the Western Areas removals. About a thousand of Johannesburg's 2 500 Chinese were thought to live in Sophiatown and Martindale, the epicentres for the forthcoming evictions. Of the area's racial and cultural mix in those days, the poet and Sophiatown resident Don Mattera recalled:

'And so were many Indian families and Chinese families [living there]. And they all played together. Lenny Lee was one of the great jazz trumpeters in Sophiatown – even before Stompie Manana. And also coincidentally, both of them were great artists, Stompie Manana who plays the trumpet is a great artist in his own right and so was Lenny Lee. He was Chinese – he was very strongly Chinese but he had broken away from the Buddhist-cum-Chinese cultural hold, so he mixed freely with Hugh Masekela who was a young *snotkop*; he grew up in front of us. And very precocious; he [Hugh] was one boy – he's 60 years old and I'm almost six years his senior – but I watched him grow. Lenny Lee, who was in my class in school and also younger than I was, he was just too much. He broke away from the mould of the Chinese culture and there was a great confluence with Sophiatown culture. And there was another Chinese, Ah Loon, who had all black women – his children today are still walking around – and so did his young brother Yap. They had two beautiful sisters and Oh, they were just crazy Chinese women, but they didn't love a Chinese life – they lived with black people; they intermingled with so-called Coloureds and Indians in Sophiatown. Then there was the Yung family, also Chinese – one of the handsomest families. They wore the best American clothes, they spoke *Tsotsitaal*, they mixed with the people. Sophiatown was that kind of melting pot: it brought all cultures, all people together.'[1]

None of the thinking, talking and protesting about the imminent evictions swayed Hendrik Frensch Verwoerd, the Minister of Native Affairs. It mattered not a jot that most Sophiatown residents owned their land and houses. Realising the need more forcibly to oppose the Government, the Western Areas Protest Committee planned a one-day work stoppage on 12 February 1955, the scheduled first day of the removals. The newspapers were filled with news, speculation and comment. When it came, the evictions were ordered and brutal: forewarned of the protest strike, Verwoerd struck two days earlier, on 10 February, sending in 2 000 police armed with Sten sub-machine guns, rifles and *knobkerries*. Defiance had been declared on the suburb's walls; WE WONT MOVE. But in the early morning of 10 February, surrounded and harried by policemen, the first 110 families targeted to be forcibly removed did not resist. The juggernaut of Apartheid had moved Sophiatown's immovable property-owners. The 'present threat against one' described by Dr Xuma had become a reality, and the many throughout the country who watched it become so, knew exactly what their futures held.

---

[1] Taped interview with Don Mattera by Gwen Ansell, June 2000, by kind permission of the Living History Archive at ABC Ulwazi.

烈火

F I R E

I am lost
in murk and darkness
as I start on my journey
to the East

from *The Lord of the East*, Song VII of The Nine Songs

FIRE

ONE
Johannesburg and Pretoria, circa 1952 to 1955

Park Station was its busy Saturday self, the centre of a web of train lines spun out across the Witwatersrand. Jewel and Mickey stood on the platform with their teammates from the Comets softball squad, waiting for the train to Pretoria. They were going up to the capital to take on another Chinese team. There, they would be met by their hosts and taken to the grounds. The Leong girls would be riding with Kit Accone, who, they knew from previous matches, would have the use of his older brother Yenny's new Packard for the day.

At first the train travelled eastwards, stopping in Germiston, before taking a turn and moving steadily north. An hour and a half after leaving Johannesburg, it arrived in the purply-blue haze of Pretoria in early November, the city and its suburbs shimmering with the blossoms of thousands of jacaranda trees. Jewel was looking forward to seeing Kit, and he was no less keen as he moved down the platform towards the visitors. Their friendship had developed into something else ever since he had asked her to dance at a wedding in Northcliff.

'Well, you dance quite well,' Kit had said to Jewel as he escorted her back to her table. He fancied himself, rightly, as a dancer, having taken ballroom and Latin American lessons in his late teens. Waltzes, tangos, foxtrots, Kit was accomplished at them all, but when he complimented Jewel she was amused and had a quiet giggle to herself. When she and Mickey were younger, they had performed many folk dances at various functions. The highpoint perhaps had been during World War Two, when they danced before a film screening that was a fund-raiser for the Chinese War Orphans' Committee. Interludes of dance and music in the interval between the supporting programme and the main feature were commonplace at the movies in those days. The big bioscopes even retained their own organists, who would play during intermission: Dean Herrick at the 20th Century and Tommy McClellan at the Metro were household names in Johannesburg.

After their dance, Kit and Jewel began seeing each other regularly. They went to movies, on picnics, and out dancing. Often they took the floor at Swallows Nest, the dinner-dance nightclub in the basement of Little Swallows restaurant, owned and run by the parents of Jewel's childhood friends Esmond, Irene and Willie, and situated in the heart of Johannesburg's Chinatown. Sometimes the band in the basement was the Chinese quartet that had Yenny on drums, with Jack Mason on piano, Victor Chang Ku on bass and Dennis Chang Ku on sax. In larger venues, it was the swing of the all-Chinese band, The Marigolds, that got things going on the dance floor. Jewel and Kit laughed over and over as they recalled the evening that the diminutive Willie Ho Hee had grabbed the baton, flourished it grandly above his head, and shouted to the already steaming ensemble, 'Come on guys, give it stick!'

Movies provided present and retrospective pleasures for the courting couple. Both had enjoyed Betty Hutton playing the legendary crackshot Annie Oakley in *Annie Get Your Gun*, filled with showstopping Irving Berlin songs. They revived childhood memories of *Lassie Come Home*, featuring child stars Roddy McDowall and Elizabeth Taylor. Jewel spoke animatedly and lovingly of *The Red Shoes*, with its ecstatically coloured expressionism and mesmerising ballet scenes; Kit listened and then, bravely, confessed that he neither understood ballet nor was moved by it. On the kinetic heights of *Singin' in the Rain* they found joyous common ground. It was on one of their first dates that they saw Gene Kelly whirling and swirling in the wet. Kit and Jewel thrilled to the sight of Kelly, Debbie Reynolds and Donald O'Connor marching over and upturning a sofa, then proceeding straight up a wall and along the ceiling and finally coming down the opposite wall; they shifted imperceptibly closer in their Royal Circle seats as Kelly performed his singing and dancing solo of the title song. Even Kit was spellbound by Kelly's balletic homage in the *Broadway Melody* segment of the film. It was on that night also that they saw the mischievous behaviour of some patrons in the more expensive Royal Circle, who casually but deliberately dropped their half-full ice cream cones on to the moviegoers below. For 2s 7d, you got a Royal Circle seat upstairs, affording a strategic aerial advantage over those in the cheaper, 1s 11d seats downstairs.

The ice-cream wars reminded Jewel of the rowdy excitement of matinees she went to with Mickey and the Song children. The obligatory reels of *Pathé News* and *African Mirror* would be followed by a pause and a tangible air of excitement. *Looney Tunes* was about to begin. The cartoon would come on, to screeching from the young audience. One of a range of favourite characters would hit the screen: Bugs Bunny, Elmer Fudd, Porky Pig, Daffy Duck, Uncle Scrooge, Mickey Mouse or Popeye the Sailor and for a few minutes the noise from the crowd would drown out the sound from the screen. Thereafter it was the turn of the weekly serial. Depending on what cinema you were in, Spy Smasher, Dick Tracy and his G-Men, Dr Fu Manchu or Alan Parker preceded interval. Kit chipped in with stories about the Empire and Orient cinemas in Marabastad, and their serials: two different versions each of Zorro and Batman, as well as Dick Tracy.

Jewel and Kit swopped these and other stories on regular picnics, which took them to the Muldersdrift haunts of her World War Two outings. Lying on a checked blanket under the willow trees, the two would talk for hours about childhood and youth and the future. Jewel told Kit about the Royal Visit, and how for the first and only time in her schooldays she had bunked classes to see the Windsors arrive at the Johannesburg City Hall for a reception.

'To see properly, I stood on one of my friend's suitcases and flattened it. She was very annoyed but excused me because I was so short. It was a dream to see Princess Margaret, whose romance with Peter Townsend we'd all followed. But Princess Elizabeth was very cold and proud; we didn't cheer for her.'

In turn, Kit regaled Jewel with tales of his motorcycling escapades, an enthusiasm that stood him in some stead with Ah Leong. Kit had a passion for large, powerful motorbikes. In some ways, they were the horses of his youth transformed into howling mechanical form. His first big bike had been a monster, an Aerial Four-Square, on which he'd had an accident. While he was recovering his mother had sold the machine.

Shamefacedly, Kit confessed to Jewel that when he found out, he had gone into the shop and smashed half a dozen Chinese tea sets in anger. Undeterred by his mishap, he bought next a Vincent Black Shadow, as fast and dangerous as its predecessor. His mother resumed her lectures on the craziness of motorcycling and begged him to switch to something safer, such as the Packards that Yenny favoured, which were traded in for a new model every year. In response, Kit enjoyed teasing his mother by exaggerating, or simply relating, his latest adventures.

There had been the wedding run that he had taken with six other Pretoria Boys. They had hit the road to the Eastern Transvaal at lunch time on a Friday, sped along through Balmoral, Middelburg and Belfast and stopped at a Chinese family's home in Machadodorp for the night. The next morning, they had flashed past Nelspruit and crossed over into Portuguese East Africa at Komatipoort, headed for the capital, Lourenço Marques. A member of the Kong family there was marrying and the Pretoria Boys wanted to celebrate with their old school friend, but only Kit made it to the wedding. The other six were arrested as they revved their way down Avenida 24 de Julho, on their way to the ceremony. Kit had the good fortune to be at the back of the motorcade, and as the traffic lights turned to amber he braked but the other Pretoria bikers accelerated through. Unsportingly, a Portuguese traffic cop leapt out from behind a palm tree and flagged down the offenders. The official affected incomprehension at their explanations that they were part of the wedding. After idling at the lights, Kit cruised past his companions, pretending not to notice them, and rejoined the procession.

Finally, however, Ah Hing's nagging became so tedious that Kit settled on a compromise: an MG TD convertible, the powder-blue roadster that carried him and Jewel to their dances and picnics and other excursions. Its chrome grille and chromed engine gleamed, mudguards curved elegantly into a running board under the doors, which were adorned by Kit's initials in small silver letters, and in the cabin Jewel was delighted to find a lined cubbyhole with a lockable lid. Her long hair under a scarf, she thrilled in the sense of freedom conferred by the open top. She also loved the engine's distinctive, throaty roar, which announced Kit's imminent arrival as he swept down Hurst Hill on his way to 27A Perth Road.

Ah Leong and Gertie heard it too, and he would mutter about the reckless young man driving too fast. Ah Leong was ambivalent about Kit. He was pleased that this apparent suitor was Chinese. Curiously, he had long ago insisted to his daughters that they marry Chinese boys. His own semi-marrying out seemed not to count as a precedent; or if it did, it was taken as read that it was a bad example. Probably the racism experienced from Chinese themselves had persuaded Ah Leong to set this course for his daughters, and when Grand Apartheid struck, with its prohibition of mixed marriages, his position seemed unassailable. But while Kit was Chinese, he was from the same clan: he, too, was *seng* Fok. In China there were age-old prohibitions against people from the same clan marrying. Furthermore, Kit's family came from Ma Kiu village, origins that presented another ancient problem. 'Sha Kiu, Ma Kiu, *da kiu*,' Ah Leong heard, again and again, in his head: 'Sha Kiu, Ma Kiu, Fight', the refrain expressing the old rivalry between the neighbouring villages in Kwangtung. Same *seng*, bad; wrong village, worse, thought Ah Leong. To those gloomy ruminations, Gertie added that Kit was a wild young man, who jived, played the saxophone and, most damningly of all, was a Pretoria Boy – and everyone in the community knew how scandalously badly behaved *they* were.

In reply, Jewel said that she and Kit were simply two people, not representatives of rival village factions. She pointed to the prickly competitiveness between Pretoria Chinese and Johannesburg Chinese on the sports field, and Pretoria's superiority there, and wondered if that had anything to do with her mother's notion of wild Pretoria Boys. Last, Jewel said that Kit was a wonderful person, whose different interests and talents made up the missing pieces in the mosaic of her life.

Kit had an even more difficult time from his mother. Ah Hing was furious that Jewel was the offspring of a half-Chinese mother and poor shopkeeper. In contrast, by this time Ah Hing was comfortably off, and was considered wealthy by the community. Yen was running the very profitable farm shop out in the countryside of Kyalami, roughly halfway between Pretoria and Johannesburg, and the old town shop in Queen Street was doing well with Kit and her there. Ah Hing virtually forbade Kit to go out with Jewel, and so the two had to devise all manner of stratagems and stories in order to be able to meet undetected. Often they would arrive separately at community occasions, their most fail-safe method of getting together.

In Ah Hing's determination to prevent any fruition of this dangerous courtship, she took to locking the telephone at night, securing it with a tiny padlock around the circular dialling mechanism. Unfazed, Kit unpicked the lock with wire from the end of a paper clip and muffled the whirr and click of the dialling ring as he made clandestine late-night calls to Perth Road. There, whenever the phone rang in this way, Ah Leong would shake his head and wonder how this relationship could be discouraged.

Sensing that Kit was neither despondent nor seeking a new girl, Ah Hing wrote to her brother in Canton. It was an angry and dramatic letter, composed in eloquent Chinese for the sake of her scholarly sibling.

'Dear brother,' began Ah Hing, 'I write to you in despair, with no one to turn to in this dark hour for my family.' She continued: 'If my late husband were here, he would be able to restore the situation, but alas he has been gone these many years, as you know. So I implore you, as a respected and influential family member, for support and help in this vexing matter.

'A terrible calamity has befallen my youngest, Fok Chong Kit. He seems to have fallen under the spell of a thoroughly unsuitable young girl from Kum Saan, a girl whose lineage, parentage and roots make her unworthy of such attention. The girl has a German grandmother! If it were not impolite to do so, I would say that her not being pure Chinese makes her an ox-head. Even if, impossibly, we allow for her being Chinese, there are several insurmountable problems. One, she is of the same *seng* as us. Two, her father hails from that blighted village, Sha Kiu. I need hardly remind you of how miserable are the people who originate from there. Three, her father, this Ah Leong, is a struggling grocer in a poor part of Kum Saan. Four, the matter of the girl's name, Hong Hgang. If I recall correctly, there was an Emperor's daughter of that name, a princess with a will of her own, who fell in love with a commoner and ran away and married him. It is a headstrong, independent name, and I will not countenance such a name in my family. Besides, who is the commoner here?

'I would value your making it clear to Fok Chong Kit the perilous nature of his obsession. There have been many occasions on which the absence of a strong, male hand has been evident in the boy's upbringing, but none so serious as in the present circumstances. I beseech you to reply swiftly and unequivocally, and look forward to your aid in this dire time.'

The reply was surprisingly speedy.

'My dear sister, you present a powerful case for the unsuitability of this union,' it opened.

'Your situation is doubly difficult because you cannot draw on the support of a husband and father to the boy. Nonetheless, things are not hopeless, and there is a distinct path to the resolution of the problem.'

Ah Hing nodded in satisfaction. She had been correct in appealing to her brother and his voice of reason. She read on.

'When two people love each other, none should stand in their way; and least of all those closest to them, who should have only the happiness and welfare of the young ones in their hearts.'

Taken aback, Ah Hing wondered at this lapse into a romantic and unwelcome vein. Had the man gone mad? She took up the letter once more, incidentally appreciating its beautifully executed characters.

'It matters not who the girl's ancestors are; it matters only what she is, and what Fok Chong Kit makes of that. The old customs about not marrying in the same clan will one day fall away; the world is bigger now. Beyond that, I do not fear that there is any danger of these two young people being too closely related by past blood.

'I have long forgotten the old saying, "Sha Kiu, Ma Kiu, *da kiu*". It has not been pleasant to remember, for it reminds me of a time of smallness and ignorant feuding. In the China that Chairman Mao is making there is no room for such insularity. We must all pull together in the same direction, for the sake of China and the Chinese. All men are brothers, and for my part I would add that all women are sisters.

'Sister, I urge you to allow your son to pursue his love, for it is clear to me that not one of the vast obstacles to this union matters in the least to him. To be so determined in the face of such is to show a love that is strong and pure; a love that should not be deflected, at least not by human intercession.'

Stunned, Ah Hing set the letter down. This was not the help she had thought would be forthcoming. The higher authority she had intended to place before Kit had evaporated. Well, not all was lost. After the opening and before the ending, the fates had placed the middle game, and romance frequently went wrong just there, when things were at their most exciting and involved. Drawing some succour from that, and remembering from *fah-fee* and *mah-jong* how easily and quickly luck can swing and fortune turn around, Ah Hing determined on playing a game of wait-and-see.

Over in Westdene, Jewel was as decided. She would persist in the relationship, despite – and because of – her parents' misgivings and Kit's mother's objections. A few years before, Ah Leong and Gertie had insisted on her passing up an opportunity to travel around Europe. There had been a cut-price student offer on a return voyage from Durban to Southampton on one of the Union Castle liners, followed by a trek around England and Europe. 'You are too young,' they told Jewel; a few years later, when her friend Moreen Viljoen invited her to Scotland, and later to Hong Kong and Japan, Ah Leong and Gertie refused flatly. Those frustrations and disappointments had been bitter, but they provided salutary warnings for Jewel to stand up for what she wanted in the more profound matter of her relationship with Kit. She had many reasons for loving Kit. He was not concerned by her ancestry. He respected her parents. She was just a person whom he loved. To herself she admitted that there was no denying the appeal of Kit as a wild boy, an erstwhile biker, and someone who connected with life through his body while she experienced life at a remove, through books and with her mind. Biker and bookworm, a classic attraction of opposites.

At the same time, Jewel accepted that Kit sometimes cut an alarming figure for her parents. They had become accustomed to his black hair swept into a ducktail hairstyle, and gleaming from the brilliantine that held it in place. But when he wore his tight-fitting leather jacket, tapered trousers and pointed leather shoes, Gertie and Ah Leong were aghast. 'Jesus, Bug,' Ah Leong – whose language tended to slip a notch in extreme circumstances – would grumble barely audibly to Gertie, 'that quiff is bad enough, but just look at those pants and shoes.'

They were more at ease, however, with the dragon band that Kit wore on the ring finger of his right hand. Cast in gold, it took the form of the head of a dragon in whose open jaws rested a pearl-shaped orb with the letter A carved in high relief. The circle was completed by a broad and irregular wavy pattern, representing the snake body that Chinese dragons are deemed to have. For an eye, the ring dragon had a small ruby inset in its ocular cavity.

When Gertie had first noticed the ring, she had been reminded at once of when she and Andrew had seen the painting of a Chinese dragon, in her father's village some 30 years before. Was that instant connection in her mind a sign, Gertie had wondered, some omen for Jewel and this young man? Legend had it that dragons could shrink to the size of a caterpillar or be so gigantic that they filled the space between the earth and the sky. It seemed to Gertie that if the feelings between Jewel and Kit grew into love, it would be of large and not small scale. And if not, the traces would remain in everyone's hearts, for was it not said that when a dragon walked away, it left behind the footprints of a tiger?

Two
Perth Road, circa 1955 to 1956

'May we buy all your bread and milk, Mrs Leong?' asked the tall man in the black cassock.

'Of course, Father Whitnall. Are they moving more people today?'

Wearily, the young man nodded in answer. Looking distractedly into Perth Road, he said, 'Soon there won't be any families left. All gone to Meadowlands. Meadowlands! Don't let the name fool you. It's barren ground, scarcely a blade of grass, hardly a tree. No running water, no toilets, no shops, no medical services.'

'Oh, Father, it must be so difficult for you, Father Huddleston and the others from the Community to witness these evictions. Here you are, 22 loaves of white, nine brown, and thirteen pints of milk. That's all I have, I'm afraid.'

'Not to worry, Mrs Leong. That should suffice for the first truckloads of people. You know, it does not become easier. Every time they move a family, it is too heart-wrenching. This morning there were two women, neighbours, wearing magnificent Xhosa headdress and traditional shawls over black dresses. They both had children clinging to them, and staring with large, frightened eyes at the policemen. The women's husbands were watching as their pathetic possessions were being bundled or thrown on to the backs of the Bedford trucks. The dignity of those Xhosa women should have shamed the police, but they just carried on loading and banging on doors further down the street.'

Gertie put the last of the milk into the large, heavy-gauge cardboard box she had used to pack the order. Dominic Whitnall had been a regular customer for some years, and then a friend of the family; since the assault on Sophiatown he had come to the shop virtually every day to buy food for the families being removed. He belonged to the

Community of the Resurrection, CR, an order of Anglican monks that had its chief priory in Mirfield, Yorkshire. In the 1940s, under Father Raymond Raynes, the CR had moved its Johannesburg headquarters from Rosettenville in the south to the heart of Sophiatown. When Raynes was elected Superior of the CR in 1943, and returned to England, he had dispatched the young Trevor Huddleston to take his place at the Church of Christ the King in Sophiatown. Huddleston had become a beloved member of the community there. Even after he was elected Provincial CR in 1949 and had to move to Rosettenville, Huddleston remained involved with Sophiatown. As the elected Chairman of the Western Areas Protest Committee, he had fought to protect his beloved Sof'town and its neighbours. It was he who alerted the Press on the morning of 10 February 1955, he who walked past the queues of displaced residents standing in the rains of that day, and he who spoke to the flocks of reporters at the scene. Among Huddleston's brethren who were based at 73 Meyer Street, Sophiatown, was Father Whitnall.

'How are the people?' asked Gertie.

'I fear their spirit is broken. "*Asi Hami*" – "We Won't Move" – is only a slogan on a wall now. On that first day, when the trucks and the armed police arrived, the people took stones and pieces of iron and banged and tapped on lampposts to protest. There is none of that now.'

Again, Father Whitnall pursed his lips. 'And yourselves, Mrs Leong? Have the Chinese any news of where they will be moved?'

Gertie slowly shook her head. 'I believe the Consul-General has taken up the case with the government. So far no area has been earmarked for us, but it can be only a matter of time. You must come for dinner again, before we have to move.'

'I will, I promise. Now I must be off. Take care.'

Scooping the box off the counter, Father Whitnall smiled at Mrs Leong and strode out of Perth Road Fruit Shop. As Gertie watched him go, she reflected sadly on how her world was in upheaval. Immediately after the war, she had been optimistic. Many of her customers had almost become friends. A good number of the boys who had fought up north brought back with them Italian wives, changing the feel of the Westdene community. Gertie had laughed when *polenta* became all the rage, for this was the selfsame yellow mealie meal that the Leongs had often eaten. She remembered fondly the welcome parties for returned ex-servicemen, and how her little shop supplied cakes, sweets and cooldrinks for those celebrations. Gertie recalled looking out over Westdene from the kitchen window and seeing flags fluttering from rooftops, the joyous announcement of a son or daughter safely back home. She and Ah Leong had found a fine helper in Lucas Mazibuko, who had been in North Africa and Italy as a stretcher-bearer. But then had come the troubles with her family, and their departure to Australia. And then had come Dr Malan and Apartheid.

Surprisingly, Cornelia and the family had returned not long after they went to Adelaide. They had found the Australians unfriendly and unhelpful, and seemingly as obsessed with questions of race as white South Africans. The whole experience was leavened only by the food parcels of Marie biscuits, Joko tea and *meebos* that Gertie and Ah Leong had sent over.

The Martinis, as they were now officially called, had an equally short sojourn in Johannesburg before setting out once again for Australia. Whatever the shocks of their time down under, they were slight compared with the conditions they discovered under Apartheid. All the fears that weighed on them before they left in 1947 had at least doubled under the new dispensation. They made for Sydney in their second migration, and there found life more convivial.

Cornelia wrote to Gertie, telling her of how a chance encounter on board had helped. Talking to a fellow passenger, Cornelia had said how she felt split, that somehow a heart was left behind in South Africa. Treat it like a divorce, had come the commonsense reply, delivered in those Australian tones that she found so odd. 'Take off your wedding ring and cast it in the sea, and start your life anew in Australia,' the woman had concluded, squeezing Cornelia's arm before walking away. And that is what she had done, she confessed to Gertie. She had twisted the ring that Martin had slid easily on to her finger more than 40 years before, twisted and tugged, eased and cajoled it until finally it came free. Holding it in her left hand, nestled in those unnaturally long fingers of hers, Cornelia

had looked at it and seemed to recall in those moments the little emporium in Chinatown, the monkey-picked tea, Martin's round face and his
ready smile. She had seen Mauritius as if through his boyhood eyes, and
she saw, unwelcomed, the mountainous waves on the night before his
fatal fall. Last, she had seen Martin's wax-white face after the life had
drained from him and before the ship's surgeon had come to take him
away. Bringing the band of gold to her lips, Cornelia had kissed it, shut
her eyes and whispered, 'Farewell, Martin my love. God be with you until
we meet in the next world.' Then, with her eyes closed still, she had flung
the ring outwards from the ship, not opening her eyes until at least a
minute had passed. It was her symbolic divorce from everything in the
past.

Gertie had been saddened by Cornelia's actions. Yet another link with
her father was irretrievably gone. Nonetheless, she continued writing to
her mother, and sending regular parcels of Cornelia's favourite foodstuffs.
Despite all the hurt and sorrow of the relationship, Gertie had never been
as grateful to have a mother as now. That realisation had come late on a
Wednesday afternoon, when Ah Leong had returned from his weekly letter-reading session at Third Uncle.

After Mao had won the civil war in China, Ah Leong had faced greater
difficulties in trying to bring Soi Sien out to Kum Saan. China had been
on the side of the Allies during World War Two, but her becoming a
Communist power sat well neither in Washington nor Pretoria. In 1950,
the Korean War had seen China support the north of that country against
the south, which was bolstered by America. American General Douglas
MacArthur had gone so far as threatening to drop atom bombs on China.
In South Africa, Malan's regime was virulently anti-Communist and
maintained ties instead with Chiang Kai-shek's Nationalist government
in Taipei. Ah Leong could neither travel to Sha Kiu nor arrange for his
mother to leave there.

A male cousin of his in the village, jealous of the money and hand-
made woollen jerseys that arrived regularly for Soi Sien, kidnapped the
old lady. He threatened to kill her if his demand for ransom was not met.
Soi Sien cautioned that it would take much time to raise the money, for
her sons and daughters were far-flung. In the interim, she appealed to the

villagers to help her raise the money. Many refused outright, others pleaded poverty, which was true. None tried to rescue her or apprehend her gaoler; the constant wars and ravages of the past fifteen years had apparently exhausted everyone's humanity. At first the kidnapper grew impatient, then edgy, and finally frustrated. Unable to wait any longer, yet unwilling simply to let the old woman go, he bound her hands together and threw her in the river. Soi Sien struggled to swim, but it was useless. She could not free her hands because the rope was too tight and she was too old and weak to stay afloat by kicking. The river in which she drowned fed the very lake that as a child she had fallen into and been rescued from by her late husband, Langshi.

Gertie was on the porch when Ah Leong came home that afternoon. He came in and said calmly to her, 'My mother is dead.' Jewel and Mickey heard the rending words and came out from their bedroom, but their father had gone through to the storeroom behind the grocery shop, where his escritoire was. Later, Gertie told them it was the only time she had seen her husband and their father cry. Two tears had expressed themselves and run down his cheeks.

Usually, a long period of mourning would have marked the passing away of someone so elderly, but Ah Leong did not want that. He told the girls to carry on life normally. In honour of the woman she had met once only, Gertie observed mourning by wearing black for three months. During that time she often remembered what Soi Sien had told her when they said goodbye. It was the anonymous but famous verse that went:

When the future looks back
It is like the present looking at the past:
Things pass by but they are never gone.

THREE
Pretoria and Johannesburg, 1956 to 1958

Kit and Jewel set off in the MG to a screening of *Carmen Jones* at His Majesty's on a Saturday evening in the early autumn of April 1956. It had taken a few years for this sensational film to make it to South Africa. Bizet's opera had been turned into an all-black musical by director Otto Preminger, and it was a minor miracle that it was showing in the country at all. Jewel had insisted on seeing it, for that reason and because she loved opera. Kit, although as wary of opera as of ballet, had not demurred and had consoled himself with the knowledge that Oscar Hammerstein II had written new and very contemporary lyrics to Bizet's music. And then there was the Dorothy Dandridge factor: the actress who played Carmen was a troubled star and movie fans were fascinated by her.

Neon letters in a vertical line several storeys high announced His Majesty's to the gathering night. Queueing at the box office, Jewel thought back to her bioscope days when only the 20th Century and the Metro would allow Chinese in. The Colosseum, with its monumental façade and reliefs of ancient Egyptian goddesses, cobras and falcons, had been barred to her. For years she had wondered as much about that exclusion as the disparity between the cinema's Roman name and its Egyptian style. The Bijou, too, was out of bounds, as was the Plaza in Jeppe Street, a building much admired by her student architect friends for its Modernist design, freighted with the theoretical ideals of the International Style. Jewel had been consoled by the grandeur of the Metro, in Bree Street, with its graduated and edged blocks that rose, step-like, towards the corner, where the large letters METRO told you that this was a cinema, not some concrete mausoleum. Inside, a massive chandelier was suspended over the foyer, drawing your eyes to the mezzanine promenade. But it was the 20th Century that most seemed to transport her into an otherworld of glamour and glitz. There, it was easy to imagine that you were in a metropolis, as the massive neon '20', with the smaller 'th CENTURY' inset towards the bottom of the nought in 20, blazed in the dark of President Street. Round the corner, a smaller '20th' topped a vertical neon sign proclaiming CENTURY. This was the Von Brandis Street side of the cinema, and it gave Jewel a frisson to think that the street had been named after Carl von Brandis, the first Commissioner of Mines in the Transvaal, to whom she was related via Cornelia. She recollected too that Gertie had often spoken about Carl, the large tabby cat that the Martin children had in Johannesburg before they left for China.

Accommodating a cinema, law chambers, and commercial tenants, His Majesty's had three towers of eleven, fourteen and eighteen storeys. It was a skyscraper, not a movie palace, but it was still an apt place of dreams to see the astounding *Carmen Jones*. Jewel was amazed and amused by Carmen's transformation from cigarette-maker to parachute factory employee. Kit was almost taken aback by the recurring di, dat, dey of Hammerstein's lyrics; later he and Jewel gleefully sprinkled their conversation with those words, which had come tumbling from the mouths of Marilyn Horne and Laverne Hutchinson. Horne had dubbed Dandridge's singing moments, but nothing could quell the fiery Dandridge in her incendiary pink skirt. Jewel had read Pauline Kael's review in *The New Yorker*, which had described the star's 'whiplash hips', and so they were. As Jewel and Kit rode back to Perth Road, the top of the MG down, they spoke about the film, wondering why the great singer Harry Belafonte, who played Carmen's GI lover, had been dubbed by Hutchinson. As they neared Westdene, they began to chatter. What lay ahead made both nervous.

'Here they come, Bug,' said Ah Leong to Gertie as the howl of the MG quieted to a burble and Kit and Jewel drew up at the alley gate.

'I wonder what Dotty Dandridge was like,' Gertie mused as she put on the kettle to prepare tea. 'Don't you think, Bug, that Giddy was looking extra smart tonight?'

'So he should,' replied Ah Leong. 'Jewel's a fine young woman. Ah, they're at the garden gate. Let me open up.'

Soon the four were seated at the kitchen table, a heavy rectangle of steel with rounded corners, painted white, as were the four steel chairs. In the corner of the room stood the faithful old cast-iron coal stove, with its brand name, Jewel, emblazoned on the oven door. As a child, Jewel had been embarrassed whenever visitors remarked on this, and for a while she had preferred Hong Hgang to Jewel. Another strategy, modifying Jewel to Julie, had brought the vicious retort of *chew-li*, pig's tongue, from the nastier children at the Chinese school. It was Kit who had banished those bad memories, when he had told her about his nickname Giddy. They had for some time now been calling each other Julie and Giddy, and the Leongs had fallen into the habit as well. Looking across at the stove, spruced up regularly with loving care and Zebra polish by Lucas, Julie speculated on which of her names – Hong Hgang, Jewel, Julie – Giddy would use when the moment came. A nickname, she thought, might not do at a time such as this.

'Another *yow cha kwai*?' said Gertie, offering Giddy a piece of this Chinese bread, that tasted like *vetkoek* but was shaped somewhat like a *koeksister*.

'No thanks, Mrs Leong. They're delicious but I am very satisfied,' he said.

'How was the picture?' asked Ah Leong.

'Dorothy Dandridge played Carmen like a wild beast,' said Julie. 'At one point she bit Harry Belafonte's wrist.'

'And they all died in the end,' joked Giddy. 'It was very sad, Carmen being killed. And it wasn't any less so for knowing the ending in advance.' He paused and cleared his throat, glancing quickly across at Ah Leong and Gertie. He thought he detected a supportive glimmer in Gertie's eyes.

'I would like to talk about a happy ending, and a happy beginning, if I may,' continued Giddy. 'Mr and Mrs Leong, Julie and I have spent many wonderful times together in the past few years. Lovely as that time has been, we would like to bring it to a close – a joyous close – by starting on something new. I feel very honoured, Mr Leong, just to be asking you this question. May I have your permission and your blessing to marry your daughter, Hong Hgang?'

'Well, my boy, this is hardly a surprise,' Ah Leong began. 'You know that at first I did not approve of your seeing one another, because you are of the same clan. Besides, there was the matter of Sha Kiu and Ma Kiu.'

'Oh, Bug, don't give the children a history lesson now, of all times,' Gertie broke in. 'Give them your answer, won't you?'

'Yes, yes, in a minute. Ah Kit, you have shown yourself to be a fair and a generous person. You hold no prejudices about status and money. You have shown respect towards me and Yok Laan. Most of all, it is clear that you honour and love our daughter. Yes, Bug, don't be so impatient. So, young fellow, my answer is: yes, you may have the hand of my daughter, Hong Hgang, in marriage, and all my blessings.'

'Thank you, sir, and you too, Mrs Leong,' said Giddy.

'Thanks Pop, thanks Mom,' said Julie, and she went round the table and gave her mother a long hug.

Ah Leong nodded at Giddy. Then he said, 'We should drink a small toast to this. I know you do not drink, and you have the long journey back to Pretoria, so just wet your lips with the *sam-shiu*.' Ah Leong rose from the table, went into the next-door lounge and came back from the cabinet with some shot glasses and a small, red, vase-shaped bottle. 'When I entered Canton as a boy, on a sampan, the old fisherman who owned the boat drank a toast with my father and me,' he explained, while pouring out tots into the glasses. Raising his, Ah Leong repeated that toast of long ago, and also of other important days in his life: '*Yum seng* – to victory, to success. In this case, to the happiness and long life of the two of you. May you have double happiness!'

Giddy and Julie, released from the tension that had hung over them ever since the evening began, embraced and kissed. They thought that the hard part was over, with only the planning of the wedding still to be negotiated, but reality turned out to be more complicated.

Ah Hing had been steeling herself for the day Kit announced his engagement. Her brother's letter had left a deep impression on her, and worn away much of her resistance to the inevitable. So on being told, early on the day following Ah Leong's consent, she presented Kit with a diamond for the engagement ring. Next, she consulted *Tong Siang*, the Chinese almanac, which listed omens, lucky and unlucky dates, and happenings. Telling Julie about this on the phone, Giddy reminded her that *Tong Siang* translated literally as 'to be able to go through with it'. And he added jokingly, 'When you get married Chinese style, you never want to get divorced because of the possibility of having to go through with it again.'

Ah Hing quickly arranged to visit her future in-laws the next weekend, and took her cousin, Mrs Jackson, with her to translate. It transpired that Mrs Jackson's interpreting skills were not necessary. Ah Hing was surprised, shocked even, by Gertie's fluent Cantonese. The older people drank tea, exchanged pleasantries and fixed a date for the wedding: 22 July 1956. It was earlier than the couple had intended, but set thus to accommodate Ah Hing's journey to Hong Kong later in the year.

Before the proper Chinese wedding, Giddy and Julie were married under the laws of the land on 26 June 1956. As they made their way to the court that day, Julie cast her mind back to a year before, when the Congress of the People had taken place in Kliptown, near South Western Townships, on 25 and 26 June. It was there that the Freedom Charter had been adopted, with its vision of a free and fair country for all, where the people would govern and share in its wealth. On another 26 June, in 1952, the Defiance Campaign's Day of Defiance had taken place on the Witwatersrand, in the eastern Cape and Natal. The conjunction of these anniversaries with her court wedding pleased Julie, and reminded her of erstwhile colleagues and friends at the institute.

Optimistically, Giddy and Julie had not reserved a slot at the Pretoria Magistrate's Court, reckoning it would not be particularly busy on a Tuesday morning. They were disappointed when they were turned away and advised to book, but King Lam Pon, one of Giddy's two best men, suggested they drive to Brits and try their luck there. No, the magistrate was not in, the clerk of the Brits Magistrate's Court told them when they arrived 45 minutes later. However, he was available: he had just gone down to the market to buy some fruit. Summoned back to court, the magistrate proved obliging. A portly man, he eased into his office with his purchases of oranges and *naartjies*, calling to the bridal party to follow him. After carefully arranging the fruit on a bookcase, he smiled at the couple and proceeded to conduct the simple ceremony with considerable affability, struggling only at the moment when he read out 'Kit Accone, born Fok Chong Kit', but recovering swiftly. King Lam and his fellow best man, Johnny Jackson, acted as witnesses. Julie had not requested a bridesmaid, and suddenly she felt this momentous event had passed too prosaically. A cheering surprise awaited her, though, because King Lam had telephoned his family, who lived in Brits, and the wedding party found itself at their home, contemplating a butter cream cake decorated with a red bow, and fine Chinese tea.

The civil ceremony and legal formalities over, Giddy and Julie devoted themselves to the minutiae and paraphernalia of the real big day. In Chinese weddings, the boy's side pays for everything but while she had given her son a diamond, Ah Hing was not going to finance the wedding. Kit's position was difficult, as he drew no salary from the shop; he had bought the MG with money from catering and other moonlighting jobs he undertook. There was nothing for it, determined Kit: he would give up a love of his life, the TD roadster, for the love of his life, Julie. The pity of selling his powder-blue joy, however, was that it realised only £600. With the wedding to finance, as well as alterations to the living quarters behind the shop to make a flatlet for him and Julie, there would be only a few pennies left. Prudently heeding that situation, Giddy and Julie settled on 90 guests at the wedding dinner. It was a small affair by the standards of the time, but it also set a precedent for more modest celebrations. As Giddy said, 'If we can break the tradition of *seng* Fok not intermarrying, we can break this one too.'

Early on the day of the wedding, Sunday 22 July, Giddy's best men came down from Pretoria to 27A Perth Road to collect all Julie's possessions, the first step in the rituals. Ah Leong had wrapped her boxes and suitcases, bags and bric-a-brac in red paper, as custom ordained. In the morning light streaming on to the porch, the bright red pile seemed alive, and was a reviving contrast to the pale straw colours, typical of the Highveld winter, that lay without.

The next arrivals came in the wedding car, driven by the *wha que kong*, the role of honour that Giddy had asked his friend Tammy to discharge. Tammy had been experiencing an appalling run at the *mah-jong* table when Giddy had asked him, during a break between games, to be the driver. Almost immediately on accepting, Tammy's fortunes had changed and he had begun to win. With the *wha que kong* came the groom and *mooien bo*, the Apricot Woman. In the old days, parents of prospective couples retained the Apricot Woman to be matchmaker and go-between, negotiating the 'price' of the wedding and establishing what gifts were required by the family of the potential bride. If the match was agreed, she would school the bride in addressing her parents-in-law and correct ways of behaviour. After the wedding, the Apricot Woman would remain in the groom's house for three days, helping to introduce the bride to her new family and surroundings and also to ease her into the new and many duties of a daughter-in-law. In the case of Julie and Giddy, *mooien bo* was present more in a ceremonial than a practical sense.

'Here we are! Here we are!' called the Apricot Woman at the porch door of the Leong home. 'Joyous day! We've come to fetch the bride!'

It was customary at this point to deny entrance to the groom, who would have to give his best men *lysee*, red paper filled with cash, to be allowed in. Julie had decided against this, though, and so Giddy immediately followed *mooien bo* into the house. Now it was time for tea and the presentation of gifts to the bride's family. But where was the third car, bearing the large red lacquer boxes that contained the gifts, and the symbolic presents of red money packets, oranges, mandarins and biscuits? Giddy whispered hurriedly to King Lam, and then looked at Julie, palms held upwards.

'No matter, no matter,' said *mooien bo*. 'Let us wait a while. Doubtless they will be here shortly.'

In this, the Apricot Woman was not far wrong. Half an hour later, the third car drew up in the yard, somewhat the worse for having swerved to avoid hitting a donkey near Alexandra Township, and then running up against a lamppost. The red lacquer boxes and their contents were undamaged, but most of the containers of biscuits had flown out the open back window, to be snatched up by the children who had descended on the accident. 'Good, good, no harm in spreading largesse on such a day,' said the Apricot Woman before ushering everyone in to tea. Already, it was nearing noon and the formal proceedings had hardly begun. Julie reminded herself to be grateful that it was not, say, a January day, when the heat in Pretoria, to which they would soon be heading, could be baking and exhausting.

Tea and cakes were served on the porch, and the couple received *lysee* from the gathering. Julie and Giddy had decided to follow the more traditional tea ceremony at Ah Hing's house only, so the atmosphere in

Perth Road was more relaxed and informal, with the company seated around the old oak table carried in from the dining room.

Tea over, it was time for Julie to bid farewell to her parents, Mickey and her boyfriend Sidney, Aunt Lil and Uncle Ah Wha, and the house she had lived in for so much of her life. The previous day, she had looked out into Perth Road and been surprised at how many memories that had stirred. In the afternoon, she had wandered in the little garden, with its winter-bare fruit trees, and thought back on the childhood games played there. Now, she bowed three times to Ah Leong and Gertie, and then repeated the salutation to family members and relatives, generation by generation.

During tea, Ah Leong and Gertie had taken from the symbolic gifts about half the oranges and mandarins and a little money, and then parcelled up the rest to be returned to the groom's family, as dictated by custom. Ah Leong and Gertie also sent back more money, to add to the suit that Gertie had already bought Giddy.

In the yard, the best men's car was stacked with Julie's possessions, the gift car had been reloaded, and the wedding car was ready to carry the bridal couple and the *mooien bo* to the groom's house. Julie and Giddy stepped into the Packard, the car engines started and the little motorcade pulled away. The young couple turned around and looked out of the rear window, and returned the farewell waves of Gertie and Ah Leong.

Ninety minutes later, the cars turned right off Vermeulen Street and into Queen, drawing up outside the corrugated iron back gate to the small dwelling behind Ah Hing's shop. Before Julie crossed the threshold, strings of crackers were fired to clear the path and dispel devils and evil spirits.

Inside, at an altar, incense sticks were burning on either side of a photograph of Fok Yu Teem. Julie brought in with her a round lacquer tray with small teacups, a traditional gift from mother to daughter presented to her by Gertie, which she would use in serving tea to her in-laws. Ah Hing greeted Julie as Ah Chiu — Pearl — having already made it clear to Giddy that she refused to call his wife Hong Hgang, which smacked too much of someone with a will of her own. Braced for this, Julie nodded and thanked her mother-in-law. Apposite to the day, Ah Hing was dressed in a red *cheung saam*, the effect of which was augmented by deep red lipstick and a touch of rouge on the cheeks.

FIRE

While greetings were taking place, the Apricot Woman tied two red cloths into bags, one for the bride's *lysee*, the other for the groom's. Now Julie knelt on a cushion with the tea tray, teapot and cups in front of her, and facing Ah Hing, who was seated on a chair. Julie poured her mother-in-law a cup of tea. Ah Hing drank in a single delicate motion, and then slipped *lysee* from her left hand into the cup, which she put back on the tray. She was replaced by another relative, and the ritual continued, with successive occupants of the chair dropping red envelopes into the cup they had just drained.

Because Giddy had married before his older brother Yen – 'climbed over his head', the saying went – a pair of Yen's trousers was hung in the doorway of the living room, and whenever he passed beneath them, Giddy inclined his head. Passing often between lounge and kitchen, Giddy bowed a great deal as the day wore on.

At last, it was time for dinner, a nine-course meal catered by Ah Chan, the community's favourite chef. This repast was for the groom's side only; a succession of teas and dinners would follow in the days and weeks ahead, hosted by different sides of the extended families related now by marriage. Practice dictated that the bride serve tea to the guests, who in return gave *lysee* or gifts such as jade rings and bracelets. While Julie circulated with her tea tray, Giddy served brandy and whisky. In this, he parted with tradition once more. Custom called for the groom to drink in response to toasts in the young couple's honour and many was the intoxicated groom who honoured that. Ah Leong was himself expert at detaining the groom at his table, proposing more and more elaborate and complimentary toasts. Having no stomach or legs for liquor, Giddy roped in his redoubtable half-sister Wendy, the daughter from his father's marriage before Ah Hing, to do the drinking for him.

Well past midnight, Julie and Giddy retired to the bedroom and lounge that he had converted from the shop's back storerooms. The wedding bed had been made up by a respected elderly couple whose union had been very fruitful, yielding five sons and two daughters. Under the pillows, they had left talismans for fertility, including Chinese dates and dried fruits.

Early next morning, Julie was woken to her new world by the muezzin calling the faithful to prayer from the minaret of the mosque a short way

243

up Queen Street. It was a thrilling, ancient sound, and one that was to punctuate her days there. Often she would walk up the quiet lane and look up at the great bulbous green dome of the mosque that was so perfectly and beautifully offset by its slender white minarets. There were other connections too, more temporal, for Ah Hing's shop and living quarters were built on ground owned by the mosque, as was the adjacent De Witt photographic studio.

Many of the marriage rituals remained to be played out. The Apricot Woman stayed in Ah Hing's home for three days after the wedding, and on the third day accompanied Julie on the obligatory return visit to her parents' home, along with Giddy, Yen, Ah Hing and the best men. In custom, the visit provided the groom's family with the opportunity of returning brides who were not virgins. More happily, it was the moment at which the groom's family presented roast pork or a whole roast pig to the bride's family. Courteously, Ah Leong divided the pork and set aside a large piece for his new in-laws to take home with them.

Four days later, on the Sunday after the wedding dinner, Ah Hing hosted a tea and dinner for her new in-laws. The next Sunday Ah Leong reciprocated. For several Sundays thereafter it was the turn of close relatives on either side to give dinners. These were sequenced in order of generation, from oldest to youngest, and ran for three months of Sundays. Each of the lavish dinners was preceded by the host's age-old disclaimer, '*Dûy mmmm jüh, laah! Jun huy mo yeh sek*' – 'Please excuse me! There is really nothing to eat!'. It was only in early November that Julie and Giddy had a Sunday to themselves, and then they packed a wicker picnic basket, Thermos flasks of tea and coffee, and tartan blankets and set off for Muldersdrift. While savouring freedom from their obligations and their enlarged family, the newly-weds knew that further family matters beckoned. Mickey and Sid were to be married on 26 December in St Joseph's Catholic Church, Mayfair, Johannesburg. As Mickey and Giddy had got on well from the first, it was natural that Julie and Giddy be involved in helping with her wedding.

Gertie was somewhat shaken by both her girls going off to start new lives within months of each other. She had also initially put up some very old-fashioned resistance to Sidney, who was Moiyean, not Namsoon.

FIRE

'Jesus, Bug, what is wrong with the boy?' Ah Leong had demanded when Gertie brought this up. Long ago, Ah Leong had discussed the so-called Hakka people, the Moiyeanese, with his father, and equally distantly he had abandoned any prejudices about them.

'You know, Bug, that they don't treat their daughters very well,' replied Gertie firmly.

'These are new times, in a new country. We are all Chinese. Give the fellow a chance, don't blame him for how his people may behave.'

Gertie fell quiet and thereafter kept her own counsel. She hoped and prayed that all would be well, and when Sidney had proposed, welcomed him wholeheartedly into the family.

At six in the evening of 4 October 1957, a group of skygazers gathered on the corner of Vermeulen and Queen Streets. Giddy, Julie, Yen, Ah Hing and William, their Chinese shop assistant, alternated between consulting their watches and looking upwards. The sky was still light, the deep blue of night some way off yet, so Giddy was worried that they would not see the small object that was scheduled to pass over Pretoria at 6.03 p.m. He knew that it would return, but to miss this very first glimpse would be disappointing.

'There! There it is!' Giddy said as an orb, blinking light in its wake, came into view and moved steadily in an arc over the city.

'It's Sputnik! Folks, we've seen the start of the Space Age!' said Julie.

Mankind's first artificial earth satellite, named 'traveller' in Russian, had made its inaugural sweep over Pretoria. Speeding through space at 18 000 miles per hour, Sputnik orbited the planet every 95 minutes until, its mission more than accomplished, it fell to Earth exactly three months later, on 4 January 1958. By then, things at Queen Street had begun to fall to pieces too. The honeymoon period between Julie and Ah Hing was long over. Slowly, Ah Hing had begun demanding the powers of a traditional mother-in-law over Julie. She made the young woman report to her whenever she was going out, and when she returned. Julie was solely responsible for the cooking, but nothing she prepared was spared criticism, or a vicious hint. Early in the new year of 1958, Julie came back with a dress from the post-festive season sale at Garlick's, one of the city's department stores. Ah Hing complained about this unnecessary expense; why was Ah Chiu indulging herself so soon after Christmas, that Christian extravagance? That was the first salvo in a war that ran deep into the winter.

'Mom, we had a king-size argument,' Julie explained to Gertie as they sat in the flatlet some months later. Gertie and Ah Leong had come up to Pretoria, with Aunt Lil and Ah Wha, all summoned by Ah Hing, as were members from her side of the family. There was to be a confab about the situation between the women at Queen Street.

In the room that had seen dinners celebrating the marriage of Giddy and Julie, the families gathered in sombre mood. Ah Hing began with a long list of Julie's faults, on each of which she discoursed at length. The melodramatic peroration accused the young woman of making the entire household suffer. Satisfied, Ah Hing sat down and sipped her cold tea.

'There is nothing for it,' Julie responded, 'but for me to make sure that the household is able to resume its old and happier ways.' Ah Hing nodded with satisfaction. Julie continued, 'Therefore, I ask that my husband look for another place for us to live while, with the consent of my parents, I return to Westdene to stay. That is all I wish to say. Now, with your permission, I am going to pack my things and return to Johannesburg.'

The silence as Julie left the room was paralysing. For minutes, no one moved or spoke. At last, Giddy stood up and said, 'Well, I must go and help Julie to pack. Why doesn't everyone have some more tea?'

Gertie and Ah Leong looked across at Ah Hing. There was nothing any of them could do, but it was clear that Giddy's mother was furious: his open support for his wife against her was humiliating. As Gertie worried about the rift being unbridgeable, Julie appeared in the doorway, carrying a small suitcase and a vanity case. Relieved, the gathering began to break up, with unusually loud and hale farewells being exchanged. Only Ah Leong and Gertie spoke softly to Ah Hing, and Julie caught a snatch of their conversation, something about 'you know young people'.

Driving back in Ah Leong's Hillman station wagon, Julie let down her façade of calm. She wiped tears from her eyes and then loosened her long hair, which fell in black waves below her shoulders. 'I don't know where

FIRE

we'll find to live, Mom,' she said to Gertie, who was sharing the backseat.
'And then there is also the threat of the Group Areas zoning in Pretoria.'

On 6 June 1958, in *Government Gazettes Extraordinary*, new Group Areas
had been proclaimed in Pretoria, other parts of the Transvaal, and
Durban. The entire central area of Pretoria and most of the suburban
municipal area had been reserved for European ownership and occupation. Non-Europeans in the centre of the city and certain suburbs were
given a year to vacate their premises. Residents in Prinsloo, Boom and
Mitchell Streets were allowed what newspapers described as a three-year
period of grace before moving. The *Gazettes* also established the places
to which those evicted might move: Claudius, an area for Indians, west of
Voortrekkerhoogte, and another for Coloureds, at Derdepoort, east of the
capital. It was only Asiatic Bazaar, on the west side of Boom Street abut-
ting Marabastad, that remained relatively untouched. Only a small part of
this densely populated, polyglot area had been set aside for Europeans,
and Non-Europeans affected by the proclamation had been given seven
years to quit the area. The proclamations also swooped on the so-called
Native freehold areas of Lady Selborne and Claremont, northwest of the
city, stripping 1 000 property owners in the former, and 200 in the latter,
of their homes.

Reacting to the moves, the Institute of Race Relations issued a mem-
orandum noting that Europeans would 'gain solidly' at the expense of
others and concluding, 'Comment on the equity or otherwise of the
proclamation is superfluous.'

Among those hardest hit were the 7 300 Indians living and trading in
Prinsloo Street, popularly called the Indian Mile, a few blocks from Ah
Hing's shop. Here for years they had run fabric, clothes, haberdashery,
shoe and luggage shops. While the threat to their livelihood and way of
life was terrible, soon it became clear that the Queen Street mosque was
also imperilled. The proclamation meant literally that the mosque could
not be owned or occupied by Non-Europeans. Demolition seemed a
likely prospect, given the fate of a mosque in Kimberley the year before.
There, the City Council had expropriated the mosque after the Muslim
community had refused to sell it, as that would have been contrary to the
Koran. A Council offer of £2 000 in compensation had been rejected on

247

similar grounds, after which the civic authority had obtained a court order permitting it to raze the building.

Alerted to the problem by protests from Imam Razack of the Queen Street mosque, and other Muslim representatives, the chairman of the Group Areas Board, Mr de Vos Hugo, said that permits would be issued for ownership and occupation of mosques in European areas as long as they were used as places of worship. Julie had cut out and kept the report in *The Star*, since it affected Ah Hing's shop and home, and also because it contained a terrible howler.

Quoting the board chairman, the story ran:

But these permits will not allow them ownership and occupation indefinitely.
'There will come a time when the Minister of the Interior will have to cancel the permits,' said Mr de Vos Hugo.
The mosquitoes [sic] would have to be moved when Moslems themselves felt that it was no longer convenient to worship at mosques in White areas.
[*The Star*, 30 July 1958]

Giddy had commented that worshipping at Queen Street would inevitably be 'no longer convenient' since Indians were being moved eight miles away from the mosque. There were reasons for Giddy's vehemence, for they enjoyed good relations with worshippers at the mosque, who often stopped by Ah Hing's shop for coconut chocolate and a cooldrink after prayers.

The Muslim community refused to accept the permit system for mosques, arguing that this would make them public property and bring about a clash between Islamic and South African law. More profoundly, Imam Razack was quoted in the *Pretoria News* as saying, 'Mosques do not belong to the sphere of human domain. They can never be sold, inherited or owned by any individual or group of individuals, since they already belong to God.'

While the Queen Street mosque stayed, many of its worshippers did not. The declared Indian area, which came to be called Laudium, was peopled by Muslims and Hindus and grew out of the forbidding and barren veld, far from the happy and prosperous places of the city centre.

The Chinese feared that they would be next. While they numbered only about 650 in and around Pretoria, the Apartheid machine would surely not ignore them. Every few weeks, newspaper reports reminded the small community of the precariousness of their position. Ah Leong and Gertie, inveterate readers of the *Rand Daily Mail*, scanned the paper every morning. Julie, her research and archival instincts still sharp, kept her own press clippings on the Chinese. One morning, during her sojourn back in Westdene, she and her parents were horrified by a small item in the *Mail*. It read:

Offence with Chinese girl alleged

In terms of the latest legislation, Chinese people are Coloured and must therefore be regarded as non-Europeans, the prosecutor submitted in a case before Mr H.J. Hardwick in the Johannesburg Magistrate's Court yesterday.

Appearing before the court charged with contravening the Immorality Act by having relations with an 18-year-old Chinese girl was Paul Stephanus Venter, 31, a railway clerk employed at Tooronga station.

Mixes with Whites

In previous evidence the Chinese girl said that she considered herself a European. She had mixed socially with Europeans as well as Chinese people in the past. Her parents are Chinese.

She admitted having made advances to Venter.

Giving evidence yesterday, Venter said that the girl came into the station ticket office. She begged him to have relations with her.

They went into the parcels office, but they only kissed. The girl was in the building all afternoon, he said.

[*Rand Daily Mail*, 3 July 1958]

'It is very sad that this young girl has to defend herself by saying she regards herself as European,' said Ah Leong. 'It's not right that you have to deny what you should be proud of being, because of the perverted laws of the land.'

Gertie thought for a moment of Cornelia and her brothers and sisters, and was about to remark that perhaps they had been correct in leaving, but she thought better of it. Things were bad enough without opening old wounds. When Julie and Giddy set out the following week to find a suitable home, they felt burdened by the story of the young girl and her railway clerk lover, and the country's other onerous laws.

None of the places they first looked at was suitable. After half a dozen blanks, an unwelcome mantra insinuated itself in Julie's mind: 'From the frying pan into the fire/ Better the devil you know/ From the frying pan into the fire/ Better the devil you know.' Then Mrs Jackson told them of a small house in Asiatic Bazaar. Why settle somewhere from which they would almost certainly be moved, asked Julie. Giddy felt that the seven-year 'grace period' in the area meant that they would have more than enough time to seek alternatives. The house was in what was popularly referred to as the Parktown of Asiatic Bazaar, so called because it consist-ed of newer buildings, made of brick. It suited their needs exactly, but for one factor: the key money. Two months' rent was required in advance, in addition to the first month's rent, a sum that they could not afford. Just as Julie began to feel defeated, another possibility presented itself. A bache-lor acquaintance of Giddy's had secured tenancy of a semi-detached house at 151A Third Street in the Bazaar, which he offered to the young couple because their need was greater. It was in good condition, with par-quet floors and copper piping in the kitchen and bathroom. Perhaps best of all, no key money was required by the Noors, the Ismaili landlords who lived in the larger semi, number 151.

Julie and Giddy moved from the Queen Street flatlet to Asiatic Bazaar in the early spring of 1958. A fortnight before, on 24 August, National Party Prime Minister J.G. Strijdom had died in office, to be succeeded on 2 September by the Minister of Native Affairs, Dr Hendrik Frensch Verwoerd. The man who had destroyed Sophiatown was in charge of the Union of South Africa.

FOUR
South Africa, circa 1958 to 1969

Asiatic Bazaar was something of a homecoming for Giddy. As a youngster, he had spent many hours in its cinemas and cycle shops and he looked forward to sharing these old haunts with Julie. Their semi was off the great trunk road of Boom Street, in Third Street. Boom ran from the zoo's easternmost border to Von Wielligh Street in Pretoria West, and branching off it was one of Verwoerd's 'black spots': the township of Marabastad, with its subdivisions of Asiatic Bazaar and Cape Location. Indians, Chinese, Coloureds and Blacks lived in this compact area, which had been proclaimed in 1888 and named after a local chief, and was a mere four blocks from Church Square, the city's centre. As close was the house of the Boer patriarch, Paul Kruger, three blocks east of the square.

The smaller streets that led off Boom were not tarred. On dry summer days red dust would filter into the shops and houses, coat people's clothing and settle in a russet film on their hair. When the Transvaal summer thunderstorms broke, and lightning serrated the air, the roads would churn to chocolate brown, detaining pedestrians by sucking off their shoes and bogging down the cars of unwary drivers. In winter the dust was worse, especially when the wind swirled almost daily and turned everything masala, cinnamon and paprika. Spring, when Julie and Giddy moved in, was the best season. The Noors welcomed them with a dish of curried fish, and Julie and Giddy began the task of gleaning more information about their neighbours, as well as the names of their five sons and eight daughters. They learnt that the Noors belonged to the Ismaili Khoja branch of Islam, which had Aga Khan IV as its Imam. The forty-ninth leader of the Ismailis, the Aga Khan was descended from the line that began with Ali and his wife Fatima, daughter of Muhammad the prophet.

On that first night, Julie looked from her front door through the semi's tall wire fence, with its climbing strands of golden shower that would be ablaze with orange flowers in late summer and early winter, and across to the large open stand used as a terminus by the Motlana bus company. Life was noisier here, filled with people and motion. The behind-the-shop seclusion of Queen Street seemed a world away, and with it the exhausting tension of the relationship with her mother-in-law. Invigorated by the change, Julie and Giddy set about meeting their neighbours and exploring the district.

In the house next door lived a Chinese family whose patriarch, Kwan Kho, was called *Makulu Kop*, Big Head, by the locals. A fat man, his belly brushed against the steering wheel when he sat in his car, so he was given to placing a handkerchief on his stomach to prevent the wheel from working a mark on to his shirt.

Directly across the road was the football-crazy Moosa family. Poppy Moosa and his sons were the originators of Sundowns football team, and as notable was the fact that his two daughters and all but one of the boys were teachers at Indian schools in Johannesburg and Pretoria. As a commissioner of oaths, Poppy did much legal work in the community.

Also on that side of the road were the fishmonger Cherry and his family, who each Friday would go round to Chinese and Catholic households to let them know of special fish in stock. Nearby lived Sherine, the second oldest of the Noor girls, and her husband Ramtula, who owned the A.B.C., the African Baking Company bakery, and the atchar factory. At the corner of Third and Boom were shops that stocked the latest American fashions, from hats to shoes, shirts to neckties, as well as women's and children's clothing.

On Saturdays, Boom Street thronged with shoppers. Customers were locals as well as visitors, many of whom came in from Lady Selborne and outlying areas to buy staple foods, fabrics, and fruits and vegetables. Because white shops in the city discouraged black patrons, the Indian and Chinese businesses in Asiatic Bazaar and Marabastad were a boon, and cheaper to boot. Buyers could also bargain with sellers, and invariably there was a *pasella* thrown in as a gratuity to the customer. That bonus was in contrast to the practice of city department stores such as Uniewinkels, where Julie had been outraged and saddened to witness a black woman not being allowed to try on a dress she was interested in buying. 'You must take it like that,' barked the attendant, finishing: 'You people cannot just sample what you want.' It was the same retailer who refused to sell embroidery silks and wools to Julie, who was at the time taking embroidery lessons with a Miss Bam, on the grounds that the embroidery teacher was English.

In the Saturday crowd, amid the so-called Non-Europeans, the occasional white face was visible, drawn by the reputation of the area for inexpensive items such as material, ribbon, cottons, beads, sequins, shirts, skirts and ready-made dresses. These passers-by stopped at the cycle shops too, where gramophones, gramophone needles and records were sold, as well as the more rudimentary bicycling essentials that gave these establishments their generic name. From these shops constant waves of sound emerged, from *maskanda* to jazz, gospel to swing, penny whistle to traditional; from Kalla's came the fullest sounds of all.

Everywhere on the pavements outside businesses, black women sold crocheted woollen caps in bright colours, toasted and boiled mealies, and roasted and boiled peanuts. Corner cafés offered hot and crispy fish and chips, *samoosas* oozing finely-ground meats and spiciness, and bottles of Shillings Guava Dew and Coca-Cola, hoisted from water refrigerators and dripping icy rivulets of water on the chin as they were quaffed.

King of all the commercial ventures in the area, however, was Makuloo Hopaan. Its name derived from *makulu*, for big, and *hoppaan*, the Chinese ginger beer-type drink that was brewed and sometimes sold as a substitute for alcohol. Owned by the Wing Sun family, Makuloo Hopaan had begun in Marabastad, and then opened up in Mamelodi, Prinsloo Street and Garankuwa. King Biu ran the parent branch in Marabastad, and ensured that it was an emporium catering to every possible customer request. In one section, mealie meal, sugar and tea were complemented by *mopane* worms; in another, bolts of fine cloth nestled alongside the strong material in dark blue and black that older African women used to make work clothes and dresses. Such was the durability of Makuloo Hopaan's heavy fabric that it was said to be guaranteed to outlive the wearer. On their first visit, Giddy revelled in showing Julie the range of goods: cottons, material, wools, knitting needles, crochet hooks, beads, bangles, bracelets, earrings, necklaces, rings, watches, ploughing implements, hoes, spanners, hammers, nails, ladders, string, ribbon, buttons, coal stoves, Primus stoves, *knobkerries*, bicycles, spare wheels, fishing rods and tackle, boots, shoes, paint, brushes, brooms, gramophone needles, dark glasses – and those were the wares in just a third of the shop!

Although Giddy did not need to argue the establishment's virtues, he was fond of recounting his youthful bet about it with Yen. The two had been working on a model aeroplane when they ran short of the specialised glue on a Sunday evening. Nothing to be done but wait for Monday, said Yen. No, I'll bet Makuloo Hopaan will have it, said Giddy. It did, and the model was finished that night.

What sealed Makuloo Hopaan's reputation was its attitude to customers. Consistency was King Biu's watchword, and almost to illustrate that, for years he wore the same tough leather apron. His customers instinctively trusted this hard-working man, and appreciated that they could deal in their mother tongues with his staff, many of whom were first-language speakers of Zulu, Sotho, Ndebele and Tswana.

Near Makuloo Hopaan was the Mariamman temple, where the local Hindus worshipped. Many storeys high, the temple had a vertiginous look, pronounced by each higher level being narrower than the last. The curved roofing near its summit contrasted pleasingly with the rectangular blocks of its façade, the intricate architecture of which was decorated by thousands of delicate symbols, each seemingly a pattern of its own, and shaded in different colours and hues.

On the other side of Boom Street was the Ismaili mosque, a simple white building. In late afternoon, each Ismaili family in the area sent a plate of food to the imam, who made this community generosity available to poor people and beggars in the area. Julie learnt that families could not begin their dinner until they had discharged this daily deed.

Across Boom Street from the mosque was Cape Location, so named because it housed Coloured people. Here the residents had turned tin shacks into homes of quaint but fierce individuality. On their Sunday morning strolls, Julie and Giddy would watch trainee ministers and young theological students from the Dutch Reformed Church conducting outdoor services here for the local children. When those ended, the sweeping assurances of religion were made more palatable by the distribution of sweets to the young churchgoers. Diverted though they were by the service, the primary reason that Giddy and Julie passed this way was Ah Chan, the Chinese chef. A little way past Cape Location brought them to his home, which doubled as a delicatessen, eating-house and take-away.

Ah Chan was purveyor to the community of Chinese ingredients and vegetables, chickens and ducks, and Cantonese food. On Sunday mornings a crowd would gather on the front porch of his house, waiting for the first batches of *dim sum* – 'touch the heart', or sweethearts – the famous Cantonese appetisers. Voices and footsteps from within would draw nearer, and then Ah Chan would be in the doorway, carrying a tray of shrimp dumplings in their translucent pouches made from wheat flour, boiling water and salad oil. His family would follow, bearing Chinese steamed buns, crammed with either sweet pork, chicken or black bean paste, spring rolls and *wun tun*. Whether fried, filled with chicken, or served as Velvet Chicken Broth *Wun Tun*, the *wun tun* were parcels of delight that lived up to, and looked like, their name, 'cloud swallows'. Ah Leong, a very fine chef, had told Julie and Giddy that the wrapped *wun tun* should resemble either wispy, fleecy clouds, or a Chinese imperial goldfish with gracefully flowing fins. After the first trays of food, came yet others: roast pork, just out of the Chinese clay oven; green peppers stuffed with crumbled fish that had been dipped in batter and fried until crisp; honey-sweet pork fillet; liver sausages, a Giddy favourite; *buk gem ghuy*, plain boiled chicken rubbed with oil. There was a story that when Queen Elizabeth II visited Hong Kong, it was this very chicken dish that she had singled out, and which subsequently became known there as Princess Chicken.

The younger Chinese had a preference for *mien*, Chinese noodles, served in various ways. There was *chow mien*, stir-fried noodles topped with either vegetables, pork or beef. *Wun tun mien* was a soup of *mien* and *wun tun*, sprinkled with diced scallions. On request only was *wor mien*, a huge steaming bowl of noodles that many chose to eat at Ah Chan's although it could be taken away if one brought one's own container. Giddy loved *wor mien* while Julie favoured rice noodles, a flat *mien* very difficult to prepare because of its tendency to stick on the wok, topped with either beef or chicken and seasoned with sesame seeds.

After such brunches, Giddy and Julie walked home either via the Mariamman temple or the Royal, one of the three bioscopes in the area, and something of a bughouse. Nonetheless, like its somewhat smarter Boom Street fellows the Orient and the Empire, the Royal got the latest films quickly. Giddy and Julie were fortunate to have three movie houses so nearby, because those in the White parts of the city did not allow Chinese in. Double features were standard in Marabastad, with an older film playing first and a new feature concluding the programme. Though the bioscopes were closed on Sundays, they were packed on Thursdays, Fridays and Saturdays. Julie and Giddy had a standing order for their seats every Thursday and would walk down to the cinemas in the early evening. When they were rushed, they would hop on the small moped that Giddy used to commute to the shop, and race down Boom Street, Julie riding side-saddle on the pillion and hanging on tightly to Giddy. Unlike Mickey, Julie was not a good pillion rider, and the times the moped was chased by dogs were the worst: then she would squeeze Giddy so tightly that by the time they reached their destination, he would say he felt as if his kidneys had been forced up into his chest. 'Julie, your grip is tighter than the kidney belt I used to wear when I rode the Vincent Black Shadow,' he would quip.

If they missed a film, there was always the possibility of catching it at one of the many drive-ins around Pretoria. North to Wonderboom, east to Menlo Park and Lynnwood and south-west to Zwartkops, went Giddy and Julie. Sometimes they even drove to the Fox drive-in near Alexandra Township, on the main road between Pretoria and Johannesburg and almost two-thirds of the way to Westdene. Often the Fox seemed to have the best films, and if a Western was showing there was no stopping Giddy. The only drive-in to which they did not go was Fountains, nestled in the green valley near Klapperkop just outside Pretoria. The city council had refused an application by the owners of Fountains, Kontinentale Films Ltd., to admit Chinese. Fountains was on ground leased from the municipality and not privately owned, and so the council argued that it would be contravening the Group Areas Act were it to allow Chinese in. About

a year after Julie and Giddy had settled into life in Asiatic Bazaar, the
council voted by twelve to six to allow Chinese at Fountains drive-in,
provided they were accommodated in a segregated area set aside for
them. Julie and Giddy imposed their own ban on Fountains, refusing to
countenance going there under such conditions.

To the young couple, this pinprick was added to others that worried
them more. There was the 'own area' threat that still hung over the community in Pretoria. Educational opportunities seemed further endangered
when the principal of Longwood House, a mixed private boarding school
in Meyerton, was ordered in September 1958 to 'get rid of' his sixteen
Chinese pupils at the end of the second of the school's three terms for the
year. Founded in 1917, Longwood drew pupils from Portuguese East
Africa, the Federation of Rhodesia and Nyasaland, and all parts of the
Union. They came because of its unusually wide-ranging curriculum,
small classes not exceeding 20 pupils, a complement of twelve teachers
for 170 pupils, and excellent results, most recently the 100 percent pass
rate in the Junior Certificate examinations of 1957. Its principal,
E.G.L. Cloete, had explained to the Transvaal Education Department that
Chinese pupils had been enrolled before the June 1957 promulgation
excluding them from European schools and had since been admitted in
ignorance of the ban. Parents of white children at the school were
angered, and gave Chinese pupils and Cloete their support. Giddy and
Julie were cheered a bit by the report in the *Sunday Times* of 28 September
1958, which quoted a letter from 'the parents of one European boy':

*When we first heard about your school we were thrilled at the thought that our
child was going to live and work with children of another race, and would thus come
to realise that underneath the skin there is no real difference in human beings.*
Please accept our sincere sympathy and regret.

Another parent had written:

*Please convey to the parents of the Chinese children at Longwood House my pro-
found regret that the Transvaal Education Department has decided on this drastic step.
I am sorry and dismayed and agree that the school will be poorer for this loss.*

A reprieve was granted when it was pointed out that the children would have no other schools to go to so late in the year, but the authorities held firm: the Chinese would not be allowed to return next year. But in mid-January of 1959, the prohibition was lifted.

'Hey, Julie, listen to this,' called Giddy, waving a copy of the *Sunday Times*. 'Mr Cloete says, "There was general rejoicing when it became known that the Department had lifted the ban and these friends would be reunited." So you see, things can work out sometimes.'

'Well, maybe,' replied Julie. 'But what kind of country will these children inherit when they grow up? Look at things today. We can't own houses anywhere. Our children need permits to attend private schools. We can't stay in hotels because of the Liquor Act. We can't have a drink in hotel bars or lounges, though "foreign Chinese" can. We still need permits to buy liquor from bottle stores. We still have to obtain trading permits. Who knows when we will have own areas imposed on us? When none of those apply, things may be a bit better.'

As the year progressed, Julie and Giddy spoke about whether to leave South Africa. A few pioneers from the community had gone to Portugal and some others were exploring British Columbia. A cousin of Giddy's had married an Englishman, and for a while 151A Third Street was filled with talk of England. Nigel, one of Giddy's fellow motoring enthusiasts, was English, and did his best to discourage the Accones from such speculation.

'It's the old country in more ways than one,' Nigel said, 'and I'd not swop the sunshine here for a lifetime's supply there of the pound seats at the yearly pantomime.'

Nigel it was who had asked whether their move to Boom Street meant that the money would be rolling in soon, and who chortled when Giddy had explained that *boom* meant tree in Afrikaans.

By early June, all thoughts of emigrating ceased. Julie was pregnant, and the baby was expected in late February 1960.

★

It had been a family Christmas camping trip, an extended version of the picnics of the war days. Ah Leong, Gertie, Ah Wha, Lil, Giddy, Julie,

FIRE

Sidney and Mickey had spent Christmas and Boxing Day together, the latter having the added significance of being Sidney and Mickey's third wedding anniversary. On the afternoon of the 26th, the family returned to their respective homes, to reconvene at Perth Road for dinner. Giddy and Julie drove back to Asiatic Bazaar, washed and changed, and then set out for Jo'burg. They were in the nine-seater Ford station wagon that took them on regular weekend trips up to Lourenço Marques. In LM, as everyone called the city, they would visit Galleria Orientale and its punctilious owner, Norman G. Man, and take delivery of goods destined for the gift shop Giddy was growing from his mother's old business. Jo'burg bound now, the Ford passed the landmark of the old Ndebele hut and eased left into a gentle curve. From out of the shadows cast by tall bluegums to the left of the road, a taxi appeared. It was driving on the wrong side, coming straight at them. Giddy wrenched the wheel to the right, changing into the oncoming lane that luckily was empty. The taxi seemed about to flash past but then twitched and veered towards them, crashing into the passenger side of the station wagon. Julie felt the shock as metal mangled metal, and heard its terrible accompaniment of grinding and tearing and screeching. The Ford began to roll over on to its left side, but even as it did so, Giddy had a glimpse in the rear view mirror and saw that the taxi was accelerating away from them round the bend.

Afterwards, it was reckoned that the station wagon rolled six times, from the six sets of red marks that Julie's lips had left on its ceiling. When the car came to rest, she was flung through the opening where the front windscreen had been, and landed some four or five feet from the car. Giddy crawled out through the passenger window, dazed and fearing the worst. He rushed to Julie, noticing that a number of cars had stopped on the other side of the road, and that people were coming over. Julie was conscious, but in great pain. Her first thoughts had been for their child, and her first words to Giddy were, 'The baby, the baby.' Giddy held Julie, desperate with fear for both his wife and his unborn child.

Looking up, Giddy saw an Indian man and woman huddled round him and Julie. 'Can you help me to get my wife to a hospital?' he asked them.

'Of course we can,' said the man.

'Thank you,' Giddy said.

'I am sorry that your wife will have to lie across the laps of our children,' said the woman. 'You see, we are on the way to my cousin's wedding, so the whole family is in the car.'

Gingerly, Giddy and the man lifted Julie off the tarmac and carried her slowly and gently to the other car. They eased her in the back door, and rested her on the children's legs. Two little boys and a girl stared down, wide-eyed, at Julie. O God, Julie prayed, please let my child live to be at least as old as these children. The car started and began its journey to Pretoria and the Marifont Maternity Hospital, which was where the Accones had booked the delivery.

Giddy first phoned Dr Danzig, their gynaecologist, and then made the more difficult call, to Perth Road. Gertie was calm, and assured Giddy that she and the rest of the family would be in Pretoria as soon as possible. At the hospital, it was established that Julie had a broken pelvis. Immobility and rest were the only cures, so Giddy arranged for her to remain there until she was able to go down to Jo'burg to be with Gertie in the fortnight immediately preceding the birth. Concern had focused early on the unborn child, but only time could answer whether it had been injured and if so, how severely. Shortly before the baby was due, Dr Danzig insisted on an X-ray to determine how it was lying in the womb, despite Julie's unease about the effects of electromagnetic rays. She thought of citing the Chinese superstition that photographs should not be taken during pregnancy because they will harm the spirit of the foetus, but dismissed recourse to beliefs that she did not share. When the X-ray was developed it showed a breech birth was in the offing, one more hurdle to the arrival of the family's first grandchild, whose gender was not known.

At 6.50 a.m. on 28 February 1960, Julie gave birth to a son, Fok Boon Nung. In his case the Mongol spot, the bluish mark on the buttocks characteristic of newborn Chinese babies, was less apparent because of bruises on his body, sustained in the accident. Curiously, wherever Julie had been worst bruised, the infant bore analogous sympathetic discolourations. But he was whole, and according to initial examinations by the doctors, unimpaired in his faculties. Julie sent silent gratitude to the powers that had protected her child, and relaxed for the first time since Boxing Day two months before. The dry, hot summer pressed against the windows of her room, and the sheets that had been crisp and cool a while before were now rumpled and sticky. Undeterred by her heat itch, Julie contemplated her good fortune, and that of her son. An old story that Ah Leong had told her came suddenly to mind, bringing fleeting sadness before augmenting her happiness. A peasant's wife in the village gave birth to a son in the early hours of the morning. At roughly the same time a rich man's wife gave birth to a girl. The wealthy parents were disappointed: they had desired a boy to carry the name of the father and of the clan. What did this daughter mean? She was worth nothing, as upon her marriage day she would be gone and of no use to the family. As dawn was breaking, the rich man stole down to the peasants' hovel and offered them much money if they would exchange their son for his daughter. They accepted. Ah Leong always remembered the terrible change of fortune that made a poor girl of a rich girl, and it helped him treasure his daughters rather than long for sons to carry on his line. Well, Julie thought, now there is a grandson who, while not bearing the Leong name, will in some way nevertheless perpetuate it.

One week after Ah Nung's birth, Julie returned home to Third Street. Soon after, she went to Queen Street to present Ah Nung to her mother-in-law, who had stayed away from the maternity home because of the ongoing feud between the two women. That was put aside for now, and Ah Hing undertook to arrange Ah Nung's *mon yute*, the one-month-old party, which traditionally fell to the father's parents to host.

As soon as Julie returned home, Gertie came down from Jo'burg to help with the baby. She had been unwell for some time, struggling to recover from a thyroid operation, but her grandson seemed to give her new purpose and energy. In the first weeks, Julie was supported by Gertie, as well as Aunt Lil and Mickey. Without them, she would never have managed, because she was still not that sure on her feet, as well as being faced with the unfamiliar demands of motherhood, compounded by the many well-wishers who came to visit. Among those were the Noors, able at last to see Ah Nung. They had been turned away from the maternity home by one of the sisters, an echo of their failed attempt to visit Julie immediately after the accident. Beaming at Julie and Ah Nung, Mr Noor turned it all into a satire of Apartheid.

'You know, I just can't get it right,' he chuckled. 'I'm the wrong colour to visit a wrinkly pink newborn boy that the authorities would classify Non-European and the Nat newspapers would say is one of the Yellow Peril. But then when I obey the rules and sit in the Non-European section of the general hospital, waiting to visit my sick old uncle, a nurse comes over and tells me, "You should be sitting in the Europeans Only side, not with the *kaffirs* and *coolies*." She's been fooled by that Ismaili complexion: what a curse to be fair! I tell her that I am, in fact, a *coolie*. What a country!'

In accordance with traditional practice, which sought to fool any evil spirits, the *mon yute* was planned for a little before a month had passed. Had the infant been a girl, the celebration would have taken place a few days after the month was up. Ah Hing set the date for Sunday 27 March, but on the Monday preceding the *mon yute*, South Africa was in the world news and Julie and Giddy took up once more the vexing subject of emigration.

Pan-Africanist Congress leader Robert Sobukwe had named 21 March 1960 as the day for the PAC to begin 'a sustained, disciplined, non-violent campaign' against the Pass. To be carried at all times by all Africans (the classification for blacks), the Pass documented the bearer's life history and rights of movement and contained the holder's fingerprints, an implication of criminality since the recording of fingerprints had hitherto been reserved for criminal suspects. Failure to produce a Pass when asked to do so by a policeman was a punishable offence. Aggravating the humiliation, whites were not subject to any similar such strictures. As Minister of Native Affairs, Verwoerd had in 1952 enlarged the Pass to a 96-page Reference Book in standard-issue covers of green or brown. Perversely, this super-Pass had been introduced by legislation that was a cunning misnomer: the Abolition of Passes Act. It was against the discrimination of the Reference Book, still popularly called the Pass, that the PAC devised a campaign of non-carrying of Passes. The idea was that prisons would quickly be filled with transgressors, bringing the country to a standstill and leading to the abolition of the Pass.

On 21 March, groups of protesters formed at Evaton, Boipatong and Bophelong, and Sharpeville. Gathered outside the local police station, the Evaton march numbered about 20 000, and was dispersed by low-flying jets that buzzed the crowd. The much smaller gathering of 4 000 from Boipatong and Bophelong made for the Vanderbijlpark police station, only to be baton-charged and broken up, leaving one marcher dead. Between 3 000 and 5 000 people converged on the Sharpeville police station. They were undeterred by the jets that had quelled the Evaton protest, and even threw their hats into the air when the planes flew low over them. But when a section of the wire fence surrounding the station gave way, and a policeman was pushed over, the police opened fire. After the shooting ceased, 69 people lay dead and 180 injured. The word Sharpeville reverberated around the world.

Giddy and Julie were shocked, and not even the *mon yute* could divert them from anguished debates about the country. But as Sunday approached, they managed to set aside ruminating on the future and focused on their son. On the morning of the *mon yute*, Ah Nung's hair was snipped by a bachelor who was considered to have good fortune. Giddy then went down to Jo'burg to fetch from Ah Leong and Gertie gifts symbolising luck, long life and happiness. These included a cock, a hen, a number of chicks, leafed stalks of fresh sugar cane and Chinese cabbages with their roots intact. The chicks signified that Ah Nung and his family would have food always while the sugar cane was used ritually when Giddy re-entered the house, dragging the stalks behind him.

In the evening came the nine-course *mon yute* dinner at Ah Hing's. Long Life Noodles featured, as did mushrooms, but the most important dish was pork trotters, flavoured sweet, sour and gingery, a dish customarily served to restore the new mother's strength. During dinner, Julie took Ah Nung around the room so that everyone could see him. Friends and relatives were very generous, giving either *lysee* or shawls, clothing and blankets. Some of the *lysee* held not money but beautiful jewellery such as a jade bangle inlaid with gold leaf, a gold bracelet and a gold tie pin.

Before the guests departed, packets containing six red eggs and pickled ginger were handed out. The eggs had been hard boiled and then dyed with food colouring, and stood broadly for fertility, and specifically for the prospects of the new parents having another child within the next year.

'I'm not sure that I'd want a second baby so soon,' Julie said to Giddy as they drove home to Third Street.

'We might not be able to afford another, either,' he replied. 'Still, things are looking up at the shop. Mom has said that I'll get it one day, so now I'm going to throw everything into it.'

FIVE

South Africa, 1960 to 1969

hree days after the *mon yute*, as Giddy began to implement new ideas
for the shop, another regime was taking hold in the world beyond.
On 30 March, the Government declared a State of Emergency, detained
more than 20 000 people and clamped down on Press freedom. Giddy
determined just to get on with his life and over the next month, new
shelves were installed and the windows of 275 Vermeulen Street, corner
of Queen, were decorated with beautiful paper and filled with striking
displays of Chinese goods. There were ivory chess sets, bamboo jewellery,
jade ornaments, fans, carved kists and crockery. Giddy commissioned
other exclusive gifts too. Badra, an Ismaili from Arusha in Tanganyika,
executed filigree inlays in small wooden jewellery boxes that he carved
himself. He also produced snug holders for carving knives, worked from
blocks of wood that were hollowed out on both sides to accommodate
their sharp contents. An elderly Xhosa man, Tshawe, decorated petite
oval-shaped wooden brooches with African scenes. Accone's, the gift
shop, had arrived.

During the next few years, while Julie and Giddy watched Ah Nung
and Accone's grow, they were almost as absorbed by national political
events and a series of crises that befell the Chinese community. Julie had
a hard time keeping her newspaper clippings up to date, so swiftly did one
matter follow another.

On 5 October 1960, a referendum was held to determine whether the
Union of South Africa should become a republic, and thus break away
from the Commonwealth. Only Whites were eligible to take part, and of
those who did, 52 percent cast Yes votes. The country formally became a
republic on 31 May the following year, realising Afrikaner Nationalism's
long-held ideal of breaking the shackles of British imperialism. But just

seven weeks before, on 9 April 1961, an attempt had been made on Verwoerd's life at the Rand Easter Show, when he survived two shots in the face.

In August 1961 an anomaly in the Liquor Act was removed, allowing 'local' Chinese to be served in hotel bars and lounges, rights previously extended to 'foreign' Chinese. Three months later began what was to be a long-running conflict over the relative treatment of Chinese and Japanese in the new republic. A fivefold increase in trade between Japan and South Africa in the preceding three years had led to a warming of Pretoria's feelings towards Tokyo, and full ambassadorial relations were being set up. The result was that Japanese were accorded full White status: they were allowed to buy houses and own land, use all White amenities, including public transport, and drink at, as well as stay in, White hotels. From Taipei, the nationalist Chinese government of Chiang Kai-shek rumbled. By default, Formosa had become the representative of local Chinese interests, as Pretoria refused to have any dealings with Mao Tse-tung's Communist government. Bob Connolly captured this new Apartheid division of Chinese and Japanese in a cartoon entitled *Great Wall of S.A. China*, published in the *Rand Daily Mail* on 28 November 1961. It showed a lone Japanese man leaning against one side of what resembled the Great Wall of China, in an area marked 'White', while dozens from South Africa's Chinese community gathered on the other side, marked 'Non-White', and looked up at the ramparts, on which stood Senator Johannes de Klerk, the Minister of the Interior, Education, Arts and Science.

The passage of Japanese visitors and residents was not to be all smooth, however. While their White status meant that Japanese could have sexual relations with Whites, they would fall foul of the Immorality Act if, for instance, they associated with Chinese, Coloureds, Indians or Africans. The maze of who was Non-European had become ever more complex, with sub-division in 1959, apart from the African category, into seven groups: Cape Coloured, Malay, Griqua, Chinese, Indian, 'Other Asiatic group' and 'Other Coloured group'. 'Other Asiatics' included anyone from any territory in Asia other than China, India or Pakistan, while 'Other Coloured' referred to persons 'whose race cannot be defined under the other six non-European groups and who are not White or African'. Presumably, though they could hardly be called European, the now 'White' Japanese no longer qualified as 'Other Asiatics'. Related to the National Party's mania for classifying and categorising, but as an aside to the Sino-Japanese situation, Julie noticed that the University of South Africa had set aside a special room for Chinese sitting the Joint Matriculation Board examinations. Her face wry, she nevertheless savoured the way that the *Rand Daily Mail* report put it on 7 December 1961: 'The University of South Africa has gone one step further than any race classification board – it has classed the Chinese as neither White nor non-White.' When would the limbo of the Chinese end, Julie asked herself.

Early in 1962, the Japanese began to explore their newly won status. They asked municipal swimming pool superintendents in Johannesburg for admission, but were told that permission would have to be granted by higher authorities. Chinese followed suit, stung by this latest discrepancy, and bearing in mind the history of unequal treatment vis-a-vis the Japanese, dating back at least to the 1928 liquor laws of the Transvaal. It fell to the Johannesburg City Council's Health and Amenities Committee to consider the requests. First, it asked the Group Areas Board for a ruling; Giddy said it was an attempt to weasel out of committing itself. The board replied that use of swimming baths could not be construed as 'occupation' and therefore the council had a free hand in deciding. Good, said Julie: legally and morally, they cannot deny Japanese if the Government deems them White. Julie and Giddy had not only principle at stake but also friendship at play in the pools saga, for they were on good terms with Mr Torada, the second secretary at the Japanese consulate, and his wife. It had begun when Torada-san had stopped in at Accone's to buy some Chinese bowls and had ended up staying for dinner. It turned out that Torada had been stationed in Kwangtung during the war, and had developed a great respect and love for things Chinese. He had never ceased to encourage his wife to learn the art of Chinese cooking, but she had not obliged. As the acquaintance between the Toradas and the Accones burgeoned, Mrs Torada came to a momentous decision: as a surprise for her husband, she would learn Chinese cuisine, if Julie would teach her. Unable to refuse such a request, Julie assented and then phoned her mother and father.

'What am I to do, Pop?' said Julie. 'I cook, but you're the chef.'

'Don't worry,' Ah Leong assured her. 'Every week we will have a rehearsal by phone for the dish or dishes you will teach her. You'll see that in the end it is only a matter of practice, judgement and developing an eye for the ingredients.'

Gertie pledged her help too, and for good measure gave Julie a copy of her old standby, *The Chinese Cook Book* by Mr M. Sing Au. It was to become much used in the months ahead, an emergency complement to the personal instruction and advice from Julie's parents. Roast duck, *dim sum*, Peking duck, *har gow* — translucent dumplings filled with diced shrimp — white cut chicken, *char siu*, rice noodles, *wun tun*, 'Slices of the Moon' — sliced cucumber salted for two hours and then dried and fried in sesame oil — all these recipes and more passed between the young Chinese woman and the young Japanese woman.

In his enthusiasm, Giddy once asked the Toradas to Sunday lunch in Perth Road. Ah Leong was gracious throughout, but afterwards asked Giddy not to repeat the invitation. Mention of Torada's time in Kwangtung had been too painful and discomfiting for Ah Leong.

In the meantime, the Health and Amenities Committee had opened Johannesburg public pools to Japanese and Chinese. Committee chairman Arthur Herold was quoted in the *Rand Daily Mail* as having said, 'In view of the trade agreements between South Africa and Japan we did not feel that we could ban Japanese from our swimming baths. It would be extremely difficult for our gatekeepers to distinguish between Chinese and Japanese as both are Mongolian types.

'In any event, we have never had trouble with our Chinese community, which is conspicuously well-behaved.'

Ah Leong felt that it was an unguardedly forthright, and therefore more telling statement. For the first time, an official had admitted the rationale for the White status of the Japanese: money. Newspaper editorials had taken the Verwoerd government to task over its motives, criticisms which Ah Leong and Gertie had enjoyed. They had admired the courage of the *Rand Daily Mail* in its leader on 24 November 1961, which they had cut out lest Julie missed it. It had concluded that the position of the Japanese in the country was 'due to rands and cents, and it exposes for what they are worth the Government's pretensions to some heaven-sent mission in distinguishing between one race and another'. The perhaps unconsciously candid Mr Herold, however, gave Ah Leong greater satisfaction.

Pools had scarcely been declared open in Jo'burg when the Management Committee of the Pretoria City Council told a Japanese swimming team that intended visiting the city that it would not be allowed to practise in the Hillcrest baths, located in the posh eastern suburbs. The South African Swimming Association took up the case, advocating for the Japanese. At the same time came the softball incident. Pretoria was to host the national softball championships in March 1962. When the Border Softball Association announced its women's team, it contained six Chinese players. The management committee declared that no Chinese would be allowed to play on any of the municipal grounds where the tourney would be taking place. So serious was the situation that Verwoerd summoned the Mayor of Pretoria to Libertas, the Prime Minister's residence, in early February 1962. There, the baths and the softball issues were discussed. On the next day, the bar on the Japanese swimmers was lifted; the ban on the Chinese softball players remained. Unlike its swimming counterpart, the South African Softball Association made no fight. It accepted the decision and directed the Border Softball Association to exclude Chinese from its team. What the national body had not reckoned on, though, was the solidarity the Border community felt with its Chinese players. By ten votes to one, the Border association voted to withdraw its team from the championships. Perth Road and Third Street were elated, and moved, by this principled act.

Soon after the sports controversies came the bus fracas. While Chinese in Johannesburg were permitted to use buses for Whites, in Pretoria only Chinese consular officials were free to board such city transport. Japanese, official or otherwise, were welcome to take buses in terms of their new White status. A diplomatic incident occurred when a bus driver refused to pick up a Japanese consular official, whom he thought was Chinese. Faced with endless embarrassing possibilities of refusing service to legitimate Japanese passengers and accidentally taking on illegal Chinese commuters, the Pretoria City Council pondered whether all Chinese should be allowed on White buses. Their deliberations were reported in the *Sunday Express* as having led to a decision to permit Chinese to ride on buses, but that proved incorrect.

'Look at this for a back-handed compliment,' Giddy called to Julie as he read the *Pretoria News* report of 5 March 1962.

No trouble expected
Chinese still not on buses
'We don't believe for a moment that the Chinese people will take advantage of the sanction given to the Japanese to travel on Municipal transport,' said the manager of the Municipal Transport Department, Mr J.M. de K Schutte, this morning.

'Wait for it, I'm going to skip down to it,' said Giddy.

> *'There has been no difficulty in the past, and we do not expect difficulty in the future.*
> *'The Chinese have not attempted to make use of municipal transport so far, and we rely on their integrity not to try to infringe the local regulations,' said Mr Schutte.*

'Aha! Suddenly they say we have integrity, and that we must use it to continue humiliating ourselves,' Giddy seethed. 'Maybe we should look at emigrating.'

'Let's not start that again, at least not until we've saved some money,' replied Julie, but she had to concede to herself that things were growing more taxing, and more ridiculous, all the time.

A mere three days after Giddy had read the latest on the bus situation, the papers ran a story so surreal that Julie felt the country had become a sideshow of the Mad Hatter's tea party. She was alerted to the news by a phone call from her mother. Gertie had been enjoying the customary early afternoon lull in the fruit shop, sitting in her little nook at the shop window and reading *All Men Are Brothers*, Pearl S. Buck's translation of the Chinese classic *Shui Hu Chuan*. Had the title been literally translated, it would have read *Water Borders Novel,* clearly neither catchy nor accessible.

'Jesus, Bug,' shouted Ah Leong, 'there is a story here called "CHINESE IS OFFICIALLY DECLARED WHITE".' Brandishing a copy of the afternoon paper, he strode over to the counter, slammed down the paper and explained.

'David Song, born in Canton, living in Durban, has had himself declared White. His lawyers seem to have found a loophole in the Government's definition of White and exploited that. The report says Song proved, through witnesses and other testimony, that he was, I quote, generally accepted as White. What's wrong with the man? Why would he want to be White? The Europeans should be so lucky as to be Chinese!'

'Calm down, Bug, you're ranting,' said Gertie, but it was no use; Ah Leong was incensed by the whole affair. A few minutes later Gertie excused herself to phone Julie.

Less than two weeks after Song's reclassification, the National Party introduced an amendment to the Population Registration Act. It placed greater emphasis on appearance than the previous Act, in which Song's case had found ambiguities and inadequacies. Now the clauses in the Act read:

'*A White person means a person, who in appearance obviously is a White person and who is not generally accepted as a Coloured person, or*

'*Is generally accepted as a White person and is not in appearance obviously not a White person, but does not include any person who admits that he is by descent a Native or a Coloured person.*'

For the Nats, the additive 'is not in appearance obviously not a White person' halted attempts by others to emulate Song. As for Song, his new status brought bizarre problems. It was pointed out that he and his Chinese wife were now living illegally, in terms of the Immorality Act, Mixed Marriages Act and Group Areas Act. His family was threatened with eviction. Hard-line Chinese who believed that Song had sold out the community felt little sympathy for someone who had deliberately 'elevated' his status, and they drew satisfaction from this singular instance of White not being right. It was a Pyrrhic victory, however, for the Nationalists seemed to be inexhaustible in their dedication to what was euphemistically referred to as Separate Development. Julie's beloved anthropology lecturer, Dr. Jeffreys, sent a letter to the papers in which, taking Apartheid to its logical extremes, he highlighted its absurdity. If the government was so concerned with 'own group' amenities, and with keeping people and their activities apart, he wrote, then surely it was imperative to provide segregated sewerage systems: nine in all, seven for the sewage of the 'Non-European' groups, one for the 'African' group and one for the 'Europeans'.

Julie had taken some part-time employment with Doc, as she and many others affectionately called him. She spent Fridays and Saturdays cataloguing his vast personal library at 19 St Andrew's Road, Parktown, the university-owned house in which he lived with his wife Kay, more formally Katharine. Giddy would deliver Julie to Perth Road on a Thursday night and come down on Sunday for the weekly family dinner to collect her. Although the separation was difficult at times, it was just as well, because Giddy had broken away from the shop. On returning from another visit to Hong Kong, Ah Hing had told Giddy that she had decided that Yen should have the town shop and Giddy the farm business in Kyalami. This Giddy did not understand, and despite asking his mother repeatedly why she had changed her mind, he received no answer. Giddy had devoted years of his life to the shop, and ploughed money back into it. More hurt than angry, he told his mother he was leaving.

If renouncing his dream was wrenching, finding a job was almost as difficult. Eventually Giddy was employed as the hardware buyer at Katzenellenbogen Wholesalers, just a few minutes' walk from his mother's. In every other respect, however, it was worlds away. Where the currency of his day had been delicate objects and rare foods, he now dealt in the banalities of hammers and nails, saws and trowels. But he had a family to support, and he found he could set aside the dissatisfactions and drudgery whenever he thought of Julie and Ah Nung, and how fortunate it was that they had survived the accident. His family was whole, and Giddy wanted to be the husband and father that he himself never knew, and that ambition enabled him to settle into a new rhythm of life, with all its exasperations and niggling slights.

There were changes at home, too, for the Aga Khan had urged Ismailis to settle in Arusha, Tanganyika, and the Noors had answered his call. Their move enabled the Accones to occupy the larger semi next door, which had a separate dining room and a roof garden extending over the ground area of both semis. The extra space was a boon, especially for Russ, the family's boxer dog. Although Russ was exercised daily at the makeshift soccer field near the retail fruit and vegetable market a few blocks down from Third Street, he possessed a seemingly inexhaustible supply of good-natured energy in need of an outlet.

Ah Nung was now at Loreto Convent in Waterkloof, a feeder school to Christian Brothers' College in Pretoria. Every year, Julie had to apply for permission for her son to attend the little school, situated in a rambling old house. The Transvaal Education Department permit posed a series of obstacles to applicants. First the head of the school had to signal approval by signing the form. Then there was the battery of questions to be answered. How far do you live from the school? How near is the Chinese school to your place of residence? Why have you chosen this school? Last came the interview at the Transvaal Provincial Administration building in Pretorius Street. Always, there was a cold man in a grey suit, with cold eyes. Always, there were the abrupt questions, further interrogating the responses on the form. Finally, the rubber stamp would hammer down on the form and the ordeal was over for another year.

In the second half of Ah Nung's Grade One year, the family was blessed with its second grandson, Ian Michael, born to Mickey and Sid on 3 August 1966. Accustomed to being the centre of attention, Ah Nung was angry and glum at first. Gertie, whom he called *Bobo*; Lil, whom he dubbed Aunt Isha; and Mickey, whom he named Aunt Mucky, had indulged him from the beginning. Mucky would piggyback him round the Perth Road garden, turning herself into a horse, complete with neighs and whinnies. Each week Isha would present him with a new toy. *Bobo* attended to his every whim, whipping up special foods for the fussy eater, telling him stories about Stone Monkey and bringing him 'midnight' snacks of warm milk and home-made biscuits. Ah Leong, whom Ah Nung called *Kongkong* (*waikong* was the correct appellation, as *waibobo* was for Gertie), took his grandchild for long walks up Hurst Hill from

Perth Road, and then repeated the route when Ah Nung, stamping his feet, refused to go back to the shop after only one ascent of the hill.

A little over a month after Ian was born, on 6 September 1966, a Parliamentary messenger, Dimitri Tsafendas, approached Verwoerd during a sitting of the House of Assembly. Tsafendas was not on official business; he had come to bring death. Slipping out a concealed knife, he stabbed Verwoerd four times before the assembled parliamentarians fully realised what was happening. The chief architect of Grand Apartheid died of his wounds, to be succeeded by the Minister of Justice, Johannes Balthazar Vorster. It was Vorster who, as an *Ossewa Brandwag* member, had been interned by the Smuts government at Koffiefontein during World War Two, along with many *OB* members who were now prominent National Party figures. More ominously, Vorster had been instrumental in suppressing political activists and threatening the Press, as well as introducing the so-called 90-Day Act of 1963, which gave police the right to hold suspects for questioning for up to three months, without access to a lawyer at any point. In becoming premier, Vorster vowed to continue carrying out Verwoerd's policies.

By the time Ah Nung was preparing for 'big school', Standard Two, he had become more accommodating of his young cousin. Julie took a while, however, to become used to the novelty of not applying for a school permit. Brother Smith, the young and determined principal at CBC, refused to sign the application. He told Julie that he would not sign any of the permits for Chinese pupils as the process was degrading, and he would decide whom to accept or refuse, not the education department bureaucracy. He added that as Chairman of the Catholic Schools Committee, he had given instructions to that effect to brother and sister schools. Brother Smith's stand brought an end to Julie's yearly applications, though not to the annual appearance by education officials performing a head-count of Chinese pupils at CBC.

As 1968 drew to a close, Giddy and Julie considered the year that lay ahead. 'Things will always be different,' said Giddy, 'but the new year holds two big changes that we already know about. Ah Nung is going to a new school and we will have to find a new home, mainly because of the Noors coming back from Arusha. It's a shame that feelings are running so high against Indians in that part of the world.'

'Well, Noors or no Noors,' said Julie, 'I think the main reason to move is what's happening in Marabastad. They've begun to move people out, and after that they will start on Cape Location and Asiatic Bazaar. There may be no further talk of an "own area" for us, but at the same time, what area can we go to? We must look around now before we're forced to go somewhere without a say.'

Every Chinese in the country was confronted by the predicament that Julie and Giddy were grappling with. While the community had success-fully resisted the earmarking and declaration of separate residential areas, the laws of the land prohibited them from living among, or being accept-ed by, people from 'other groups'. The season was less than festive as Julie and Giddy mulled over their situation.

When the new year began, it brought another unforeseen event into their lives. On New Year's Day 1969, Ah Hing suffered a stroke. She was taken to hospital in a coma. Despite having left the shop, Giddy was on good terms with his mother; indeed, he had visited her almost every day, either going to or returning from work. As he sat at her bedside, he had no regrets about his decisions nor any cause to berate himself for his actions. Nevertheless, he was distraught. His mother had fed, clothed and educated him and Yen, working on her own while carrying the terrible memory of her husband's sudden demise. Whatever her flaws, she was the sole parent he had known. Nor could Giddy have wished for a better example of single-mindedness and hard work. Above all, he reflected, she had fulfilled the promise she made to herself that, one day, she would be able to live well and dress stylishly. It was as such thoughts turned in his head that Ah Hing slipped quietly away.

There were many customs to be observed for the funeral, and in the weeks following. On the day, the immediate family gathered at Ah Hing's Vermeulen Street house to which she had moved from the cramped quarters behind the shop. Yen and his wife Peggy, Giddy and Julie, and the brothers' half-sister Wendy had a mid-morning meal together. Instead of the required simple fare, however, they were confronted by food for happier occasions. Inexplicably, the cook had sent round roast duck and roast pork. Their repast over, the family drove to Johannesburg, where there was a viewing of the body at the Cantonese Club in Chinatown prior to burial. The familiar smell of incense laced the air, and at the top of the room Ah Hing lay in an open casket, of which Ah Nung had been forewarned. It was the boy's first experience of death, and he found it difficult to look at his grandmother, whose waxen complexion contrasted shockingly with the sanguine appearance to which he was accustomed. Because Julie and Giddy had done their best to prepare him, very little about the day was unexpected, but nothing was easier for that. He kept imagining the piece of silver, or silver coin, that he had been told the eldest son places in the dead person's mouth, to smooth the way to the next life.

White packets, each containing a five-cent piece, were given to all the mourners at the club. This money had to be spent before they returned home, as did the five cents they received in red packets after the funeral. The custom was literally to buy something sweet to remind themselves of the deceased's good qualities. However, by tradition no one in the immediate family, Ah Nung was told, spent the money.

Square leaves of paper, with embossed smaller squares of gold or silver, were on hand to be burnt. Ah Nung was puzzled by the crude containers in which the papers were set alight: four-gallon tins that usually held cooking oil. The papers, he knew, represented money for Ah Hing on her journey in the other world.

At the cemetery, the coffin was lowered and a mound of earth thrown over it. The so-called permanent wreaths, with their strangely coloured plastic flowers under Perspex bubbles, were piled on top. Yen and Giddy placed a wooden stake with Ah Hing's name in Chinese characters at the head of the grave. Then the closest family members gathered at the foot of the grave and bowed three times. The large candle that had been lit on arrival at the cemetery was taken by Yen, honouring the belief that the smoke would lead the spirit home.

That night, a seven-course dinner was held for the close family at Yen's home in Johannesburg. In remembrance, there would be a dinner every year on that day, and for the next six weeks there were similar gatherings, with ever-widening circles of Ah Hing's relatives and friends.

Two days after the funeral, Ah Hing's sons burnt two of her finest *cheung saams* at the cemetery. The grave diggers were so acquainted with this custom, designed to ensure the deceased has apparel in the afterlife, that they supplied the brothers with a small drum in which to burn the long dresses. Back home that night, Giddy told Julie that he felt somehow relieved after the clothes-burning ceremony. The two of them drove to his mother's house and put out food for her spirit, as well as her favourite Western drink, Coca-Cola.

Then, perforce, they turned their attention to finding a new home, for the Noors would be returning from East Africa in just six weeks, and before that, Ah Nung would be beginning at his new school. Their search produced a house in the north-west of Pretoria, between Hercules and Claremont. It was in a Non-White enclave about to be declared White, surrounded by ultra-right wing Afrikaners, but it had a small garden, trees and grass. Whenever Ah Nung went to play at the homes of school friends, he would revel in rolling on their lawns, and his parents worried that all he had at home was the rooftop garden with its cement surface and potted plants and trees. Excited by the prospect of some greenery in their home environment, Julie and Giddy went to the local Group Areas office in Munitoria, the hulking rectangle of cement and glass that was the Pretoria City Council.

'*As jy daarin trek, meisie, sal ek jou bed, ketel, stoof en jou gat in die straat skop,*' said the short, fat, heavily bearded man behind the desk. Before Julie and Giddy could respond, he pushed his chair back and walked into the adjacent annexe, shutting the door behind him.

Humiliated and angry, Julie could not help crying. As she and Giddy walked towards the lifts, they passed a rotund, bearded man in a long-trousered safari suit.

'Is anything the matter?' he asked.

'Yes ... that, that fat pig,' Julie spat out.

'Who?'

'Him ... in the office.'

'What happened, madam? Please come into my office and explain.'

Julie, unwilling at first, was persuaded by Giddy.

'My name is Nel. I am the head of what is called Non-European Housing Affairs,' the man explained in his office. 'First, may I offer you some tea?'

A while later, restored and a little fortified by the tea, Julie recounted the incident. 'The Group Areas official said that if I moved into the house, he would kick my bed, kettle, stove and me into the street.'

'Actually,' said Giddy interrupting quietly, 'he said also he would kick your backside and he called you girlie.'

'I do apologise for his behaviour,' said Nel, who was evidently angry. 'Allow me to make it up by issuing you with an Open Permit, which will allow you to live anywhere in the city that you like. And please be in touch with me should you meet any problems.'

Julie and Giddy were grateful, rather than jubilant. Essentially, the well-meaning gesture was empty since there was no prospect of their being allowed to live where they chose, but it was enough that the permit gave them some means to continue looking for a house. Indeed, a few days after the Munitoria visit, they received a call from the housing department offering them a number of houses in Claremont.

'Poor Mr Nel exceeded his authority,' said Giddy. 'Imagine if we had tried to move into one of the eastern suburbs like Brooklyn, or Hatfield, or somewhere even grander like Lynnwood, or Muckleneuck, or Waterkloof! Waterkloof – old *skuld bult*, debt ridge. Ha! That would have been the property equivalent of David Song's reclassification.'

'Yes,' agreed Julie, 'it would have been a precedent. I'm happy with this option, though, except for one thing. You know, Gid, that they are moving people out of Claremont and Lady Selborne, Coloured and black homeowners. In all likelihood we will be getting one of their houses.'

When they went out to Claremont, they found all the proffered houses in terrible condition. None had electricity, running water and toilets. Candles, Primus stoves, a backyard tap and a long-drop lavatory outside were how people had lived, not out of choice. Best of the four houses was a solitary, square house, with a huge old poplar tree that shaded its whole southern side. At the very edge of Claremont, surrounded by veld on three sides, it had a curiously appealing insularity. Here, at 902 Achilles Street, Giddy and Julie found four families living, and sharing a kitchen. One of the mothers was in when they visited, and she and Julie exchanged a look of empathy.

'Don't be sad about us,' said the Coloured woman. 'We are moving where they say things will be better, there in Eersterus. You will like this place, it has a nice feel, my dear.'

Julie thanked her and wished her well, and then gently pulled Giddy by the sleeve. Outside, passing under the tree, she whispered to him, 'I don't know if I can go through with this. It's not the house, it's moving the people who live there.'

'Look at it this way. They have no choice but to move. The people here are tenants in a place where they don't have any basic amenities. Maybe the woman is right and Eersterus will have lights and water. But we aren't evicting her, the government is. Whether we take the house or someone else does, it won't change what happens to those families back there. It's the way Apartheid makes dominoes out of people.'

'We condone that if we move here,' said Julie.

'I'm not going to argue with you. But just think. Ah Nung will have grass, and trees, instead of the cold, dusty cement upstairs at home.'

Over time, Julie became reconciled to the idea. There were, after all, only four weeks till the Noors returned. In that month, they would have to get the house into some sort of livable condition. Help came from many sides. Kenny Shaw, the father of Ah Nung's great school friend Peter, was a quantity surveyor for the council, and he helped expedite the provision of electricity and laying of water pipes. Kenny's head of department, Mr Breytenbach, moved things along too, and finally, when only institutional inertia stood in the way of the taps producing water, another Munitoria bigwig, Mr Kingsley, came down to bawl out the council workers. In the midst of all this, Giddy spent weekends and most nights after work painting and repairing, and installing ceiling boards. Some of his painstaking ceiling work was undone in seconds when the electrical contractor came in to do the wiring. It was then that Giddy heard, and then saw, the erstwhile Springbok rugby hooker Gys Pitzer crash through the ceiling boards and stop just short of the floor, pulled up by his safety harness.

As he worked assiduously on their home, Giddy felt increasingly comfortable. He really liked the place, with its fresh air and view of the eastern, tail end of the Magaliesberg. The base of those hills was about half an hour's walk away, he reckoned, and he vowed that he and his son would walk up them often in the time ahead. It was the strangest of circumstances, this haven in the midst of Nationalist territory, with Daspoort and Danville to the south-west, and Hercules, with its extreme conservative demagogue Jaap Marais, two minutes' drive away. Northeast, along the big arterial of Paul Kruger Street, lay Wonderboom, the remarkable wild fig tree that was centuries old and, with its many subsidiary growths and branches, spread out over almost an acre. We have our own wonder tree here, thought Giddy, as he sipped a Coke in the cool of the poplar, during a break from tiling the bathroom.

Achilles Street was not quite ready when the Noors came home. But books, clothing, furniture, crockery and other household effects had been moved from Asiatic Bazaar to Claremont by the end of February. In the midst of the comings and goings, Ah Nung's ninth birthday slipped past, but Julie and Giddy promised him a grand party later in the year, when he and his friends would be able, for the first time, to play outdoors.

Summer eased into its last days as the Accones settled in. The mornings were clear and there was a curious absence of red dust. Out of the kitchen they could see, not the neighbouring semi's wall, but the sun rise. On the south side of the house, protecting it, was the poplar, its trunk many rings thick. Looking north, the family saw mountains that seemed like a gigantic sea frozen in motion, cliff faces cresting steep south slopes, which swept downwards in an ever more gentle wave to the broad valley floor and their home. It had been a long journey to this patch of paradise that seemed to reach, with the purity of fire, from the earth to the sky. Here, Giddy and Julie thought, it was as if they were living all under heaven.

EPILOGUE

The weight of this sad time we must obey,
Speak what we feel, not what we ought to say.
The oldest hath borne most: we that are young
Shall never see so much, nor live so long.
– *King Lear*, Act V, Scene iii, lines 325 to 328

On holidays at the coast, Ah Leong would stand looking eastwards over the Indian Ocean, hands clasped behind his old but upright back: east towards China, towards the home he had left when not yet a teenager, certain in his youthful optimism he would return soon. He never set foot on Chinese soil again. He spent the last 73 years of his life in Namfeechow.

At the end of July 1981, Ah Leong and Gertie closed the Perth Road shops and moved to a house over the road from 902 Achilles Street. Throughout 1984, *Kongkong*'s health deteriorated and on 26 October, minutes after seeing the doctor, he collapsed and died in a shopping centre. Thankfully, Gertie and Julie were with him, but the sudden and public manner of his passing were terribly traumatic for them.

None of the harshness and disappointments Gertie endured made her bitter or unforgiving. When Cornelia visited for the last time in 1967, she came expressly to ask for Gertie's forgiveness for the way she had treated her. It was granted unhesitatingly. Six months later, Cornelia died of a heart attack in Sydney.

On the night of the lunar eclipse of 11 August 1999, Gertie died after a few weeks during which she had hardly been conscious. At the same time, Giddy had been battling lung cancer, discovered only two months before.

The family did not tell him that Mom, as he called her, had died. His own condition was worsening rapidly, and he had lost the use of his legs as the cancer spread. By Friday 13 August, it became apparent that death was imminent. A little before 4 a.m. on 14 August, Giddy winked, an action that probably demanded immense energy and will, for he had been too ill to communicate for the past day. Shortly after, he left life, at only 67.

Having had a tough childhood, with no idea of the limits of fatherly indulgence, he erred very much on the side of the bountiful. That extended to his caring for 'Mom' and 'Pop', Gertie and Ah Leong, for whom he bought the house opposite his and Julie's for their retirement.

Giddy bought Ah Nung a Chinese chess board and set and marked on tiny adhesive labels in his clear, strong script, the names in English of each of the pieces. He was a young boy's dream father, except that his son was rather bookish. Undeterred, he took Ah Nung fishing, flying kites that he would make, playing with radio-controlled aeroplanes and boats. The fishing and the radio-controlled fads converged splendidly in a boat designed to take their fishing lines way out into Hartebeespoort Dam. Giddy christened the boat Tanya, after their second child, who was born on 26 October 1971, and who really understood and valued his outdoor pursuits and talents.

Julie moved from the Claremont house and its faithful poplar tree on 28 February 2001, the day of Ah Nung's birthday and eighteen months after Giddy's death. Ah Nung came by that day, more to bid a shared goodbye than to mark his birthday. But there was cake, and tea, and a final walk around the garden that had been little more than bare soil when they first moved in. Mother and son circled the property, stopping at the Christmas tree that now was almost as tall as the poplar but once had been a sapling in a tin drum, brought down from Perth Road. They moved on to the old mulberry trees that had fed the family's silkworms each season, and back to the shade of the poplar, for a last look at the pomegranate that sheltered beneath it.

I know what Julie said to Ah Nung that day. And I know because I am Fok Boon Nung: in other words, Ah Nung. For all my life the name I have used has been Darryl Accone, the western-style name given me at birth: first name first, surname last. My unused middle name, Ford, is the only slight clue to another identity. It is a conversion of my clan – my *seng* – name, from what it is in Chinese: Fok.

My Chinese name states first my clan name, then my personal name. Looking back, I suppose I could say that what I've done has been to use my public name or 'style' name, as it is called in Chinese, for all these years.

Accone is an Italian-sounding name. Our family has never established how we acquired it as a surname. Was there some immigration official of northern Sicilian descent who admitted my father's father to this country and, unable to cope with a barrage of Chinese names, simply bestowed his own on the hapless immigrant standing before him? Certainly, that happened with my uncle Sid's family, who became Johnsons, and with a cousin of my father, who went by the splendid name of Frederick Jackson. But Accone? It even fooled – embarrassed, in actuality – the Catholic priest who was approached to baptise me at the rather advanced age of five. 'You Italians,' he chastised my mother over the phone. 'Always leaving things late. Late to be baptised, late to confess – except on your deathbeds.' Well, he was rather jolted when he met us and realised his entirely reasonable assumption was, unfortunately, flawed.

My grandfather would tell us grandchildren many tales of his brief boyhood in China. As the first-born grandchild, I had to listen to those more often than my cousin Ian and sister Tanya. Reiteration did not always mean retention, sadly, and now I regret the impatience and easy boredom of youth and its continual quest for the new. But of the retellings, what remains indelible is that things were always bigger and better in China. Snakes were longer, summers hotter and more humid; the rivers were broader and an incomparably beguiling colour. For an eleven-year-old, such must have been the world, and its image remained perfectly preserved, captured forever in the amber of Ah Leong's memory and forming the substance of yearning dreams.